The Grotesque in Contemporary Anglophone Drama

Ondřej Pilný

The Grotesque in Contemporary Anglophone Drama

Ondřej Pilný
Department of Anglophone Literatures and Cultures
Faculty of Arts
Charles University, Prague
Czech Republic

ISBN 978-1-349-70276-3   ISBN 978-1-137-51318-2 (Ebook)
DOI 10.1057/978-1-137-51318-2

Library of Congress Control Number: 2016943519

© The Editor(s) (if applicable) and The Author(s) 2016
Softcover reprint of the hardcover 1st edition 2016 978-1-137-51317-5
The author(s) has/have asserted their right(s) to be identified as the author(s) of this work in accordance with the Copyright, Designs and Patents Act 1988.
This work is subject to copyright. All rights are solely and exclusively licensed by the Publisher, whether the whole or part of the material is concerned, specifically the rights of translation, reprinting, reuse of illustrations, recitation, broadcasting, reproduction on microfilms or in any other physical way, and transmission or information storage and retrieval, electronic adaptation, computer software, or by similar or dissimilar methodology now known or hereafter developed.
The use of general descriptive names, registered names, trademarks, service marks, etc. in this publication does not imply, even in the absence of a specific statement, that such names are exempt from the relevant protective laws and regulations and therefore free for general use.
The publisher, the authors and the editors are safe to assume that the advice and information in this book are believed to be true and accurate at the date of publication. Neither the publisher nor the authors or the editors give a warranty, express or implied, with respect to the material contained herein or for any errors or omissions that may have been made.

Cover illustration: © jvphoto / Alamy Stock Photo

Printed on acid-free paper

This Palgrave Macmillan imprint is published by Springer Nature
The registered company is Macmillan Publishers Ltd. London

Acknowledgments

In writing this book, I have benefited from discussions with many friends and colleagues who generously gave of their time and insights and shared their work with me. I am particularly indebted to Martin Procházka, Clare Wallace, Keith Hopper, Shaun Richards, Tilman Raabke, Michael Raab, Werner Huber, Nicholas Grene, and John Harrington. My work owes much also to the wonderful and truly engaging conferences of the German Society for Contemporary Theatre and Drama in English (CDE) and the Irish Society for Theatre Research (ISTR), and to the many stimulating debates with my students.

I would like to express my special gratitude to Roy Foster, who facilitated a research stay at Hertford College, University of Oxford for me while I was working on this project, and who was such a wonderful host. I am equally grateful to the Moore Institute at National University of Ireland, Galway for providing me with a research fellowship at an early stage of my research, to Patrick Lonergan for hosting me in Galway, and to Shelley Troupe for helping out with numerous practical matters. My thanks are due to Tim Crouch for his generosity in letting me read the manuscripts of his most recent plays and use them for this volume.

I am much obliged to Linda Jayne Turner for meticulous copy-editing, and to Paula Kennedy, Peter Cary, Jenny McCall, April James, and all the staff at Palgrave Macmillan for their trust in the project and for their commitment to bringing this book to publication. I would also like to thank the anonymous readers for their carefully considered comments, which have all been extremely useful.

v

As ever, I am very grateful to my parents for their unwavering support of my work and, last but certainly not least, my wife Hana and my children, who had to live with the grotesque for long enough, and were exceedingly patient. It is they who sustain me.

Early versionst of some parts of this book were published as follows:
Parts of Chap. 1 appeared in 'On the Politics of the Grotesque in Contemporary Drama', in Ondřej Pilný and Mirka Horová (eds.), *'Tis to Create and in Creating Live. Essays in Honour of Martin Procházka* (Prague: Faculty of Arts, Charles University, 2013), pp. 87–95 and 'Jan Grossman, Prague Structuralism, and the Grotesque', in Martin Procházka and Ondřej Pilný (eds.), *Prague English Studies and the Transformation of Philologies* (Prague: Karolinum Press, 2012), pp. 184–97.

Parts of Chap. 3 appeared in 'Then Like Gigli, Now Like Bette: The Grotesque and the Sublime in Mark O'Rowe's *Terminus*', in Donald E. Morse (ed.), *Irish Theatre in Transition: From the Late Nineteenth to the Early Twenty-First Century* (Houndmills: Palgrave Macmillan, 2015), pp. 137–46.

Parts of Chap. 4 appeared in 'The Grotesque in the Plays of Enda Walsh', *Irish Studies Review*, 21 (2) (2013), pp. 217–25.

I am grateful to the publishers for their permission to reprint the material.

Research for this book was supported by the 'Programme for the Development of Research Areas at Charles University, P09, Literature and Art in Intercultural Relations,' sub-programme 'Transformations of the Cultural History of the Anglophone Countries: Identities, Periods, Canons', and a grant provided by the Department of Foreign Affairs and Trade (Ireland): Cultural Relations with Other Countries Programme.

Contents

1 Introduction: The Grotesque and Contemporary Drama   1

2 Engaging Monsters: Philip Ridley   29

3 Wild Justice: Mark O'Rowe   57

4 Life in a Box: Enda Walsh   81

5 Mutabilities: Suzan-Lori Parks   103

6 Imagine This: Tim Crouch   131

7 Afterword: The Grotesque and Spectatorship   163

Index   171

CHAPTER 1

Introduction: The Grotesque and Contemporary Drama

I

Theatre in English has been marked by extreme diversity since the early 1990s, ranging from a static rendering of bare narrative in many monologue dramas to site-specific performances using state-of-the-art media technology. This book is dedicated to text-based theatre, which has progressively become characterized by the blending of established genres. It aims to show that in the work of some of the most exciting contemporary playwrights, this generic combination is associated with the grotesque.

Reviewers have highlighted the presence of the grotesque in the work of young British, Irish, and North American authors such as Sarah Kane, Mark Ravenhill, Tracy Letts, Philip Ridley, Martin McDonagh, or Enda Walsh. However, a play or some of its features have mostly been labelled grotesque without any indication as to what exactly is meant by the term, apart from "bizarre but extremely engaging", and where it is that the grotesque might take us. The objective of the present volume is to discuss the grotesque in Anglophone drama on the basis of a thorough examination of the concept, with a particular emphasis on the work of dramatists whose plays have been applauded by audiences and reviewers alike but who have suffered relative neglect by scholars. It is my contention that the reasons for the absence of more extensive commentary prominently include the use of the grotesque, given that one of its chief effects is leaving the beholder puzzled.

© The Editor(s) (if applicable) and The Author(s) 2016
O. Pilný, *The Grotesque in Contemporary Anglophone Drama*,
DOI 10.1057/978-1-137-51318-2_1

The grotesque is an aesthetic category whose origin has been outlined by virtually every art historian or literary scholar to have written on the subject. Around 1480, the remains of Emperor Nero's Domus Aurea were excavated in Rome, a grandiose palace that was to reflect Nero's image as a sun god. The excessive residence was found to be decorated by ornaments that freely combined elements of the animate and inanimate worlds, whose incongruity in the eyes of the Quattrocento gave rise to a reaction typical of the grotesque: a mixture of disgust and attraction. The ornaments became universally referred to as *grottesche*, as they were found in what by then was an underground space resembling a cave (Harpham 2006, pp. 27–32). Complaints by the guardians of the principles of classical aesthetics remained unheeded and a grotesque style came into vogue that lasted a number of decades. As early as 1484, Pinturicchio decorated a loggia in the Vatican with *grottesche*, and was followed by numerous prominent artists of the time, including Raphael, who created grotesque designs for several Vatican loggie with Giovanni da Udine between 1515 and 1519. Subsequently, the fashionable style spread across Europe, endorsed by the courts of the Habsburgs and King Francis I of France (Connelly 2012, pp. 32–4).

While the term was not coined until the late fifteenth century, grotesque images had been abundant in Western art ever since its very beginnings. To stay with Ancient Rome, we find evidence with Vitruvius, who launched a famous attack in his *De architectura* (ca. 27 BC) on those who chose to 'decorate the walls with monstrous forms'. He rallied: 'how can the stem of a flower support a roof, or a candelabrum a pedimental sculpture? How can a tender shoot carry a human figure, and how can bastard forms composed of flowers and human bodies grow out of roots and tendrils?' (qtd in Connelly 2012, p. 27). Horace also condemned the free amalgamation of the incongruous in ornaments in his *Ars Poetica* (published sometime during the last two decades before the Christian era), referring to them as a 'sick man's dreams [...] empty of substance, no single form relating head and foot'. (qtd in Connelly 2012, p. 26). Both Vitruvius and Horace objected to grotesque ornamentation because it was unnatural, at variance both with nature and with Classical harmony—all this still before the Domus Aurea, which was built after the fire of Rome in 64 AD. Similarly, early Christian art and architecture frequently features grotesque images, be it in the form of ornaments, marginalia in illuminated manuscripts, or indeed the numerous composite monsters or leering faces that appear both in the interior and on the exterior of Gothic cathedrals, well before the term entered general usage.

In her wonderfully comprehensive study of *The Grotesque in Western Art and Culture* (2012), Frances Connelly describes how the concept has gradually broadened its meaning. Originally used for the style of ornamentation associated with Nero's palace in the 1480s, it was back in the early 1500s that a slightly different kind of ornamentation emerged in Europe and was referred to as grotesque: the arabesque or the moresque, an 'abstract vegetal design' of Islamic origin that became widely imitated and developed by European artists (pp. 54–5). By the seventeenth century, the word 'grotesque' was most often used to refer to a particular type of caricature and also to the capriccio both of which foregrounded the body. These were exemplified by the carnivalesque commedia dell'arte drawings of Jacques Callot from the 1610s, and later in their different ways by William Hogarth's caricatures (1730s– 1750s) or Francisco Goya's *Los Caprichos* (1793–1799). In Romanticism, the grotesque began to be linked to the emotions of horror and repulsion, following from the earlier nightmarish visions of painters such as Martin Schongauer (*The Temptation of Saint Anthony*, ca. 1480–1490), Hieronymus Bosch (ca. 1450–1516) and Pieter Bruegel the Elder (ca. 1525–1569), who had been working in the tradition of the *diablerie* and often depicted the monstrous (Connelly 2012, pp. 19, 99–109, 120). This wide scope of reference amply supports Connelly's assertion that the grotesque is historically and culturally specific (pp. 13–14); at the same time, any contemporary use of the term will inevitably bear distinct echoes of all its previous applications.

Like any complex aesthetic category, and particularly given the historical variety of its meaning, the grotesque is a term that threatens to wear thin through being conceptualized too broadly. Generally speaking, the grotesque is primarily defined by the blending of radically incongruous elements, together with the simultaneous repulsion and fascination it triggers. The grotesque is also fundamentally puzzling—as noted earlier— to the extent that it 'confounds language and logical sequence', opening 'room to play' where meaning is created by the beholder (Connelly 2012, p. 12). The danger that this overall definition entails in a study dealing with the theatre lies in the temptation to regard, for instance, any incongruous mixing of genres in a play as grotesque, making the term virtually synonymous with 'experimental' or even 'avant-garde'. Further specification is clearly needed; this must consist in stressing that the grotesque is always concerned—in the words of Justin Edwards and Rune Graulund— with 'questioning and unsettling assumptions about what is human and what is not human' (Edwards and Graulund 2013, p. 86). This concern is often communicated through an emphasis on the human body, as in Bakhtin's carnival, but frequently also by an examination of the intellect, particularly through focusing on individuals whose thought processes are incongruous with what is considered to be acceptable or normal.

Although the outline of the different types of the grotesque in Western art and culture presented by Frances Connelly is accurate and will be used as a constant point of reference throughout the present study, the nature of the material covered here still solicits a refinement of one of Connelly's categories—the monstrous grotesque. There is no doubt that the monsters depicted on the margins of medieval manuscripts or in Gothic cathedrals are grotesque, as are the monsters in Bosch's *The Garden of Earthly Delights* (1510), Henry Fuseli's *The Nightmare* (ca. 1781), or the monstrous creature in Salvador Dalí's *Soft Construction with Boiled Beans (Premonition of Civil War)* (1936), vastly different as their nature and contexts are. Similarly, Frankenstein's monster in Mary Shelley's novel (1818) may be regarded as grotesque, a being created from an assortment of body parts that combine in 'a mishmash of disparate elements made terrible by "horrific contrast" between the beautiful and the vile' (Edwards and Graulund 2013, p. 53). However, not everything that is monstrous is also grotesque. Much recent drama features graphic depictions of extreme violence; to give a few examples, consider the rape scenes in Howard Brenton's *The Romans in Britain* (1980) or in Mark Ravenhill's *Shopping and Fucking* (1996), the depiction of rape and war atrocities in Sarah Kane's *Blasted* (1995), or indeed the vivid description of the evaporated human bodies in a fallout shelter in Iraq after the explosion of a US drill-bomb in Heather Raffo's *Nine Parts of Desire* (2004). Yes, monstrous violence *can* be made grotesque, as in the dark comedies of Martin McDonagh. However, these images are obviously not: they remain merely horrific. A dividing line is needed to distinguish between the two forms of the monstrous. This may be plausibly drawn by reference to mimesis and genre: monstrous images that clearly relate to human atrocity, be it in direct documentary fashion as in Raffo's play, or in the context of realist scenes as in the other plays just mentioned, are never grotesque.

As already apparent from the debates concerning grotesque ornamentation in Ancient Rome, the grotesque is always defined against a norm; it 'does not exist except in relation to a boundary, convention, or expectation' (Connelly 2003, p. 4). It does not stand in direct opposition to the norm, however: it occupies a liminal position and 'is more like a catalyst, opening the boundaries of two disparate entities, and setting a reaction in motion' (Connelly 2012, pp. 8–9). Since it challenges accepted norms, it is always inappropriate; it may be perceived as offensive, dangerous, and may cause destruction. In Connelly's apt phrase, it embodies 'the threat of images to mortally wound what is known, what is established, what is accepted'. As such, Connelly asserts, the grotesque has been appropriated in the modern era 'as the weapon of choice for social protest and a voice for those oppressed by traditional social boundaries, or made monstrous by them' (Connelly 2012, p. 18). These uses of the grotesque are of eminent interest in the present volume, which aims to discuss in detail the ethics and politics pertaining to the grotesque in contemporary drama.

Yet not all plays that feature the grotesque foreground ethical or political issues, and even some of those that ostentatiously do so may not really voice any kind of protest, as I will attempt to demonstrate shortly. However, the grotesque does harbour a profound potential for true audience engagement, in the sense of the emancipation of individual audience members promoted by Jacques Rancière in his influential essay *The Emancipated Spectator* (2008). Rancière joins the ranks of those thinkers and practitioners who regard clear-cut political art as futile. He argues that the assumed connection between watching a play about social or political injustice and taking action is dubious; he asserts that 'There is no straightforward road from the fact of looking at a spectacle to the fact of understanding the state of the world; no direct road from intellectual awareness to political action' (Rancière 2011, p. 74). In other words, there is no guarantee that the spectator will interpret a work of art as socially critical or political in the way intended by the artist, or that he or she will act upon it either. According to Rancière, the power of art lies in its capacity to 'rework the frame of our perceptions and the dynamism of our affects. As such [it] can open up new passages towards new forms of subjectivation' (p. 82).

This emancipatory power of art had in fact already been identified by John Ruskin in his celebrated discussion of the grotesque. Ruskin wrote that,

A fine grotesque is the expression, in a moment, by a series of symbols thrown together in bold and fearless connection, of truths which it would have taken a long time to express in any verbal way, and of which the connection is left for the beholder to work out for himself only; the gaps, left or overleaped by the haste of the imagination, forming the grotesque character. (Ruskin 1903, p. 132)

Ruskin's emphasis on the essential role of the imagination in interpreting the grotesque is precisely what Rancière requires of his 'emancipated spectator', watching a complex work of art, as the only means that may lead to the rectification of injustice. Rancière's notion may be idealistic, given that he himself acknowledges that the result of the engagement of the spectator's imagination cannot be predicted. Both Ruskin's and Rancière's argument besides presuppose belief in a basic set of shared moral values. Nevertheless, the appeal to the critical reasoning and imagination of the individual is perhaps the best that contemporary art can hope for, and is very much present in the grotesque.

The starting point for examining the effects of the grotesque in its association with ethics and politics in this study of contemporary drama is a basic contrast between two influential perspectives on the subject. In his pioneering work, *The Grotesque in Art and Literature* (1957), Wolfgang Kayser regarded the grotesque as essentially bleak and terrifying. He defined it as an expression of a fundamental 'alienation of the world' (Kayser 1966, p. 52). According to Kayser,

> The grotesque world is—and is not—our own world. The ambiguous way in which we are affected by it results from an awareness that the familiar and apparently harmonious world is alienated under the impact of abysmal forces, which break it up and shatter its coherence. (p. 37)

The unhinging of the familiar world that is communicated by the grotesque has a tendency to inspire insecurity and terror in the audience: 'We are so strongly affected and terrified because it is our world which ceases to be reliable, and we feel that we would be unable to live in this changed world' (pp. 184–5).

Taking a different perspective to Kayser, Mikhail Bakhtin has highlighted the centrality of laughter to the grotesque in his celebrated *Rabelais and His World* (1965). In his view, the grotesque involves 'the lowering of all that is high, spiritual, ideal, abstract' to the material, earthly level (Bakhtin 1984, p. 19). This degradation is always positive according to Bakhtin, however, since in the grotesque, 'The world is destroyed so that it may be regenerated and renewed' (p. 48). The grotesque thus has 'power to liberate from dogmatism, completeness, and limitation' and the role of laughter on the way to this liberation is essential (p. 44).

The difference in opinion between the respective scholars stems from the nature of the material focused on as well as the circumstances in which they were writing. Bakhtin was concerned primarily with medieval and Renaissance literature and culture, and his concept of the grotesque is linked with the 'folk', the ordinary people whose grotesque laughter is to bring about liberation from an oppressive political regime. Bakhtin may have taken a rather idealistic view of the extent to which the peasants' revelry would have in fact been capable of subverting the social hierarchy or the political status quo of the day (see Connelly 2012, p. 88), but his argument must also be read as an oblique strategy to challenge the Communist rule in the Soviet Union, which had been in place for more than three decades when he began writing. Kayser, on the other hand, focused primarily on the period from Romanticism up to the 1950s. He first conceived of his book in 1942 and wrote most of it in the atmosphere of a spiritually and materially decimated Germany immediately following World War II. The liberatory potential of the grotesque was barely touched upon in his study, and laughter was mentioned sporadically. Kayser described laughter only as 'involuntary', 'filled with bitterness, [...] mocking, cynical, and ultimately satanic' (p. 189).

My own view is that Kayser's and Bakhtin's perspectives form useful end points on a broad scale of effects that grotesque works may have as regards engaging the audience in an ethical or political sense. At one end of the scale is Kayser's bleakness and terror that paralyzes and potentially engenders bitterness and cynicism, at the other end is Bakhtin's anarchic merriment that brings about change and freedom. While the impact of the plays discussed in the following chapters is inevitably dependent not only on the precise nature of the grotesque that each of these features, but also on the context of their staging and interpretation, they will all be positioned within this scale. As regards laughter, its nature and effect can be measured in a similar way, whenever it does actually occur. I tend to agree with Ralf Remshardt—the author of the only existing study in English dedicated to the grotesque in theatre—in that laughing at the grotesque is always inappropriate in a sense: laughter counteracts the horror generated by the grotesque but it is simultaneously a reaction that is chillingly aware of its own 'callousness' (Remshardt 2004, p. 85). According to Remshardt, the nature of such laughter reflects the principal generic base of the grotesque in modern drama, which is not comedy but in fact tragedy; indeed, most contemporary grotesque dramas can be described as a blend of tragedy with farce (p. 92).

II

Before embarking on a discussion of the contemporary era, several important manifestations of the grotesque in modern theatre need to be pointed out, as they have exercised seminal influence on subsequent playwriting and theatre practice. First, there is the explosive merging of puppet theatre with serious drama by Alfred Jarry in his Ubu plays. In a recent biography of Jarry, Alastair Brotchie has entertainingly detailed how the author and his friends orchestrated their first production of *Ubu Roi* in 1896 as an attack on what they regarded as the stale conventions of both naturalist and symbolist drama. The clamorous emergence of the monstrous Père Ubu on the scene through the fireplace, with padded belly, brandishing a toilet brush in place of a sceptre and uttering his infamous 'Merdre!' has entered theatre history as not only a notorious outrage but also a truly revolutionary moment. Using a lack of resources to his advantage, Jarry emphasized the crudity of set and costume, and had his principal player mime action like entering through a non-existent door in the fashion of zero-budget amateur theatre; this angered audience members and critics as much as the vulgarity of the show (Brotchie 2011, pp. 123–70). While the event may have been viewed by its perpetrators as a prank to some extent, in his detailed analysis of the play, Ralf Remshardt has argued that Jarry inaugurated a tradition in which grotesque theatre 'reviles and assaults the audience', going beyond satire as 'a social corrective' (Remshardt 2004, p. 182).

Staging the world as a puppet universe, Jarry's method corresponds with Wolfgang Kayser's emphasis on alienation as the most fundamental feature of the grotesque. Moreover, Kayser gives a useful summary of dramatic precedents to Jarry in his discussion of pre-Romantic and Romantic drama that centres around puppet-like characters (Kayser 1966, pp. 40–5, 195, n. 26). Apart from relatively well-known works such as Jakob Michael Reinhold Lenz's *The New Menoza* (1774) or Georg Büchner's *Woyzeck* (1837), Kayser's list includes Hans Dietrich Grabbe's play *Jest, Satire, Irony, and Deeper Signification* (1826), a freewheeling piece that provided inspiration for Jarry's 'pataphysical dramaturgy' (Remshardt 2004, p. 184). Jarry has gone a step further with his brand of the grotesque, however, since his theatre truly proposes 'the representability of human relations in the context of a Punch-and-Judy show gone berserk' (Remshardt 2004, p. 168). Furthermore, most commentators on *Ubu Roi* have noted that the play deliberately parodies Shakespeare's historical plays and Racine's tragedies by using their elements in the context of amateur theatrics and the puppet show. This early foregrounding of citationality, crude and approximate as it may be, has become an important precursor for subsequent manifestations of the grotesque in the theatre.

An entire grotesque style was developed by a group of Italian playwrights between 1916 and 1925. It was known as the *teatro del grottesco* and its authors also depicted human beings as puppets. Whereas for Jarry, the grotesque of German Romanticism served mostly as an incidental model regarding form, the *teatro del grottesco* followed directly on from these German Romantics as far as the existential dimension of the puppet universe was concerned. Writing in 1928, Adriano Tilgher described the principal belief behind the work of the Italian group as 'The absolute conviction that everything is vain and hollow, and that man is only a puppet in the hand of fate. Man's pains and pleasures as well as his deeds are unsubstantial dreams in a world of ominous darkness that is ruled by blind fortune' (qtd in Kayser 1966, p. 135).

The most famous were Luigi Chiarelli—the subtitle of whose play *The Mask and the Face. A Grotesque in Three Acts* (1916) provided the name for the movement—and Luigi Pirandello. Their focus was unrelentingly on depicting the self as split between different identities and masks, resulting in the abandonment of any unity of character (see Kayser 1966, pp. 135–7). Pirandello became one of the most important innovators in early twentieth-century theatre with his masterpiece, *Six Characters in Search of an Author* (1921), the initial reception of which was almost as tumultuous as that of *Ubu Roi*. The play includes grotesque scenes enacted as pantomime, and the monstrously grotesque character of Madame Pace, described as an 'Apparition', 'a gross old harridan wearing a ludicrous carroty-coloured wig with a single red rose stuck in at one side' that makes the Actors and the Producer jump off the stage in fright (Pirandello 2000, p. 713). However, it is Pirandello's radical deployment of metatheatricality that develops the emphasis of the *teatro del grottesco* on the fragmented nature of the self, enhances the disorienting quality of the play, and leaves the audience 'on the brink of losing foothold on reality' (Kayser 1966, p. 137). Ever since, metatheatrical elements such as multiple plays-within-plays and various kinds of role-playing within these have loomed large on the palette of authors of the dramatic grotesque.

The conviction that the world is ultimately a bleak place has also been ascribed to the theatre of the absurd, although this ignores the essential role of humour in the works of Eugène Ionesco, Jean Genet, and the early plays of Samuel Beckett. Developing after World War II, the theatre of the absurd is a grotesque genre par excellence, since its central principle is to create a puzzling mélange of the incongruous. According to

Martin Esslin's well-known delineation, plot and dramatic structure are shattered in the theatre of the absurd and characters are disfigured and/or resemble puppets. Instead of mirroring reality, absurdist plays seem to reflect dreams and nightmares, and language is often reduced to 'incoherent babblings' (Esslin 1968, pp. 21–2). Esslin's umbrella definition inevitably comes across as only approximate due to the vital differences between the works of the individual playwrights discussed in his book: for instance, compare the nonsensical language of Ionesco's *The Bald Soprano* (1948) with Beckett's *Endgame* (1957) where language is overloaded with meaning, or the political dimension of Genet's *The Balcony* (1952) with Pinter's 'comedies of menace', which relate to politics very obliquely, if at all. Problems of definition aside, there is still no doubt that the theatre of the absurd has been recognized as perhaps the most influential genre of post-war theatre, and its multifaceted use of the grotesque has been widely emulated by contemporary playwrights.

Esslin famously saw the theatre of the absurd as a radical embodiment of the absurdity of existence. For him, absurdist plays voiced 'the attitude most genuinely representative of our own time', a time in which 'the certitudes and unshakeable basic assumptions of former ages have been swept away' by the war, having been 'tested and found wanting' (Esslin 1968, p. 23). However, when absurdist works were first allowed to be performed in the countries of the Eastern Bloc (incidentally also in the early 1960s when Esslin published his seminal study), they were mostly interpreted as allegories of life under the totalitarian regime. The views of the influential Czech director Jan Grossman may serve as an example of this. Grossman was affiliated with the Prague theatre Na zábradlí (On the Balustrade), which was then the local hub of absurdist theatre, with the young playwright Václav Havel serving as his assistant. Grossman's most powerful productions included Alfred Jarry's *Král Ubu* (King Ubu, 1964), Havel's *Vyrozumění* (The Memorandum, 1965), and an adaptation of *The Trial* by Franz Kafka (*Proces*, 1966). For Grossman, the theatre of the absurd focused 'on a single basic phenomenon: the uniformity, banality, forcing into line, and standardization' brought about by an excessively bureaucratized and dogmatically ideological political regime (Grossman 1999, p. 138; my translation). As such, the theatre of the absurd was to unravel the parochialism that lay at the heart of society, a 'state of mind' that was responsible for 'manipulating the world and exploiting, degrading and depreciating all values' (p. 138). Grossman continued:

The parochial mentality is truly embodied [in the theatre of the absurd]: its imaginings, dreams and interpretations seem to be rooted in a climatically favourable environment, where they proliferate as tropical vegetation out of all proportion. [...] Objects grow over into an unnatural dimension, as do the people, albeit in a different sense. Made by humans, things slip out of human control, cease serving people, and devour them instead. (p. 138)

Passages such as the preceding demonstrate Grossman's keen awareness of the grotesque aspects of absurdist works, which is also apparent in the vocabulary he used to comment on them. Contrary to many early reviewers of absurdist plays in Western Europe, who complained of the alleged nihilism and lack of engagement in this new strand of theatre, Grossman and his fellow practitioners behind the Iron Curtain conceived of the genre as profoundly political and socially critical. Grossman wrote that 'The theatre of the absurd is analytical and produces, if you wish, a cold diagnosis. As a matter of principle, it does not offer solutions. Nevertheless, I would argue that its adherence to such principles does not stem from a certainty that the solution does not exist, but rather from the conviction that the solution will never be *given* to us in any way by anybody anywhere' (p. 141).

Although certainly not viewing the genre as nihilistic, Martin Esslin perceived it as a radicalization of the angst of the existentialists (see Esslin 1968, pp. 23–5). Grossman, on the other hand, saw the roots of the theatre of the absurd in realism. He asserted that while absurdity was created by hyperbole, 'only that which has been first stated with precision may be hyperbolized' (Grossman 1999, pp. 138–9). Absurdism was to be regarded as a form of hyper-realism, epitomized by Franz Kafka standing alongside Alfred Jarry as an ur-father of the theatre of the absurd (p. 139). Consequently, Grossman's brilliant absurdist version of Jarry's Ubu did not assault the spectators, as the original production did, nor could it be seen as vituperation that went beyond social satire (see Remshardt 2004, p. 182). What it did instead was to point out an overwhelming social malaise by confronting the patient 'in the most drastic manner with his potentially imminent destruction. Not in order to bring this destruction about, but rather to prevent it from happening' (Grossman 1999, p. 141). As part of its political mission, the production emphasized that, in Remshardt's succinct phrase, in a grotesque world, human relations 'can be expressed only in the primitive metaphors of power and desire' (Remshardt 2004,

p. 250). A central device in Grossman's *Král Ubu*, as in his other absurdist productions, was the use of various gags. Appropriated from slapstick (and very much present in the early plays of Samuel Beckett), the technique was the subject of a philosophical essay written by Václav Havel only months before the opening of *Král Ubu*. Havel saw the gag as 'deliberate nonsensification' of a faulty reality, which was to result in liberatory laughter (Havel 1963, p. 8; my translation). He also asserted that 'A sense of absurdity, the ability to estrange, absurd humour—these are likely the ways in which the contemporary man achieves catharsis. This may possibly be the only method of "purification" that is adequate to the world we live in' (p. 8).

The fact that audiences in Czechoslovakia shared Grossman and Havel's perspective on the theatre of the absurd as a hyper-realistic depiction of the grim truth about their lives was evident in the general banning of the genre from the stage by the authorities (as were Grossman, Havel, and numerous other theatre practitioners) after the Warsaw Pact invasion of the country in 1968.[1] This example only further confirms the observation of recent commentators such as Geoffrey Harpham (Harpham 2006, pp. xxiv–vi) and Frances Connelly (Connelly 2012, pp. 13–14) that the grotesque must always be interpreted in the context of a given period. Moreover, it shows that the same grotesque features or tropes may be interpreted in very different ways within the same era, depending on the political and social circumstances. Finally, the diverse contemporaneous perspectives on the theatre of the absurd testify to the importance attached by theorists of the grotesque to the fact that its meaning is created only in the act of reception: while being a structural feature of works of art, the grotesque is primarily defined by the effect it has on its beholders (see Connelly 2012, p. 2).

III

Surveying recent Anglophone drama, it is the grotesque nature of the theatre of the absurd that has left perhaps the strongest and also the most variegated legacy. Consider, for instance, the use of language and monstrosity in Caryl Churchill's *The Skriker* (1994) on the one hand, or the radical scepticism concerning the expressive power of words voiced in Martin Crimp's *Attempts on Her Life* (1997) on the other, a play in which the self of the protagonist fails to be embodied in seventeen different narrative attempts. The distinct mark of absurdism is also evident in Edward Albee's exploration of the limits of tolerance in *The Goat, or Who Is Sylvia?*

(2002), which weaves a goat into the fabric of human relations, or, very differently still, in the entrapment of characters in grotesque routine in Enda Walsh's recent plays. A line may be traced from Pirandello's use of multiple levels of play through the metatheatricality of Beckett's drama to the grotesquerie of the play-within-the-play in the works of Enda Walsh again, and—although not at all in the same vein—Suzan-Lori Parks or Tim Crouch. The precedent of Jarry's puppet theatre with live actors is highly evident in the comedies of Martin McDonagh (see Pilný 2006b). However, the work of authors such as Philip Ridley or McDonagh is also indicative of the new, vivid forms of the grotesque that have emerged since the 1990s in plays that have shocked their audiences by their aggressive displays of physical and verbal violence. Following Aleks Sierz's pioneering book on British drama in the nineties, such works are customarily referred to as 'in-yer-face theatre', an umbrella term that is useful and at the same time reductive precisely in the same manner as Esslin's coinage, the theatre of the absurd. What is remarkable is that these excessively violent plays tend to foreground seminal issues of ethics, politics, or social justice. A preliminary scrutiny of this phenomenon is therefore apposite here.

A particular brand of cinema and drama that is best described as 'grotesque entertainment' appeared in the mid-1990s. Films such as Quentin Tarantino's *Reservoir Dogs* (1992) and *Pulp Fiction* (1994) or Danny Boyle's *Shallow Grave* (1994) not only achieved a cult status, but came to be enjoyed by mass audiences, inspiring a whole wave of epigones who have since been attempting to capitalize on the same formula. The emergence of these films coincided with the advent of the 'in-yer-face' wave in the theatre. The plays in this category fall within a broad scale in terms of the depth of the engagement with the issues vehemently flagged in them. This scale ranges from mere entertainment provided in plays such as Tracy Letts's *Killer Joe* (1993) or the extremely popular plays of Martin McDonagh set in rural Ireland, through the disorienting 'visceral spectacle' (Wallace 2006, p 189) presented by Sarah Kane, up to the use of the grotesque as a device of social and political critique as seen in works by Mark Ravenhill.

Grotesque entertainment involves the staging of graphic violence, offensive language, and ubiquitous black humour, including laughs at the expense of characters who might not be particularly intelligent. While rooted in realism, the structure of the works blends disparate genres and thematic elements (see Pilný 2006b). The violent aspect of the plays and films confirms Remshardt's observation that grotesque transgression, and crime in particular, is never arbitrary there but rather 'most acutely logical', and is simultaneously 'deeply horrifying' and 'farcically funny' (Remshardt 2004, pp. 230–1). Violence in these works is not devised merely to frighten: its ultimate aim is the exploitation of the seductive nature of the grotesque by inducing laughter, regardless of how repulsive the action is. Any pondering of morality, justice, or politics is secondary in grotesque entertainment to its combination of outrageous dramatic action and plot with the social and mental distancing of the characters.[2] One vivid example is Tracy Letts's *Killer Joe*. This dark comedy focuses on a family subsisting in a trailer home on the outskirts of Dallas, Texas. The characters are depicted as stereotypical 'white trash'. The play revolves around a plot devised to kill the mother and cash in on her life insurance policy; a corrupt policeman is hired to effect the murder and a twenty-year-old daughter is given to him as a 'retainer', whom he freely uses as a sex toy. The shock element is already introduced in the opening scene, which has a dishevelled woman walking around naked from the waist down; the play revels in the display of bloody violence, and features a scene of enforced fellatio involving a chicken leg.

Killer Joe was a hit in the UK: it won a Fringe First at the Edinburgh Festival in 1994, was subsequently produced at the London Bush Theatre in January 1995—the same month as Sarah Kane's momentous and upsetting first play *Blasted*—and finally transferred to the West End. The reviewers were somewhat insistent on interpreting *Killer Joe* as a moral play, arguably in particular contrast to *Blasted*, which was universally savaged as gratuitous (see Sierz 2000, p. 54). The reading of the play as a work of extreme realism that involves an element of social critique was supported by Tracy Letts's subsequent proclamations to the effect; he claimed that 'it's risky material but it's about what's happening here and now. It's scary but these people really exist. Domestic violence is a popular issue since O. J. Simpson put it on the agenda' (qtd in Sierz 2000, pp. 55–6). Notwithstanding the anachronism of Letts's assertion—O. J. Simpson's domestic violence first made headlines in June 1994 following the murder of his wife and her friend, which is almost a year after the US première of *Killer Joe*—it was Aleks Sierz who came to poignantly qualify the perception of the play:

> The popularity of *Killer Joe* had little to do with its morality and everything to do with its resemblance to a cult film. Like a movie, it offered the thrill of sex and violence; like a Jacobean drama, it excused the excess by thoroughly punishing the villain. Its morality acted as an alibi, licensing the audience's enjoyment. (Sierz 2000, p. 56)

This is a powerful description of how the conventional use of morality in the play vindicates the audience for giving way to the seduction of the grotesque without engaging their minds. Moreover, the marked difference between the audience members and the characters in social status, lifestyle, and in the case of the UK, also of location, allowed for a relatively unproblematic enjoyment of the play, including laughter at the dimness of the characters' wits. Clearly, *Killer Joe* does not really enter into any serious discussion of ethical or social questions, which is typical of grotesque entertainment.

While Martin McDonagh's series of five plays with an Irish setting spurned an extensive and very significant debate concerning the representation of Ireland on stage,[3] his work ultimately falls into the same category as *Killer Joe*. *The Lieutenant of Inishmore* may serve as an example. Premièred by the Royal Shakespeare Company at Stratford in 2001, the play focuses on a conflict that arises from the disappearance of a pet cat belonging to the terrorist Padraic, who even 'the IRA wouldn't let in because he was *too* mad' (McDonagh 2001, p. 7). Like McDonagh's earlier 'Leenane Trilogy' (1996–1997) and *The Cripple of Inishmaan* (1996), *The Lieutenant* is marked by a blatant appropriation of the rural Ireland postulated by the Irish Literary Revival, which it refigures in a brutally humorous sitcom-cum-gangster-movie vein. Characteristically for McDonagh both as a playwright and as a filmmaker, it builds on an intricate plot involving many an unexpected twist. Another typical feature of McDonagh is *The Lieutenant*'s clever use of a plethora of citations: as well as the overt gesturing towards J. M. Synge through its language and geographical location, the play appropriates motifs from, for instance, Quentin Tarantino's *Reservoir Dogs* (such as the torture scene involving a psychopath and his reflections on it) or *Bonnie and Clyde* (Padraic and Mairead as the romantic outlaws in Scene 8). The setting, the obtuse characters, and the farcical nature of their interaction also represent a continuation of McDonagh's earlier work.

The ostentatious engagement of the play with terrorism might indicate that *The Lieutenant of Inishmore* is intended to be political. Indeed, several theatres in the UK initially refused to stage it, afraid of a backlash against what they perceived as dangerous mockery of Irish Republican paramilitaries. Moreover, a number of productions of the play that followed in the wake of the 9/11 attacks were inevitably seen in the light of that event: McDonagh's play was said to alleviate the tension by depicting terrorists as ridiculous, simple-minded lunatics. Nevertheless, the involvement of *The Lieutenant* with politics is in fact no different to that of *Killer Joe* with pressing social issues: the play's likeness to a cult film, its embracement of basic justice (the main villains are killed) combined with the a priori alienation of the audience in terms of social status, location, and IQ cancel out any urge to take political issues seriously, and enable audiences to merely enjoy the grotesque spectacle. This is possible despite the author's declared intention to put the audience to test as to how much blood and violent sounds may be tolerated on the stage: McDonagh hailed *The Lieutenant* as having 'more gunshots and squibs going off on stage than any play you've ever seen' (qtd in O'Hagan 2001). True, the frequency of gun blasts will be trying (and possibly annoying) in any production; however, it is not that easy to achieve the level of gruesome realism that was presumably intended—in most productions, at least the dismembered corpses will be glaringly fake and thus also ludicrous, diminishing somewhat the horror that emanates from the grotesque and contributing to the ultimate perception of the play as an outrageous, but still inconsequential comedy.

The Pillowman (2003, National Theatre, London), McDonagh's first work on a non-Irish subject to have reached the stage, is a much more intricate play in terms of structure. It focuses on a writer in a fictitious totalitarian country who is being interrogated by the police because of the nature of his short stories; it soon turns out that the stories involve gruesome murders of small children and that someone has been using them as a model for real killings. A number of the writer Katurian's stories are enacted as part of the play, which serves largely as a device to introduce further twists in the play's spellbinding plot.

Despite the complexity of *The Pillowman*, McDonagh still merely expands the dramatic blueprint utilized in his "Irish" plays. What he adds is the foregrounding of the question of artistic responsibility and the value of art. All fundamental issues are entangled in a puzzling mélange, however: the initial motif of the persecution of artists is negated when it transpires that the problem with Katurian's writing is unrelated to politics. The ensuing murder enquiry seems to pose the grave question of whether an author who writes violent stories of slaughter is to blame when someone uses them as a set of instructions for an actual murder. This is followed by the presentation of Katurian as a writer who argues that literature is of more value than human life, including his own and his brother's. Katurian is eventually shot—only to be soon resurrected, in an uncanny moment that finally indicates that the whole story of Katurian's interrogation may have been sheer fiction from the outset. The moral, political, and artistic dilemmas introduced earlier are thus unravelled and found to be essentially irrelevant.

In effect, *The Pillowman* is dominated by an unscrupulous manipulation of the characters as puppets. First, Katurian is introduced as a passive victim, but already in Act I Scene 2 he is pulling the strings of the other characters (a fact that is comically stressed by the child's corpse sitting 'bolt upright in bed' in the re-enacted story; McDonagh 2003, p. 34). A similar situation occurs in Act II Scene 2 (the drastic re-enactment of 'The Little Jesus'), and ultimately at the very end of the play, which, in a feat of unabashed authorial ventriloquism, unveils Katurian the puppeteer as merely a puppet himself, as his corpse with a 'bloody, bullet-shattered head' stands up and delivers the dénouement (p. 102). The finale reveals the central role of the manipulative creator of the play, who uses his puppets to shunt the audience to and fro in a way that is similar to his treatment of the play's characters.

I have already noted Wolfgang Kayser's observation that the reduction of characters to puppets became a principal feature of grotesque drama from the very onset of Romanticism and that, in the Romantic grotesque, the world was frequently presented as a puppet play in which the puppets are operated by an uncanny, incomprehensible force that has replaced God (Kayser 1966, pp. 41–4, 91–2). We have also seen how the Italian *teatro del grottesco* developed the topos of the world as a puppet play through its use of metatheatricality, causing profound disorientation of the audience due to the multiple levels of illusion and play-within-the-play and exuding existential despair over who the puppet master actually is (Kayser 1966, pp. 135–9). Martin McDonagh's *The Pillowman* may therefore be viewed as the development of an established brand of the grotesque. Nevertheless, existential angst over the incomprehensible forces that govern our estranged world is far from being an issue in McDonagh's work: characters and audiences are being manipulated for the sole purpose of entertainment, one which is frightening and hilarious at the same time. Humour is an essential ingredient, and ranks high among the reasons why McDonagh has been so attractive to audiences worldwide. The laughter that McDonagh's plays and films induce is very similar to that triggered by *Killer Joe*, or indeed the 1990s films by Tarantino or Danny Boyle, however. It is that 'inappropriate' laughter associated with the grotesque, as described by Remshardt (pp. 81, 85): it functions as an antidote to the horror, but those who are laughing are aware that they should not be doing so.

Sarah Kane's *Blasted*, first performed at the Royal Court Theatre Upstairs in 1995, came to be regarded as 'the most notorious play of the decade' in the UK (Sierz 2000, p. 93). Set in a hotel room in Leeds, it features three characters: Ian, a journalist in his forties, his ex-lover Cate, who is in her early twenties, and an unnamed soldier. Ian is abusive, racist, homophobic, rampantly nationalist, and self-destructive; he is also dying of cancer. Cate seems at least initially vulnerable and not very bright. Ian tries to force Cate into having sex with him and eventually rapes her. After she has left, the soldier enters and tells Ian gruesome details of killing and war; then he rapes him, sucks his eyes out, and shoots himself. Cate re-enters with an abandoned baby, which soon dies. Cate buries it under the floorboards and departs. The blinded Ian is left to scavenge for food. The audience watch him masturbate, try to strangle himself, defecate, ultimately eat the dead baby, climb into its grave, and die. In the final scene, Cate is bleeding from her womb and is seen to feed a revived Ian bread, sausage, and gin; the final words of the play are his 'Thank you' for her act of charity (Kane 2001, p. 61).

The exhibition of extreme violence in *Blasted* notoriously sickened the early reviewers, most of whom almost hysterically panned the play. A more considered reaction ensued only after Edward Bond and Harold Pinter expressed their support for Kane (Sierz 2000, pp. 94–8). The general consensus amongst critics now is that the exceptionally negative initial comments were prompted not merely by the aggressive presentation of physicality and violence, but also by its combination with Kane's attack on traditional dramatic form, causing the play to be seen as gratuitous, rather than uncompromisingly experimental. The violence may be unflinchingly realistic; however, as Clare Wallace aptly summarized, 'while the play is "about" manipulation, violation and war, it simultaneously deals with an interior terrain, which is structured by the logic of dream and association' (Wallace 2006, p. 211). *Blasted* is at heart anti-mimetic, consisting of a free association of images, and as such has its roots in expressionism rather than naturalism; indeed, most directors tend to stage its second half as a dream sequence or a nightmare (Wallace 2006, pp. 191, 211). The combination of excessive physicality and monstrous violence on the one hand and expressionist technique on the other also typifies its brand of the grotesque.[4]

Blasted patently presents a world Kayser refers to as shattered, alienated, radically disorienting, and ultimately terrifying (Kayser 1966, pp. 37, 184–5). Its engagement with ethics and politics is evident, but the nature of this engagement is profoundly complicated. The stormy initial reception of the play inevitably triggered a debate about its 'morality' or 'amorality'. Of course, Kane's detractors regarded exposing the audience to such shocking scenes as amoral. Conversely, there is no doubt that the play foregrounds an examination of the relationship between private interpersonal violence and war atrocity, and the soldier's narration of the latter is based on footage of the war in Bosnia, which was constantly being shown on television screens at the time and with which most of the British public failed to engage in any way (see Sierz 2000, pp. 100, 104). As Kane herself argued, 'My play is only a shadowy representation of a reality that's far harder to stomach' (qtd in Sierz 2000, p. 106). So far, the most plausible view on the matter of morality has been offered by Ken Urban, who proposes interpreting Kane's work as a 'quest for ethics' (Urban 2001, p. 37). As regards *Blasted*, he argues that the play shows 'the possibility that an ethics can exist between wounded bodies, that after devastation, good becomes possible' (p. 37). Still, this seems a rather optimistic interpretation of the play's final scene, particularly as Ian is already dead.

A play that may be seen to occupy the opposite end of the scale to grotesque entertainment in terms of engagement with ethics and politics is *Shopping and Fucking* by Mark Ravenhill (1996). Together with Kane's *Blasted*, Ravenhill's first major play became truly iconic of 'in-yer-face theatre'. Described by Aleks Sierz as a 'controversial shockfest' (Sierz 2000, p. 122), the play also abounds in vulgarity and violence and openly displays drug use, gay sex, and rape. It focuses on young middle-class Londoners who instead of enjoying a good life at the heart of a prosperous society find themselves stuck with absolutely no sense of direction. As Sierz put it, everything around is fundamentally corrupt and with that knowledge, 'there is little to relieve the pain and the tedium except shopping and fucking' (Sierz 2000, p. 132). Consequently, even relations among the closest of friends and lovers are perceived as commercial transactions: you don't fall in love, you shop for a lover. The world that is realistically depicted to the audience indeed 'is—and is not—our own world', to return to Kayser (p. 37), and its alienation is frightening. A seminal grotesque element in the play consists in the scope of its citationality, which ranges from the Bible, *Romeo and Juliet* and *The Three Sisters* to, famously, the Disney cartoon *The Lion King*, while the names of three of the principal characters—Robbie, Mark, and Gary—are those of the members of the teen pop group Take That (see Rebellato 2001, pp. x, xix).

What is more than obvious is the play's emphasis on the exposed body, a feature it shares not only with *Blasted* and other works classified as 'in-yer-face', but importantly also with the Bakhtinian grotesque. Bakhtin argues that in Rabelais,

The stress is laid on those parts of the body that are open to the outside world, that is, the parts through which the world enters the body or emerges from it, or through which the body itself goes out to meet the world. This means that the emphasis is on the apertures or the convexities, or on various ramifications and offshoots: the open mouth, the genital organs, the breasts, the phallus, the potbelly, the nose. The body discloses its essence as a principle of growth which exceeds its limits only in copulation, pregnancy, childbirth, the throes of death, eating, drinking, or defecation. (p. 26)

In *Shopping and Fucking*, the physical or narrated presence of orifices, including the rectum and the vagina, is truly in excess, as is that of various protuberances, including naked breasts and particularly the penis. Moreover, bodily fluids and excretions of all kinds abound, starting with vomit and continuing with blood, urine and, yes, tears. However, Ravenhill parades the body in what is very close to a vision of purgatory or hell: his is not the bawdy Rabelaisian carnival discussed by Bakhtin but a dystopian version of it, involving group rape and injurious sexual practices and—like Kane's early work—designed to be shoved in the audience's face (Ravenhill wrote the play for 'a close-up audience of 65 people'; qtd in Sierz 2000, p. 127). While the play undeniably features humorous scenes, very few spectators will be laughing at the bodily aspects. Bakhtin's carnival transforms 'All that was frightening in ordinary life [...] into amusing or ludicrous monstrosities' (Bakhtin 1984, p. 47). In Ravenhill's version, the emphasis is on the violation of the body, as in Kane's, which is even more extreme. Kane's inferno is indeed comparable to the hell depicted by Hieronymus Bosch, and perhaps more ghastly since its terrors are the work of humans only. Unlike Kane's profoundly ambiguous merging of exterior and interior landscapes, however, Ravenhill's dystopia points out its origin in free-market capitalism. As the author eventually confirmed, the play was written as an implicit critique of Margaret Thatcher's dictum that 'There is no such thing as society.' In his view, if Thatcher were right, the world of this play would be what we would be left with (Sierz 2000, p. 132).

What the individual characters tend to veer towards in their despair and radical alienation is the telling of stories. The purpose of these is most traditional: to help their narrators and/or recipients find their bearings. In Aleks Sierz's words, 'the evident longing of [the] characters [...] for narratives that make sense of the world, links the play with an older tradition of committed drama' (Sierz 2000, p. 133). The powerful presentation of the alienation caused by the dominance of commerce together with its victims' yearning for guidance thus disclose the grotesque in *Shopping and*

Fucking as a device of political critique. However, Ravenhill's cheerless development of the carnal elements of the carnival indicates that achieving the desired social renewal is virtually impossible. Similarly to Sarah Kane's *Blasted*, the depth of the crisis is apparent in the ambivalence of the play's closing scene: Mark, Robbie, and Lulu may be able to share their meal for the first time, but what they are eating is still ready-made junk food purchased in a chain store.

IV

This book aims to examine how the grotesque may be seen to solicit engagement with vital present-day issues, and seeks to place the effects of contemporary forms of the grotesque on the broad scale between Kayserian despair and Bakhtinian liberation. Its discussion of English-language dramas from the past three decades excludes works that ultimately yield mere entertainment, such as the plays of Martin McDonagh. There is certainly nothing wrong with theatre providing only a good night out[5] but examining the effects of these works would not be relevant to the present context.

Grotesque elements have been a staple feature of hilarious contemporary satire that has forged a theatrical analogy to television series such as *Yes Minister* and many others: Steve Thompson's comedy from the British parliament entitled *Whipping It Up* (2006), Tim Loane's uproariously dark treatment of Northern Ireland's politics in *Caught Red Handed* (2002) and *To Be Sure* (2007), or David Mamet's Oval Office farce *November* (2008), to give only a few remarkable examples. This brand of overtly political drama is also omitted, since its discussion would lead to rather self-evident conclusions, given that it mostly harnesses the grotesque to a straightforward message.

The following chapters are dedicated primarily to authors whose challenging work has in my view not received sufficient critical attention to date. This necessitated the exclusion of a number of celebrated playwrights who would definitely be eligible for a study of the contemporary grotesque. These include Sarah Kane and Mark Ravenhill, whose work has been appropriately addressed in almost every book about British drama in the nineties, as well as older playwrights such as Martin Crimp, the subject of two outstanding recent monographs: *The Theatre of Martin Crimp* (2006) by Aleks Sierz and *The Plays of Martin Crimp: Making Theatre Strange* (2012) by Vicky Angelaki. There is also no detailed discussion here of Caryl Churchill, the relentless experimentalist and pivotal figure in British political drama, or the master of the grotesque in American theatre, Sam Shepard, both of whose oeuvre has been treated in a number of book-length studies and has had a separate Cambridge Companion volume dedicated to it.

The present monograph focuses on five playwrights who came to prominence in the 1990s or the 2000s and have already created a significant and original body of work: Philip Ridley, Mark O'Rowe, Enda Walsh, Suzan-Lori Parks, and Tim Crouch. The selection of these particular authors is the result of extended preliminary research in drama that has been referred to as grotesque and that engages with matters of ethics, politics, and social justice. The principal criterion in narrowing the focus to the five dramatists—apart from the relative scarcity of critical analysis— was to choose material that employs the grotesque in a variety of different ways, with the intention of examining a range of works by the same author, tracing the apparent continuities, developments, and resonances. Rather than merely offering a discrete argument pertaining to each of the selected dramatists, however, the analysis also features a comparative dimension that juxtaposes the different practice of the individual authors, particularly in terms of attitude to and impact on audiences.

The sequencing of the chapters is chronological and thematic at the same time, with some degree of temporal overlap that is due to the authors being contemporaries. The thematic ordering proceeds from plays in which the grotesque is associated with the presentation of violence to the use of the grotesque in a re-examination and re-writing of history and the employment of the grotesque in radical work with dramatic form.

The book opens with an extended discussion of Philip Ridley, who has continued to shock his audiences ever since his first major play, *The Pitchfork Disney*, opened in London in 1991. Widely praised for his lush imagination but also angrily dismissed because of his confrontational use of extreme violence in dramas such as *Mercury Fur* (2005), Ridley tends to throw spectators into the abyss of an uncontrollable grotesque, towards discoveries concerning the unsavoury elements of the world they inhabit. Ridley's work involves an unfaltering examination of morality and politics, and as a rule leaves the audience facing painful ethical quandaries that have been interpreted both as nihilistic and as emancipatory in their nature.

The following chapter is dedicated to Mark O'Rowe, who has gradually moved away from the grotesque entertainment of the gangland comedies he began writing in the mid-1990s to a peculiar resuscitation of neo-Jacobeanism in three remarkable monologue dramas: *Howie the Rookie*

(1999), *Crestfall* (2003; revised 2011), and *Terminus* (2007). The narratives of these plays combine harrowing content with highly aestheticized language, and involve supernatural and mythical elements. O'Rowe's riveting use of monologue often gestures towards the association of the grotesque with the sublime, a link that has been important for the perception of the grotesque since the late eighteenth century. On the other hand, O'Rowe capitalizes on human fascination with horror and the lurid to the extent that he has been repeatedly accused of glorifying violence.

The dramatic oeuvre of Enda Walsh is discussed next, as a prime example of blending the farcical with the tragic. The pivotal role of the grotesque is manifest not only in the nature of the stories that are told in plays such as *The New Electric Ballroom* (2004), *The Walworth Farce* (2006), and *Penelope* (2010), but also in Walsh's distinctive use of citationality, the interweaving of several levels of dramatic action, pathological interaction between characters confined in limited spaces, and the dark yet at the same time explosive humour present in his work. Walsh's latest original drama, *Ballyturk* (2014), demonstrates the playwright's increasingly pronounced association of the grotesque with mortality and death. The apparent bleakness of the juxtaposition is examined in the context of Walsh's emphasis on slapstick gags which have come to prominence in his drama of inevitability.

The use of the grotesque in Suzan-Lori Parks's powerful dramas testifies to Frances Connelly's assertion that it may function as an efficient strategy for those oppressed by rigid social boundaries or conceptualized as monstrous or abject by these (Connelly 2012, pp. 18, 144). Parks's principal concern as a dramatist has been with African-American experience and its erasure from US history. My discussion of her work centres on the pseudo-historical tragedy *Venus* (1996), which revolves around the perception of the black female body as grotesque, and on the multifaceted Lincoln–Booth dramas, *The America Play* (1994) and *Topdog/Underdog* (2001), in which grotesque re-enactments of the assassination of President Lincoln serve to highlight the significance of the present over any mechanically reproduced narratives of the collective past. The closing section of the chapter examines the first instalment of Parks's epic cycle of plays, *Father Comes Home from the Wars (Parts 1, 2 & 3)* (2014) in which a grotesque treatment of *The Odyssey* serves to engage with the journey of African Americans from slavery to emancipation.

The last chapter focuses on Tim Crouch, one of the most gifted and most challenging authors to have emerged in the early twenty-first century. Crouch has embarked on a vigorous search for a new kind of estrangement in theatre, stripping theatre to its fundamentals and articulating a categorical refusal of mimetic representation in favour of an active employment of the spectator's imagination. Crouch's radical use of the grotesque is already apparent in his first play, *My Arm* (2003), in which the bizarre story of a boy who raises his arm and refuses to put it down is performed with random objects in the role of characters. Scrutinizing the relevance of art in the face of trauma and death, Crouch uses an unrehearsed actor to perform the role of a grieving father in *An Oak Tree* (2005), guiding him or her through the play like a caring puppet master. Crouch's most controversial play, *The Author* (2009), turns the tables on the audience by abolishing the stage space and blurring the boundaries between performers, characters, and spectators in a disturbing examination of responsibility pertaining to the consumption of images of violence. The latest play to date, *Adler & Gibb* (2014), continues the playwright's critique of the commodification of art and the fetishization of the artist voiced in his earlier work; this 'dematerialised' drama (see Crouch 2014) that requires rich visual and physical components in order to take place confirms the centrality of paradox to Crouch's practice. Crouch's grotesque dismantling of the conventions of theatre is performed in order to solicit true audience engagement in the sense outlined by Jacques Rancière. However, Crouch poses the question about the transformative potential of theatre—and art in general—in a much more forceful and wholehearted manner.

The book closes with an afterword about the audience. As outlined earlier, the impact of the grotesque is closely tied to the act of reception (see also Kayser 1966, pp. 180–1). The manner in which meaning is created in theatre is notoriously complex, and given that the playwrights discussed in this book have universally emphasized the role of the individual in imaginatively interpreting the gaps opened up by the grotesque, the work of semioticians on how meaning is created in theatre must be complemented at least by a brief summary of the current state of research into individuals' response to theatrical performance.

A final disclaimer is required here concerning the origin of the selected dramatists. The fact that I have chosen to examine two English, two Irish, and one American playwright is not intended to indicate that the grotesque is somehow more at home in a particular tradition than in another. To assert that the grotesque is typical of a national culture (be it within a limited period) always runs the grave risk of national stereotyping; besides, it is never possible to provide unambiguous evidence. This is not to contradict the assertion made earlier that the grotesque is always interpreted within a specific historical, political, and cultural context. The relevant contexts are delineated in the following discussion of individual works as closely as possible; it will be apparent that the interpretative frameworks for contemporary theatre are as frequently national as they are global.

Notes

1. For further details on Grossman's productions and views, see Pilný (2012).
2. This definition of 'grotesque entertainment' has recently been elaborated upon by Greg Thorson in his study of McDonagh and Letts. Somewhat inconsistently, Thorson concludes that 'The "new grotesque" of McDonagh and Letts serves as a metaphor for contemporary life' and a vehicle of representing contemporary society (Thorson 2009, pp. 68–9).
3. The seminal essay collection edited by Lilian Chambers and Eamonn Jordan (Chambers and Jordan 2006) provides an indispensable overview of the debate. See also Pilný (2006a), where I have argued that McDonagh's "Irish" plays may be viewed to satirize the predominant discourse of Irish drama criticism, a matter that is only of peripheral interest in the context of the present study.
4. Kane's two subsequent plays intensify the use of stunning grotesque motifs as part of the author's effort to dismantle naturalism: *Phaedra's Love* (1996) features flying genitals and vultures, and in *Cleansed* (1998) the stage is invaded by rats and is supposed to have a sunflower grow out of the ground. Both plays thus present unsurmountable obstacles to any director who might wish to stage them in a naturalist fashion.
5. As a matter of fact, the present author chose to translate Martin McDonagh with considerable delight.

Works Cited

Bakhtin, M. (1984). *Rabelais and His World* (1965) (Hélène Iswolsky, Trans.). Bloomington: Indiana University Press.
Brotchie, A. (2011). *Alfred Jarry: A Pataphysical Life*. Cambridge, MA: The MIT Press.
Chambers, L., & Jordan, E. (Eds.). (2006). *The Theatre of Martin McDonagh: A World of Savage Stories*. Dublin: Carysfort Press.
Connelly, F. S. (Ed.). (2003). *Modern Art and the Grotesque*. Cambridge: Cambridge University Press.
Connelly, F. S. (2012). *The Grotesque in Western Art and Culture: The Image at Play*. Cambridge: Cambridge University Press.

Crouch, T. (2014, May 5). Interview. *Aesthetica*. Retrieved September 25, 2015, from http://www.aestheticamagazine.com/interview-with-tim-crouch-writer-and-director-of-royal-courts-adler-and-gibb/
Edwards, J. D., & Graulund, R. (2013). *Grotesque*. London: Routledge.
Esslin, M. (1968). *The Theatre of the Absurd* (1961) (Rev. ed.). Harmondsworth: Penguin.
Grossman, J. (1999). Uvedení *Zahradní slavnosti* [Opening of *The Garden Party* by Václav Havel] (1964). Reprinted in M. Klíma, J. Dvořák, & Z. Jindrová (Eds.), Jan Grossman, *Texty o divadle—první část* [Texts on the Theatre, Vol. 1]. Prague: Pražská scéna.
Harpham, G. G. (2006). *On the Grotesque. Strategies of Contradiction in Art and Literature* (2nd ed.). Aurora, CO: Davies Group.
Havel, V. (1963). Anatomie gagu [The Anatomy of the Gag]. *The Václav Havel Library Online Archive*. Retrieved November 7, 2012, from http://archive.vaclavhavel-library.org/Functions/show_html.php?id=156819
Kane, S. (2001). *Complete Plays*. London: Methuen.
Kayser, W. (1966). *The Grotesque in Art and Literature* (1957) (Ulrich Weisstein, Trans.). New York: McGraw-Hill.
McDonagh, M. (2001). *The Lieutenant of Inishmore*. London: Methuen.
McDonagh, M. (2003). *The Pillowman*. London: Faber and Faber.
O'Hagan, S. (2001, March 24). The Wild West. *Guardian*. Retrieved June 15, 2003, from http://www.theguardian.com/lifeandstyle/2001/mar/24/weekend.seanohagan
Pilný, O. (2006a). Disconcert and Destabilise the Prisoner: Martin McDonagh. In O. Pilný, *Irony and Identity in Modern Irish Drama* (pp. 154–169). Praha: Litteraria Pragensia.
Pilný, O. (2006b). Grotesque Entertainment: *The Pillowman* as Puppet Theatre. In L. Chambers & E. Jordan (Eds.), *The Theatre of Martin McDonagh: A World of Savage Stories* (pp. 214–223). Dublin: Carysfort Press.
Pilný, O. (2012). Jan Grossman, Prague Structuralism, and the Grotesque. In M. Procházka & O. Pilný (Eds.), *Prague English Studies and the Transformation of Philologies* (pp. 184–197). Prague: Karolinum Press.
Pirandello, L. (2000). *Six Characters in Search of an Author* (1921) (John Linstrum, Trans.). In W. B. Worthen (Ed.), *The Harcourt Brace Anthology of Drama*, (3rd ed., pp. 703–723). Fort Worth, TX: Harcourt Brace.
Rancière, J. (2011). *The Emancipated Spectator* (2008) (Gregory Elliott, Trans.). London and New York: Verso.
Rebellato, D. (2001). Introduction. In M. Ravenhill, *Plays: 1* (pp. ix–xx). London: Methuen.
Remshardt, R. E. (2004). *Staging the Savage God: The Grotesque in Performance*. Carbondale: Southern Illinois University Press.

Ruskin, J. (1903). *Modern Painters, Vol. III* (1856). In E. T. Cook & A. Wedderburn (Eds.), *The Works of John Ruskin, Vol. 5* (pp. 1–439). London: George Allen.

Sierz, A. (2000). *In-Yer-Face Theatre: British Drama Today*. London: Faber and Faber.

Thorson, G. (2009). *The New Grotesque: The Theatre of Martin McDonagh and Tracy Letts*. Saarbrücken: VDM Verlag Dr. Müller.

Urban, K. (2001). An Ethics of Catastrophe: The Theatre of Sarah Kane. *Performing Arts Journal, 23* (3), 36–46.

Wallace, C. (2006). *Suspect Cultures: Narrative, Identity and Citation in 1990s New Drama*. Prague: Litteraria Pragensia.

CHAPTER 2

Engaging Monsters: Philip Ridley

I

The Pitchfork Disney, Philip Ridley's first full-length play, premièred at the Bush Theatre in London in 1991, directed by Matthew Lloyd. It tells the story of Presley and Haley Stray, twins in their late twenties whose lives seem to have frozen in their teens when their parents disappeared. They live bolted up in their flat in deliberate seclusion, feeding on chocolate, medicine, and fantasies in which they cast themselves as survivors of a nuclear apocalypse who must keep the dangers of the outside world constantly at bay. Their stalled existence is disrupted when Presley invites in Cosmo Disney, a glamorous eighteen-year-old wearing a bright red sequin jacket. Cosmo makes his living as a performer eating cockroaches and other vermin; his first act on stage is to vomit ('Have to get it out of my system', he comments. Ridley 2012, p. 32). Considerable sexual tension develops, since while Presley is clearly attracted to Cosmo, the latter finds himself drawn to his twin sister. With the conflict of desire approaching its climax, Cosmo's menacing companion Pitchfork Cavalier enters: he is very tall, has an awkward gait and apart from the same glitzy jacket, he also wears a black leather bondage mask. He appears to be mute, castrated, and evinces superhuman strength. When Presley and Pitchfork are sent off to buy more chocolate, Cosmo lets the sleeping Haley suck his finger and reaches orgasm. At this point, Presley returns and, enraged, breaks

© The Editor(s) (if applicable) and The Author(s) 2016
O. Pilný, *The Grotesque in Contemporary Anglophone Drama*,
DOI 10.1057/978-1-137-51318-2_2

Cosmo's finger, symbolically depriving him of his manhood. At the end of the play, the siblings are left alone in the flat again, embracing and telling each other that they are scared.

Reviewers were confused by *The Pitchfork Disney* and were appalled by the nightmarish violence of the stories narrated by the Strays; lacking a frame of reference for Ridley's grotesque spectacle, they almost universally rejected it (see Ridley and Sierz 2009, p. 111). However, the play brought to the theatre large audiences of mostly young people: theatre scholar Dan Rebellato remembers seeing the play fresh out of university and regarding it as 'a ferociously funny and unsettling vision of a 1990s culture shot through with uncertainty, absence and loss' (Rebellato 2011, p. 428). By the 2010s, Ridley has become established as an influential playwright and pioneer of in-yer-face theatre (Sierz 2012, pp. 90, 111), and the gradual acceptance of the in-yer-face style has resulted in the revivals of his early work playing to critical acclaim both in the UK and internationally. Scholarly attention has remained sparse nonetheless, amounting to less than a dozen articles and book chapters to date. Moreover, almost every new play has met with further controversy; in the words of Aleks Sierz, 'Ridley continues to divide opinion: depending on your point of view, he's either Britain's sickest playwright or a singular, prolific, and amazingly visionary genius' (Ridley and Sierz 2009, p. 109).

Apart from being a dramatist, Ridley is a successful visual artist who studied painting at St Martin's School of Art in London; as both Sierz and Rebellato have argued, the outrageous and provocative imagery in his plays comes across as less outlandish when viewed in the context of the contemporaneous arts scene in which his talent matured and which included the likes of Damien Hirst and other members of the 'Brit pack' (Sierz 2000, pp. 42–3; Rebellato 2011, p. 426). Another interpretive context in which Ridley's imagery appears more natural is that of surrealist cinema: as Rebellato has pointed out, his drama shows an influence of radical film makers such as Luis Buñuel and Jan Švankmajer (Rebellato 2011, p. 426). Yet to dismiss Ridley's work as that of a visual artist turned amateur writer (a treatment of which he has complained—see Ridley and Sierz 2009, p. 111) would be factually incorrect at best, since his writing career has developed parallel to his painting and photography: prior to the first production of *The Pitchfork Disney*, he had written and performed several of his monologues, written three radio plays, published a novel and a collection of short stories, scripted and directed a short film entitled *The Universe of Dermot Finn* and the award-winning horror feature

The Reflecting Skin (starring Viggo Mortensen), and authored the script for the acclaimed 1990 film about the larger-than-life East End gangsters, *The Krays*. A significant part of Ridley's output has been dedicated to children: to date, he has written ten children's novels as well as two children's plays, and six dramas for young audiences.

Ridley's stage work for adults has been characterized by an unrestrained blending of the incongruous: popular culture from the late 1950s/early 1960s, various brands of comic books, classical literary texts, everything from Greek tragedy to motifs and techniques that echo playwrights as profoundly different as Tennessee Williams and Harold Pinter. The disparity of these elements has been typically underlined by the stark contrast between the dilapidated settings of his plays and the extravagant costumes and heightened language of many of his characters. The stories the characters tell give further evidence of how lush Ridley's imagination is: they paint mesmeric, starkly coloured pictures of lyrical beauty, while often describing scenes of brutality and apocalypse. As a rule, Ridley's plays have a strong propensity to simultaneously trigger laughter and disgust. All of this makes Philip Ridley an obvious candidate for a discussion of the grotesque in contemporary drama. Indeed, the term 'grotesque' has been making a regular appearance in reviews of Ridley's work; however, it was only in 2011 (that is, twenty years after *The Pitchfork Disney*) that Dan Rebellato first suggested a serious exploration of Ridley's plays through the prism of the aesthetic of the grotesque. Given that his essay was commissioned as an entry for a theatre handbook, there was little space for Rebellato to go beyond an interpretation of Ridley as depicting an estranged world that has a deeply unsettling effect on the spectator, in line with Wolfgang Kayser's seminal discussion of the concept (Rebellato 2011, p. 432).

This chapter will provide a more detailed consideration of the grotesque in six of Ridley's plays for an adult audience, produced from the early 1990s up to the late 2000s: *The Pitchfork Disney*, *The Fastest Clock in the Universe* (1992), *Ghost from a Perfect Place* (1994), *Mercury Fur* (2005), *Leaves of Glass* (2007), and *Piranha Heights* (2008). My selection is determined not so much by a focus on a clearly defined period but rather by the fact that Ridley as a playwright has frequently changed style (see Rebellato 2011, pp. 427, 437): although virtually all his dramas feature realistic settings and have their generic base in naturalism, his subject matter has determined that a number of his plays after 1999 tend to follow the conventions of naturalism and/or standard psychological drama more closely, while grotesque elements become marginal or are absent altogether. Such is the case of *Vincent River* (2000) or *Dark Vanilla Jungle* (2013), a two-hander and a monologue drama, respectively, dealing with trauma; *Tender Napalm* (2011), a two-hander that examines the deepest layers of a long-term relationship; or the very different multiple-character play *Shivered* (2012) in which Ridley presents a bleak panorama of the effects of global capitalism and war on a family.

The aggressive nature of Ridley's grotesque has led to periodical allegations of gratuitous excess, and the playwright was repeatedly accused of ending his plays on a note that Michael Billington has called 'fashionable nihilism' (Billington 2005). In contrast, the few scholars studying Ridley's drama to date have all viewed his vision as fundamentally moral. Their observations are in line with Ridley's own idea of the theatre as transformative and redemptive in its effect. In his view, theatre is a ritualized activity in which the playwright acts as a 'witch doctor', whose job it is 'to tell a story to make [the audience] less afraid, or at least feel that they can deal with the monsters. [...] The story aims to make sense of fear'. Good theatre is always moral in this perspective, regardless of how immoral the particulars of its subject matter may be (Ridley and Sierz 2009, pp. 112, 114). Since my interest in the present volume is to explore the relationship of various forms of the grotesque to ethics and politics, close attention will be paid both to Ridley's assertions and to the way in which interpreters such as Ken Urban, Aleks Sierz, and others have made their case.

II

The typical setting of Philip Ridley's plays is a home or a habitation in the East End of London that features furnishings and/or memorabilia of the past: of the works discussed here, *The Pitchfork Disney*, *Leaves of Glass*, and *Piranha Heights* are set in East End flats, and the action in *The Fastest Clock in the Universe* unravels in a room above a disused factory. Sometimes, the place has suffered considerable damage, as with the flat in *Ghost from a Perfect Place*, which has partially burnt down, or in *Mercury Fur* where the flat is completely dilapidated and eventually set on fire. These spaces correspond to Ridley's subject matter, and the decrepit nature or final destruction of many of them indicates 'a profound vision of social calamity' (Rebellato 2011, p. 429).

The very specific location of Ridley's work in what has traditionally been a fairly rough part of London, associated with poverty and criminality at least since the 1880s, might indicate that Ridley is intent on relating his work to the life of the underprivileged by way of social commentary. Indeed, Ken Urban has made a detailed and persuasive argument concerning Ridley's first three plays and how they reflect the social and political issues of the day in Britain. In Urban's view, Ridley's characters are sick with nostalgia, which makes them dismiss the present, abdicate on the future, and live their lives in stories of a mythologized past. 'The recurrence of nostalgia in Ridley's plays', Urban argues, 'reflects larger, ongoing debates about nostalgia in British culture, from Thatcher's call for a return to Victorian values to the rise of Tony Blair's New Labour party and its championing of Cool Britannia, which looked back to the 1960s Swinging London as its model' (Urban 2007, p. 326).

The Tory attitude to immigration, notoriously embodied in Thatcher's 1978 television interview in which she referred to immigration as 'swamping' England, is thus reflected in *The Pitchfork Disney* by Haley Stray's hysterical dread of foreigners: 'They're dangerous, Presley. Dangerous and different. They beat up women and abuse children. They don't do things the way we do. They hate us. They'd kill us all if they had the chance' (Urban 2007, p. 336; Ridley 2012, p. 27). A similar point may be made about Cosmo Disney's rampant homophobia and its origins in diehard conservatism: 'They should all be gassed. Homosexuals. All of them. Or herded into one place. Like a big stadium. Have a bomb dropped on them' (Ridley 2012, p. 51). Sherbet Gravel's love of 'traditional things' in *The Fastest Clock in the Universe* in turn parodies 'the neo-Victorian nostalgia of Tory propaganda: the centrality of family, the importance of proper signifiers for the holidays (the turkey, the chimes, the singing of carols), and the love of the past as it never was' (Urban 2007, p. 333).

Moving on to the New Labour era in the UK, Urban has shown how quick Ridley was in critiquing *its* particular brand of nostalgia at what was only its onset in 1994. Much of the 'coolness' of Blair's Britain of the 1990s, with its ostentatious foregrounding of popular culture and music, was based on a nostalgic recreation of the Swinging Sixties, a myth that is savagely dismantled in *Ghost from a Perfect Place*: following on from his film script for *The Krays*, in this play, Ridley pulls apart the image of the noble gangster of the East End, and shows it as a place still shaped by a legacy of violence, organized crime, and deprivation (Urban 2007, pp. 337–40). All three plays thus ultimately reveal that what is underlying these forms of cultural and social nostalgia is violence (Urban 2007, p. 336).

However, Urban also duly notes that Ridley's plays never comment on this—or any other—political context directly (p. 336). Local references to London are sparse, and even *Ghost from a Perfect Place*, which may be said to be based in a particular urban mythology, 'wear[s its] East End references lightly' (Rebellato 2011, p. 426). The stories told by individual characters in the plays are often reminiscent of fairy tales (Rebellato 2011, p. 428), placeless gothic stories, plots of horror films, or scenes from science fiction. The names of the characters function as a further distancing device from social realism: in *The Pitchfork Disney*, they gesture towards a globalized blend of popular culture (1950s and 1960s American rock 'n' roll, Disney cartoons, Marvel and DC comics, and *Cosmopolitan* magazine), while as Urban has pointed out, the surname of the siblings has a symbolic ring to it: the Strays are 'perpetually lost children' (p. 326). In *The Fastest Clock in the Universe*, the names of Cougar Glass, Captain Tock, Foxtrot Darling, Sherbet Gravel, and Cheetah Bee all bear resemblance to nicknames originating within a closely knit group of people, such as teenagers or criminals (or indeed characters in a comic book), but some of the surnames also carry a tinge of symbolism: the heartless and cruel Cougar is called Glass, Sherbet's surname reflects her worldly nature, and the Captain's name echoes the tick-tock of a clock. Slightly different again, the character names in *Ghost from a Perfect Place* all revolve around the opposites of fire and water: Torchie Sparks, Miss Sulphur, and Miss Kerosene stand opposed to Travis Flood, and Rio Sparks symbolically combines the two elements. Still, Ridley retains a reference to popular culture through a link to Rio Rita and her female team of superheroines from the 1980s Femforce comics.

All in all, there is more than enough in Ridley's plays to indicate that their East End setting functions largely as a mere spring board for reflections that have a more general impact, a loosely conceived microcosm that provides an image of the contemporary era in general. This is not to contradict Urban's well-pitched reading of Ridley in the context of 1990s Britain. Rather, the observation is offered by way of expanding the interpretive context of Ridley's work, a step that is warranted further in view of the successful productions of Ridley's drama across the European continent and in the United States.

III

As outlined in the introductory chapter to this book, any form of the grotesque is fundamentally puzzling, since it always rips open the boundaries of aesthetic convention and subverts the beholder's expectations. There is no doubt that this is precisely the effect that *The Pitchfork Disney* had on its early audiences. Its emancipatory potential remains much less clear however. Watching any decent production of the play certainly provides an intense emotional experience, and what is just as intense is the sense that the Strays have trapped themselves in a pathological world of fantastic stories, which prevents them from moving on in any way. While the moral judgment of such an existence is relatively straightforward (as also indicated in Urban's interpretation summarized earlier), it does not come across as the actual heart of the play. The chief element of this unsettling drama in my view is linked with the deployment of fear. *The Pitchfork Disney* caters to contemporary audiences' desire to be scared (what Cosmo refers to as 'man's need for the shivers'; p. 67) and simultaneously parodies it. This is brilliantly captured in Pitchfork Cavalier's exit scene. Pitchfork—whose character resembles both Dr Frankenstein's monster and Freddy Krueger of *A Nightmare on Elm Street* (see Sierz 2012, p. 96)—has been menacingly moving towards Presley and is now standing in front of him; Presley is whimpering with fear:

> **Presley** … Murder.
> *Suddenly,* **Pitchfork** *lunges forward.*
> **Presley** *flinches but –*
> **Pitchfork** *grabs* **Cosmo's** *overcoat from the back of the chair.*
> *Pause.*
> **Pitchfork** *walks towards door.*
> *At door,* **Pitchfork** *turns to face* **Presley***.*
> *Pause.*
> **Pitchfork** (*violently, very loud*) BOO!
> **Presley** *jumps, drops medicine and dummy, covers mouth with hands.*
> **Pitchfork** *exits.*
> **Presley** *suppresses a scream.*
> *Finally, it squeezes its way out. It is heartbreaking, terrible.*
> (pp. 95–6)

The scene is terrifying and funny at the same time, sending up the spectators' expectations of brutal violence but still scaring them with a mere childlike interjection. Rather than triggering moral, political, or emotional emancipation, Ridley's play is bound to leave its audiences dazed and perhaps amused by the shock, yet also with an ultimately indeterminate sense of 'absence and loss', to return to Rebellato's account of his own experience.

The emancipatory potential of the grotesque appears to be more prominent in Ridley's second play, *The Fastest Clock in the Universe*. Premièred at the Hampstead Theatre in London and again directed by Matthew Lloyd, it featured a young Jude Law in the role of Foxtrot Darling. The play focuses on thirty-year-old Cougar Glass who lives in panic over ageing and insists on periodically celebrating his nineteenth birthday. On this particular birthday, he is planning to seduce fifteen-year-old Foxtrot and subsequently discard him. His 'sugar daddy' (Urban 2007, p. 332), forty-nine-year-old Captain Tock, becomes a grumbling accomplice in the plan, as he harbours an unfulfilled desire for Cougar. Things get complicated when Foxtrot arrives at the party in the company of his girlfriend, Sherbet Gravel, who is pregnant. A prolonged struggle over Foxtrot ensues between Cougar and Sherbet, at the end of which Cougar assaults the young woman, ferociously punching her in the belly and making her miscarry the child.

The reception of the first production of the play was as outraged as that of *The Pitchfork Disney*, although as Aleks Sierz has noted, much of the clamour curiously centred around images of cruelty to animals rather than on the fact that a teenage boy is being seduced on stage (Sierz 2012, p. 102), not to mention the battering of a pregnant woman. The amplification of onstage violence is indeed one of the main differences from the earlier play, which in fact limited itself only to the breaking of Cosmo's finger, sickening as that may have been. Combined with the drastic nature of some of the narrated images, *The Fastest Clock in the Universe* comes close to Jacobean tragedy in its 'extremism', 'heightened language and grotesque action', as Sierz has argued (Sierz 2012, pp. 100–1). The Jacobean grotesque with its fundamental imagery of blood and savage violence is embellished by Ridley's use of birds: the realistic elements of the set are undermined by the ubiquity of 'stuffed birds, china birds, paintings of birds', which are intended to give the room 'an atmosphere somewhere between museum and aviary' (Ridley 2012, p. 105). Furthermore, live birds keep intruding from the outside in a fashion reminiscent of Alfred Hitchcock's famous cinematic treatment of Daphne du Maurier's story (see Sierz 2012, p. 101), and eventually start to shriek deafeningly during the characters' savage fight.

Following Ken Urban's argument about the role of nostalgia in Ridley's work, Cougar comes across as an exceptional case of a nostalgic who insists on living his life in one particular moment of his past, having smashed all the clocks in the house and taking care to have every single grey hair dyed by Captain Tock. His preference by way of hairstyle is for the quiff, a fashion associated with the 1950s Teddy Boys and rock 'n' roll (but nostalgically subject to periodical revivals in England, including in the 1990s). The more serious pathological effects of Cougar's condition include paedophilia, since his seductive power over teenagers seems to provide a confirmation of his youthfulness, and also his hatred of women, who to him primarily stand for the power to reproduce. Sherbet's miscarriage thus represents an adamantly desired destruction of the future (Urban 2007, pp. 332–3, 335).

Cougar's actions amply testify to the basic moral message of the play foregrounded by Urban, which is that insistence on being stuck in the moment leads to brutality (p. 336). The idea is further underlined through Cougar's unrelieved emphasis on physical beauty that—apart from satirizing humanity's obsession with appearance and fashion—juxtaposes Ridley's play with Oscar Wilde's moral tale of Dorian Gray. In fact, one of the reviewers of the first production, Lee Levitt, referred to Cougar as 'a Dorian Gray for the 1990s' (qtd in Sierz 2012, p. 99). Although Cougar's fixation involves no interest in art whatsoever, the parallel concerning the unnatural and immoral desire not to age is unequivocally strong: it is as if Cougar decided to become an immortal picture of his youthful self and this had turned him monstrous.

The dénouement of the drama is delivered in the form of a static scene in which Captain Tock finishes his fairy tale of the Prince, the Blind Girl and The Fastest Clock in the Universe. While the spectators are digesting the shocking violence that they have just witnessed, the Captain discloses that the Fastest Clock is … love. As Ken Urban aptly points out, the clichéd lesson of the tale—that love is blind and timeless—becomes absurd in the context, since it is 'the Captain's love that is truly blind: blind to Cougar's inhumanity' (p. 335). One may add that conversely, it is the lack of true love in his life that has made Cougar how he is—inhuman.

The grotesque is harnessed to a similarly strong moral point in Ridley's third full-length drama, *Ghost from a Perfect Place*, which centres on the stultifying consequences of mythologizing the past. The play was once again directed by Matthew Lloyd and opened at the Hampstead Theatre in 1994. In the first scene, Travis Flood, dressed in a black shot silk suit complete with a silk handkerchief and gold cufflinks, arrives at an appointment with a young prostitute called Rio, bringing her a bunch of white lilies. Instead, he meets her grandmother Torchie, with whom he begins to reminisce about the good old days in Bethnal Green. Torchie tells the visitor about her daughter Donna who died giving birth to Rio at the age of thirteen, and when Travis suddenly remembers who Torchie is, Rio enters. Contrary to what had been agreed, Travis not only refuses to have sex with her but also refuses to pay her, at which point she proceeds to torture him with the help of her fellow gang members, Miss Sulfur (who is seventeen) and Miss Kerosene (aged twelve). Travis encourages them throughout, and just as he is about to be killed, he discloses to Rio that he is her father. Rio dismisses her companions and together with Travis re-enacts the scene of her mother's rape. When the re-enactment is over, she is ready to kill Travis, but since her grandmother enters, she releases him instead. He walks away towards a bonfire that had been lit by the girls' gang.

While this play is closer to conventional realism than the preceding two, and its plot follows a pattern familiar from Charles Dickens (see Sierz 2012, p. 105), it is dominated by the prolonged grotesque scene of a spic-and-span gentleman being tortured by a gang of blonde girls in gold lamé miniskirts, who stub cigars in his face and perform ritual chants to 'Saint Donna'. Consequently, this scene became pivotal to all reviews, which were once again almost entirely negative; among those most outraged was Michael Billington, who described the play as 'degrading and quasi-pornographic in its use of violence' (qtd in Sierz 2000, p. 42). As Ridley has observed in retrospect, however, much of the negativity had to do with casting, as the role of Travis Flood was played by the revered Shakespearean actor John Wood. This gave the torture scene an unintended taste of generational revolt (qtd in Sierz 2000, p. 45).

Whatever the initial outcry of the critics, *Ghost from a Perfect Place* is the play in which Ridley has focused most on attacking the notion of living in an idealized or fictionalized past. Both Torchie and Travis revel in stories of the days when the East End was ruled by honourable gangsters like Travis and his men, who had style and a noble heart, kept order in the streets, and were helping out the poor. Torchie's nostalgia is so spectacular that, in the words of Ken Urban, she comes across as 'a caricature of the working-class Londoner, who would not be out of place on an episode of *EastEnders*' (p. 339). In corresponding manner, Travis—the 'ghost from the perfect place' of the past—is popular culture's sentimental image of the noble criminal. (In fact, Ridley satirically has him spending his retirement days in Hollywood.) However, their stories are soon dismantled, as it turns out that for Torchie, living in an idealized past has been a way of coping with the trauma of having lost both her daughter and her husband, who has been in a coma ever since Donna's death, following a failed suicide attempt.

By the same token, when Travis realizes that fate has confronted him with the effects of the rape that he committed, he admits that the autobiography that he has come to London to promote is sanitized and deliberately rose-coloured, and discloses that the reason why he left for America was that he had informed on his gangster friends. Travis's moral awakening is triggered not only by Torchie's condition but also by witnessing that Rio has taken refuge in a fantasy, too: her strategy of coping with life is based on a mock-religious cult of her mother in which Donna has features both of a saint and of a comic book superhero. The worship of Saint Donna is ultimately geared to incite Rio's gang of girlfriends to wreak havoc and terror on all and sundry. This form of violent self-assertion becomes one of the causes of the neighbourhood remaining a wasteland and a place of crime and abject poverty. Faced with the impact of the careless brutality of his previous existence, Travis realizes his need for retribution, as the director Matthew Lloyd has emphasized (qtd in Sierz 2000, p. 44): the reason he eggs on his torturers is precisely that he desires justice to be carried out on him.

The principal ethical point that violence breeds more violence is made very clearly in *Ghost from a Perfect Place*, and consequently, Sierz has described the ending of the play as optimistic. In his view, the exorcism of hypocritical fictions is bound to result in a better future (Sierz 2000, pp. 44–5). But are things really as clear-cut? Travis's self-inflicted punishment is likely to have been accomplished by walking to his death in the girls' bonfire, as indicated by its final flare outside. However, as Andrew Wyllie has asserted, Torchie is unlikely to relinquish her fantasy world. 'She cannot afford to let loose her grip on nostalgia' since '[t]he reality of her life is simply too unbearable to be acknowledged' (Wyllie 2013, p. 68). The main issue, of course, is the effect on Rio of meeting her father: she gets to relive the trauma of her mother's rape in its re-enactment, and the perpetrator is punished. But does this amount to a catharsis that will prevent Rio from replacing her invented story of Saint Donna by another one of a similar nature? Ridley himself claims that the ending should be regarded as 'neutral': Rio can now make a choice but the fundamental question for the author is whether she is better off than her grandmother, who does not know the truth (qtd in Sierz 2000, p. 45). Accordingly, the final scene gives no indication as to what the right choice for Rio may be.

IV

If none of Ridley's earlier plays had been for the faint-hearted, *Mercury Fur* turned its facets of violence up to an even higher level. Indeed, its shock effect was likened to Sarah Kane's *Blasted*, a play with which it has more in common than just the commotion that it created, as we shall see. Set in a derelict flat in a London tower block in the unspecified future, it focuses on a group of youngsters who survive by assisting rich clients to make snuff movies involving children. The audience witness teenage brothers Elliot and Darren preparing the current 'Party Piece', that is, a drugged ten-year-old boy, for sexual torture and execution by dressing him up in a golden suit as a child Elvis Presley. They are being helped by Elliot's transvestite lover Lola, her twenty-one-year-old brother Spinx, and a fifteen-year-old boy called Naz who has recently found shelter in a neighbouring flat. Also on the scene is the Duchess, a blind woman of thirty-eight dressed as a fairy tale Ice Queen whose mind appears to be trapped in a fantasy world of old-style aristocracy.

Outside is a post-apocalyptic world devastated by riots, a country that had been bombed by the government with sand and butterflies. The butterflies are hallucinogenic and intended to pacify the population by having them experience their deepest dreams, be it of pleasant experiences or of murder or suicide. The current 'Party Guest' arrives: he is a man in his early twenties wearing an expensive business suit. After he has run through the scenario of his sadistic Vietnam War fantasy with his suppliers, changed into a military outfit, and broken the boy's thumb by way of a test, it turns out that the victim is too weak to participate. When the boy collapses and dies, Naz is forced to take his place. As Naz is being tortured in the offstage bedroom, Elliot and Darren decide to intervene and end up shooting the Party Guest. In the play's finale, government airplanes begin to drop bombs on the city and Elliot and Darren, being the last to leave, set the place ablaze. With the flat burning and the bombs exploding outside, Elliot aims a gun at Darren and deliberates whether to shoot him.

Mercury Fur caused a scandal even before it opened, since Ridley's publisher refused to print the text due to its treatment of child abuse. The play premièred on 10 February 2005 at the Drum Theatre in Plymouth and then moved on to the Menier Chocolate Factory in London; it was directed by John Tiffany and starred the upcoming Ben Whishaw as Elliot. While the acting and the production were almost universally applauded, many reviewers and audience members were predictably shocked, both by the violence and by the savage language used by the characters, which involves a formidable level of vulgarity and racist and xenophobic abuse. The experience was made even more uncomfortable by the fact that walking out was possible through a single exit, only accessible by crossing part of the stage space (see Taylor 2005; Harpin 2011, p. 108).

The perception of the play as outrageous had much to do with the choice of artistic medium and genre. *Mercury Fur* is a dystopia, which has been noted by almost all the commentators, and even reviewers hostile to the play, such as Michael Billington or Matthew Sweet, expanded on the fact by comparing it to *A Clockwork Orange* by Anthony Burgess (see Billington 2005; Sweet 2005). However, *A Clockwork Orange* is not a stage play but a novel, and while the level of physical, sexual, and verbal violence it features was regarded as somewhat extreme at the time of its publication in 1962, it was relatively quickly accepted as a masterpiece. Coincidentally, *TIME* magazine included the book in the list of the 100 best English-language novels published since 1923 in the same year that *Mercury Fur* was produced. Stanley Kubrick's film adaptation of the novel released in 1971 notoriously met with much more controversy; but again, by the beginning of the new millennium, the film was celebrated as a milestone of modern cinema. *A Clockwork Orange* is only one of many works of acclaimed dystopian fiction that feature graphic details of a degraded society, and the same holds true of film of course; moreover, even the ghastly subject of making snuff movies has appeared in numerous major cinematic releases ever since the late 1970s, some of them involving children (such as Joel Schumacher's *8mm* of 1999, starring Nicholas Cage).

What the reaction to *Mercury Fur* indicates is that by introducing this calibre of degradation and brutality on the stage of a theatre, Ridley was still breaking a taboo. Discussing the issue, Ridley pointed out that in theatre, horrific violence is acceptable only in Greek tragedy or classics like Shakespeare's *King Lear*. 'If I'd wrapped *Mercury Fur* up as a recently rediscovered Greek tragedy', he asserted, 'it would be seen as an interesting moral debate like *Iphigenia*, but because it is set on an east-London housing estate it is seen as being too dangerous to talk about' (qtd in Gardner 2005). Moreover, the violence depicted in Ridley's drama was not just extreme but its victim was a child; and although Anne Harpin has recently compiled an extensive list of contemporary British plays that have dealt with child abuse, she emphasized that, unlike *Mercury Fur*, 'The majority do not feature on-stage, real-time acts of cruelty' (Harpin 2011, p. 106).

What contributes to the disturbing effect of the play apart from these generic transgressions are the grotesque elements of Ridley's dystopia: within the framework of what is essentially a well-made play (staged by most directors, including John Tiffany, in naturalist fashion), Ridley presents the audience with a glaringly incongruous mixture of vivid costumes, ranging from the hoodies and track suits of working-class teenagers to drag or a fairy tale-like, icy evening robe and white fur coat. He adds his trademark of fantastic stories, which this time include not only accounts of nightmares, fractious memories, and narratives that resemble fairy tales but also the Duchess's account of her past, which is similar to the plot of *The Sound of Music* (as noted both by Paul Taylor and Matthew Sweet in their reviews—Taylor 2005; Sweet 2005). The grotesque structure is completed with psychotropic butterflies dispensed to the consumer in a way reminiscent of a Catholic priest administering the Host to a member of his congregation.

This is surely a disorienting concoction; what prevents it from being dismissed as hotchpotch is the firm plot line that inexorably leads towards sadistic child abuse, together with the way in which the real-time violence is linked to the apocalypse outside. Here, Ridley follows the same pattern as Sarah Kane in *Blasted*, along with the use of imagery from TV news footage: his images come from the first Gulf War (including the looting of the National Museum in Baghdad, which in the play significantly becomes the British Museum), Rwanda, and the Vietnam War and would have been familiar to many an audience member in 2005 (see Gardner 2005; Wyllie 2013, p. 72). Like Kane, Ridley is intent on exploring the relationship of violence between individuals and war atrocity, and like Kane, his stance is that to condemn the display of extreme violence in the play as sickening and immoral amounts to grave hypocrisy, since what the spectators have just been following at home on television was, for instance, the shooting of 334 hostages including 186 schoolchildren by terrorists in the town of Beslan in Ossetia (see Ridley and Sierz 2009, pp. 114, 117).

Ridley's profound engagement with politics and ethics is also evident in the way in which he has the government in the play manipulate the population through the distribution of drugs (following the remarkable precedent in Aldous Huxley's 1932 dystopian novel, *Brave New World*), and ultimately send in troops in order to solicit peace. The use of the army bears an obvious and uncanny resemblance to the 2003 invasion of Iraq by the Bush administration backed up by Tony Blair: as the Party Guest puts it, the soldiers will 'be here to help [...] We need the fucking bombs and soldiers to bring some fucking order back' (Ridley 2009, p. 187). The underlying implication that a government that plays globocop abroad may at some point use a similar approach against its own unruly citizenry may sound intemperate, but it is not entirely irrational. Finally, a plain political point is made by the fact that the impoverished youngsters live by fulfilling an affluent, well-connected businessman's perverted sexual fantasies. Very much in the spirit of his critique, Ridley has the Party Guest emphatically agree with the deployment of the army against the unrest and at the same time making sure that he will not be present in the place of conflict when it occurs: in the Party Guest's eloquent phrase, 'I ain't part of this shit' (p. 187). While the references to politics are broad enough to make *Mercury Fur* resonate for audiences in other countries (which has been evidenced by its successful productions outside the UK), for British spectators this was an uncomfortable state-of-the-nation play, as Sierz has observed (Sierz 2011, pp. 65–6); the discomfort was further enhanced by the fact that the tortured boy is Pakistani.

Vital to all of Ridley's plays, the ability to tell stories assumes a central role in *Mercury Fur*. First, the play deals with the erasure of memory. Reflecting a contemporaneous survey among sixteen-year-olds in the UK, many of whom lacked a basic knowledge of modern history and placed, for example, the Vietnam War before World War II, Ridley has Darren enthusiastically relate a story of how President Kennedy fought a war over Marilyn Monroe with Hitler and, 'dropping all this napalm and stuff [... and] a couple of atom bombs' on Germany, he 'turned all the Germans into Chinkies' (p. 114). Darren's comical and at the same time cautionary version of history is a product of his addiction to the butterflies, whose long-term effect is that they wipe out memory. In a metaphorical sense, the magic insects represent the tabloidized contemporary media, which focus on the lurid and the entertaining instead of maintaining and cultivating the collective memory of history.

When discussing the play, Ridley has underlined the essential connection between the narrative of history and the narrative at the root of individual identity: '*Mercury Fur* is about what happens to people when you take away their history. The first thing that goes is a sense of identity. And once your identity and storytelling start to go, the next thing that goes is a sense of morality: you cease to be able to decide what is right or wrong' (Ridley and Sierz 2009, p. 114). The ethical consequences of a skewed sense of history do not need to be dwelt on, and are amply demonstrated in Ridley's play. However, Ridley's assertion makes a significant conceptual leap by linking *any* kind of storytelling with morality. This link is problematized even in Ridley's own earlier work, as we have seen in our previous discussion of the harmful impact of taking refuge in mythologized stories of the past. What *Mercury Fur* actually demonstrates is not so much that telling stories is *moral*, but that it is *human*, in the sense that the characters in the play are groping about for stories that would provide them with basic bearings in their shattered world, and consequently with some sense of identity. Thus, Ridley's play replicates a point that was strongly made by Mark Ravenhill in *Shopping and Fucking*, another drama with pronounced dystopian features (see Chap. 1 and Sierz 2012, p. 56).

The fundamental connection between storytelling and humanity occurs also on a collective level in *Mercury Fur*, as the characters make repeated references to a variety of foundational narratives of Western civilization. These include the myth of the Minotaur, which is partially retold by Elliot. In an interview, Ridley spoke about his intention to make Ariadne's thread stand for the thread of stories that is to lead humanity away from the monster of the Labyrinth (Ridley 2005). Judging by the existing commentaries, the symbol is communicated too subtly to be recognized; nevertheless, the issue of humanity versus monstrosity is foregrounded in the same scene by Darren's amusing pondering of the precise nature of the Minotaur: if there were enough humanity in the creature, Darren argues, 'this Theseus might have been able to have a chat with the Minotaur. I bet the Minotaur—if it was a man with a bull' s head—wanted to get out the fucking Labyrinth too' (p. 157). Despite Darren's humorously unlearned phrasing, the idea represents a powerful metatheatrical comment, given the foreseeable tendency of the audience to regard the characters as monstrous: since the Minotaur was indeed part human, what is suggested is that humanity should help him out of the Labyrinth and correspondingly, the spectators should sympathetically engage with the characters of the play.

On a more subjective note perhaps, the image sets up a resonance with other grotesque renderings of the story of the Minotaur by various artists, such as Pablo Picasso's famous etching entitled *Minotauromachia* (1935). There, against the backdrop of a surreal image of death in warfare, an unperturbed girl stands holding a candle and flowers (both of which prominently feature in Ridley's play), facing the approach of a threatening Minotaur whose outstretched and outsized human arm is reaching for the candle. The scene is observed from a safe distance by one male and two female onlookers. While the outcome here is just as ambivalent as in Ridley's play, the firm stance adopted by the girl is the clear focal point of the image. Moreover, it is not without interest that Picasso used this picture as a comment on the growing turbulence of his time, and incorporated its elements—including the Minotaur—into *Guernica* two years later.[1]

The issue of engaging the monstrous is also crucially reflected in Ridley's progressive foregrounding of the humanity of the characters in *Mercury Fur*. Albeit the emotional attachment between the two brothers is reasonably clear from the onset, as is the love relationship between Elliot and Lola, the gradual humanization does not commence until the crucial point when the audience are made aware that the Duchess is Darren and Elliot's mother. This occurs shortly after the conversation about the Minotaur discussed previously. It is only now that the spectators realize that most of the characters they are watching are actually members of an extended family (Spinx being Lola's brother). Moreover, Darren and Elliot almost immediately acknowledge their filial relationship to the disturbed Duchess for the first time by trying to protect her from hearing the sounds of the torture. Subsequently, Spinx discloses how he rescued Darren and his mother from a hospital that was under attack and how he cared for the two as well as for the injured Elliot.

The unravelling of the emotional attachment among the family members is followed by the central development in the play, which, as Rebellato has asserted, is that the brothers evolve 'a moral conscience through the course of the action' (Rebellato 2011, pp. 439–40). This process is difficult, however, and its practical implications are ambivalent due to the nature of the ethical dilemmas faced by the brothers. When the intended victim of the torture dies and Elliot and Darren are being persuaded by Spinx to use Naz in his stead, they are reluctant, since Naz is someone they had got to know in the meantime. Nonetheless, it turns out that by sacrificing Naz, they will gain information from the Party Guest that is bound to save their lives and the lives of their loved ones in the ensuing bombing. What is the ethical course of action here? The brothers initially opt for the lives of their loved ones, but after witnessing a lengthy moment of torture, they intercede and kill the Party Guest. For Rebellato, this represents the triumph of morality in the play (p. 440), and Anne Harpin is certainly right in asserting that making the audience watch for an extended time 'a choreography of glances on stage, looks of horror and shame passed between Lola, Darren and Elliot to a soundscape of brutality' bears a powerful message concerning the ethics of witnessing (Harpin 2011, pp. 109–10). Nevertheless, Ridley follows the scene by yet another moral conundrum: as Elliot listens to his brother musing on whether this planet is 'fit for human life' (p. 200) and watches the pandemonium outside, he takes out a gun. Should he shoot Darren in order to spare him from the horrors of existence in this hell? This dilemma is left unresolved. Moral conscience has certainly returned—but acting on it proves to be exceedingly difficult.

V

Leaves of Glass, Ridley's subsequent drama, may be seen as the middle part of 'a trilogy of plays on the subject of brotherly love' (Sierz 2012, p. 226), completed by *Piranha Heights*. Apart from their focus on the interaction of two brothers, the three dramas also share a cryptic way of alluding to a canonical literary work in their title: Leopold von Sacher-Masoch's *Venus in Furs*, Walt Whitman's *Leaves of Grass*, and Emily Brontë's *Wuthering Heights*. However, the plays are very different in almost all other aspects. After the forcefully grotesque *Mercury Fur* and its confrontational violence that takes place in a disused tower block, *Leaves of Glass* comes with a style couched in kitchen-sink realism, involves little real-time violence, and is set in a series of middle-class homes. The play was first produced at Soho Theatre in London in 2007, directed by Lisa Goldman, and again starred Ben Whishaw in a celebrated performance. It focuses on the relationship of Steven, the successful owner of a company that cleans graffiti from buildings (played by Whishaw), and his younger brother Barry, a visual artist battling with a drinking problem. Both brothers are haunted by the traumatic loss of their father, who committed suicide when Steven was fifteen and Barry was ten. The theme of the lost father was already sketched out in *Mercury Fur*, and while being yet another feature that brings Ridley's work close to the early plays by Mark Ravenhill, it in fact develops Ridley's concern with the absence of parents in his previous work, such as in *The Pitchfork Disney* (see Rebellato 2011, p. 428).

Ridley's use of the grotesque is more subdued in *Leaves of Glass* and chiefly centres on interlacing a family drama with images of war atrocity and terrorism on the one hand, and gothic stories on the other. No less importantly, a set of recurring images is strategically positioned throughout the play: a tree, a leaf, and stars are the most vivid of these. The precise nature of how all these elements resonate together functions as a puzzle which is slowly unravelled, teasing the imagination of the spectator. Ridley's desire for the audience's imaginative engagement is in fact made explicit about two thirds of the way into the drama, which is structured as a series of loosely connected scenes. At this point, Barry shows some of his drawings to Steven and comments: 'They're a sequence. You see? Individually they don't make much sense. [...] But when you put them next to each other and ... it'll start to balance out. Make sense. The same images occur in all of them. Hidden somewhere. You see? A tree here ... Roots ... A leaf' (Ridley 2009, p. 254). What the author is doing here is giving a clue to those who still may be clueless by foregrounding his symbols and the fact that these connect the individual scenes as well as the plot. But there is a trick involved at the same time: while trees and leaves are frequently referred to in the play, roots are not, or at least not literally. Moreover, Barry's list does not feature stars—one of the most recurrent and most vivid images in the play. Ridley's meta-comment therefore seems to indicate that the meaning of the symbols, and indeed the mixture of the various expressive elements, is intended to remain confounding to a certain extent.

Another symbolic presence is that of glass, as even the provocatively enigmatic title of the play indicates. Glass occurs prominently in Barry's story of US nuclear tests prior to the Hiroshima bombing, which melted the earth into a glassy surface. At the end of the play, it appears in a reference to the double glazing in the family's new house, and in the potent image of glass leaves hanging on a glass tree. Another symbolic function associated with glass is apparent in the way a number of important moments in the play refract one another, featuring a reversal of the characters' roles. Crucially, this involves the relationship of the brothers in which the roles are first reversed, and then they return to their previous state before the tragic outcome, reflecting the brothers' struggle. Steven is initially the dominant of the two; he is rational, seems to be well-intentioned, and his life is neatly organized, in contrast to Barry, who is teetering on the brink of a nervous breakdown, his life is in shambles, and he is in the grips of self-destructive alcoholism. In the middle of the play, Steven is the one who is breaking down and drinking, he has driven his pregnant wife to leave him, while Barry has got his life back on track and is trying to talk sense into Steven. However, as the brothers end up fighting a final battle over their joint memories and Steven comes out victorious, it is

Barry's life that is crushed again, this time literally. It is not until the final scene of Ridley's play that these symbolic references and ways of mirroring are united in a complex metaphorical image of a world of glass, and their meaning is fully disclosed.

As Steven and Barry are attempting to come to terms with their father's death, they gradually give voice to their childhood memories. Like all of Ridley's narrators, they are captivating storytellers and their stories possess an intense lyrical beauty. And, typically for Ridley again, their private memories are juxtaposed with stories of brutal violence pertaining to the world outside. In *Leaves of Glass*, these include scenes from World War I, Nazi concentration camps, the Vietnam War, and as mentioned earlier, the dropping of the atomic bomb. Most controversially, perhaps, a story that Barry tells early in the play features an aestheticized description of a suicide terrorist attack, an image of substantial resonance for a British audience in particular after the attacks on the London public transport system of July 2005. While the linking of the private and the public in this manner generally functions in the same way as in *Mercury Fur*, indicating a fundamental connection between individual and collective violence and trauma, the stories of warfare told in *Leaves of Glass* include several more specific associations with Steven and Barry's family, such as the discussion of Enola Gay as the mother of the pilot who dropped the atomic bomb on Hiroshima. This underscores the essential difference between the two plays as regards the nature of the family: whereas the awareness of family relations serves as a means of humanizing the characters in *Mercury Fur*, the family in *Leaves of Glass* is truly poisonous and destructive. Barry depicts family life in terms of the Kennedy assassination:

> Full of lies and deceit and spin ... and mind-fucks. Each one of us is either sitting in the back of the car waiting for a bullet. Or sitting at a window waiting to pull the trigger. Or loading a gun waiting to shoot the man who pulled the trigger. The trick is—while all this ... this bloody madness is going on—to comment on how beautiful Dallas looks in the sunshine. (pp. 287–8)

Barry's summary is uncannily succinct: while a lot of the conversation among the family members seems to consist of friendly banter and understatement, the audience in fact witness Steven and his mother Liz whitewash Steven's assault on his pregnant wife and see Liz refer both to suicidal depression and to nervous breakdown as a 'fluey bug thing' (pp. 280–2, 303) in her refusal to acknowledge the facts. But what is most horrific is how Steven, who is first encountered as a pleasant and supportive individual, turns into a monster. Driven by his envy of Barry's talent as an artist, he is discovered to have been intent on destroying him from his early childhood. He first lies to Barry as a boy and insinuates that their father is dismissive of his art, causing Barry a lifelong insecurity concerning the quality and the purpose of his work. Although he feels guilty about what he did, Steven completes the process after Barry has been cured of his alcoholism: he decimates him emotionally, hands him a bottle, and ultimately drives him to suicide. The play closes with Steven, Liz, and Steven's wife Debbie denying the nature of Barry's death and Liz enthusiastically praising Barry's work, which the audience know she was contemptuous about. It is in this context that the nature of Steven's job is unravelled to be symbolic. As Sam Marlowe pointed out in his review, Steven's work in cleaning away street art suggests 'wip[ing] away the filth of memory' (Marlowe 2007, p. 22); however, the symbolism is really twofold, since as becomes apparent from Steven's role in the death of his brother, his intention is to eradicate art generally, and as Barry had argued earlier in the play, a world without art means a place of grey desolation and brutality that is akin to a concentration camp (Ridley 2009, p. 234).

As outlined, the family in *Leaves of Glass* are suffering from the trauma of the father's suicide. Steven and Barry's intent on voicing their memories at the onset might indicate that the result will be a gradual coming to terms with the loss. Nevertheless, in the toxic context of these particular family relations, 'the therapeutic potential of the act of remembering is defeated', to use Andrew Wyllie's words (Wyllie 2013, p. 73). Over and above that, it is only now that we come to discuss the most terrible revelation in the play's plot: there is another trauma lurking behind the loss of the father. Both Steven and Barry are driven to the edge at various points of the play by having uncanny visions of a ghost. We learn from Steven at an early stage that his brother keeps seeing the ghost of the father; in turn, Steven becomes possessed by the ghost of a little boy, who eventually turns out to be his brother, aged ten and drawing a leaf, which was the moment that had driven Steven to lie to him about their father's attitude to his artistic talent. In the ultimate confrontation between the brothers, which, most appropriately for its gothic nature, takes place in the cellar and is lit by antique candelabra, the brothers narrate the real story behind Barry's vision of 'Mr Ghost': he is revealed to be an old English teacher of their father's, to whom Steven prostituted Barry after the father's funeral, and who may or may not have abused the father as well. Steven falsifies every important detail of Barry's version of the events, and as the truth is largely still beyond telling for Barry, he is defeated by Steven's denial of what had happened (pp. 290–7). However, enough information is communicated for the audience to glean the most potent reason why Steven decides to destroy Barry now for good.

With Barry's death, the appalling deed that Steven had committed is swept back under the carpet in a chilling scene of family harmony that is based on lies. The dominant image of the scene is in ironic contrast to what the audience know about the characters: it is that of a beautiful glass tree given to the mother by Steven, on which she had been hanging a new glass leaf at the end of every week. The symbolic meaning of glass here is primarily that of life melted into hardened matter, like after an explosion of an atomic bomb, since the leaves are associated with Barry in their strong resemblance to the leaf drawn by him as a child, and Steven purchased them from the money received every Friday for prostituting his little brother to the paedophile English teacher. Yet, Liz says that it was the tree that saved her life after her husband's death (pp. 293, 297, 304). The striking beauty of the image thus simultaneously testifies to the violence perpetrated on the artist and to the redemptive power of art; Barry remains in the house to haunt the family eternally.

Comparing the play with *Mercury Fur*, Lyn Gardner emphasized that in contrast to the visceral violence of the earlier work, the violence in *Leaves of Glass* 'is perpetrated with twisted memories, words, looks and silences'—but it is 'no less dangerous' for that (Gardner 2007). It is of interest that Ridley spoke of the subject matter of twisted memories in relation to Tony Blair's Labour government that was also 'wrestling truth and defeating it' (Ridley and Sierz 2009, p. 115). While this has had some resonance with audience members of the first production in the UK, the main strength of this highly accomplished play lies in providing a deep insight into the psychology of the characters without absconding on a peculiar use of the grotesque, which makes *Leaves of Glass* seem like a revisiting of Tennessee Williams merged with an inspired graphic novel.

VI

Piranha Heights followed *Leaves of Glass* within a year, opening at Soho Theatre in London in 2008 and again directed by Lisa Goldman. The fraught relationship of the two brothers, Alan and Terry, which is at the centre of the play in many ways replicates that of Barry and Steven in *Leaves of Glass* but the roles are reversed: here, the older brother, Terry, is the artist with a drinking problem, opposed to the younger Alan who is a married man with a dysfunctional family life. The brothers are fifteen years older than in the preceding play (which makes them forty-two and thirty-seven, respectively); their mother has just died and at the opening curtain, they are arguing about which of them has the right to inherit the tower block flat where they have come to sort out her possessions. The stage is set for a conventional kitchen-sink drama but with the intervention of Lilly, a fifteen-year-old girl dressed in a hijab with niqab and speaking fake Arabic, things immediately spin out of control and the play is unravelled for what it really is: an English farce married to violent nightmare.

The brothers stop squabbling over family memories after the arrival of Lilly's aggressive boyfriend nicknamed Medic, pushing a pram with their 'baby'—that turns out to be a plastic doll. Medic attacks both brothers in turn, and eventually attempts to strangle Terry, with Alan's consent. The violence escalates when Alan's fifteen-year-old son Garth appears, culminating in a Mexican standoff between Garth, Medic, and Lilly. As the three guns go off simultaneously amidst much screaming and shouting, the chandelier falls down. No-one is hurt and Medic proceeds to mutilate the plastic doll and cut its head off. Alan subsequently discovers the family treasure, consisting of their grandmother's jewellery symbolically hidden behind a family photograph; while he intends to use it for him and his son to start their life over, Garth seizes the jewellery and runs away with Medic to create a new world together. The ultimate result of the savage turmoil is the reconciliation of the brothers; but since they are at a loss as to how they will go on living without their mother, Ridley has Lilly step into her role in a final comic twist. Dressed in the mother's clothes, Lilly emerges from the bedroom asserting: '[...] oh, why the worried faces? Come and tell me all about it. You know there's no problem your mum can't make better' (Ridley 2009, p. 387).

Piranha Heights once again tackles some of Ridley's principal themes. The detrimental effect of living in imagined stories is demonstrated on Lilly who constructs her identity as that of a Muslim refugee. The past that she recounts is full of atrocity and gruesome detail, but at the same time it is clearly culled from contemporary media reports about Islamist fundamentalism. This is indicated not just by the clichéd elements in Lilly's account but also by her "Arabic" vocabulary (the first word she speaks is 'fatwa' and her utterances gradually turn into obvious gibberish). Moreover, her story involves misremembered facts of history, as apparent from her reference to a bomb explosion at Bethnal Green tube station.[2] The veracity of Lilly's narrative is ultimately undermined by the baby being a doll. In his effort to help, Terry urges Lilly and Medic to acknowledge the falsity of their invented existence, arguing that we should not hide from what we do not want to deal with. Regardless of Terry's plea, Lilly does not surface from her fiction until she is ruthlessly rejected by Medic; her genuine grief over the dismemberment of the doll, absurd as it may be, emphatically points out the malignity of taking refuge in fantasies.

As in *Leaves of Glass*, the contest among the brothers in which they strive to rewrite family memories breeds violence, and similarly to several of Ridley's earlier plays, *Piranha Heights* shows the consequences of the absence of a father, in that Garth's violent nature and recourse to fantasy are a direct result of being neglected by Alan, who has also been abusive and dismissive of his mother. In this context, it is possible to agree with Lyn Gardner that beneath Ridley's 'bitterly funny black humour is an almost wistful sense of the human need for kinship and family, and a recognition that fantasy is both a refuge and a weapon for the mortally wounded in a world built on lies' (Gardner 2008). In accordance with his view of the theatre as transformative, Ridley orchestrates the play as a cathartic whirlwind in which, as the violence grows, the lamps in the room are knocked down one by one and are left flickering on the ground, with the climactic shootout and the mutilation of the doll taking place only in skewed light, some of which is provided by a thunderstorm raging outside. When Garth and Medic run away to shape a new world, the lamps are duly replaced and stop flickering, and the storm abates. This might indicate that the exorcism of delusions and lies has been accomplished. However, a positive interpretation of such nature is undermined both by the final twist in which Lilly embodies Alan and Terry's mother and the fact that Garth and Medic's new existence plainly will be as perpetrators of gratuitous violence fed by wild fantasies.

What is more important still is that any consideration of the 'need for kinship' and honest engagement with reality is complicated by the superabundance of the grotesque in the play. Its ingredients are similar to Ridley's previous work, but in *Piranha Heights* they proliferate out of all proportion. This happens to the detriment of the plot and of the consistency of character psychology, which is clearly attempted. Everything is simply somewhat over the top, from Terry's artwork including a picture of a radioactive donkey turned Donkey-Man in 'ironic homage' to

Spiderman (Ridley 2009, p. 324), to the pivotal fairy-tale-like narrative in which Pinocchio is transformed through lying into Elephant Man and then into a tree in presumed metaphorical fashion, and, crucially, the way in which not only Medic's but also Garth's exceedingly idiosyncratic and aggressive behaviour makes them come across as raving psychopaths. Indeed, one of the play's early reviewers captured the overall effect by describing *Piranha Heights* as an 'exercise in theatrical hysteria', which ultimately has nothing but short-term impact (Wise 2008, p. 19). The last play of Ridley's loose trilogy is no doubt the most exuberantly grotesque, but it also warns of the dangers of excess that may preclude other aspects of the work, including any redemptive potential.

VII

I hope to have demonstrated that the grotesque in Philip Ridley's plays always serves to engage a variety of vital ethical, social, and political issues, and therefore cannot be dismissed as mere grotesque entertainment. Similarly, the playwright's use of extreme physical and verbal violence is never gratuitous and is always fundamentally tied to these issues, confrontational as it may be. While the estranged world depicted in his plays is often very bleak and interlaced with terror, which corresponds to Wolfgang Kayser's view of the grotesque (see Chap. 1), the accusations of nihilism levelled at Ridley are unfounded precisely because of the unfaltering examination of morality and politics in his work. The grotesque in Ridley's drama rips apart the conventions both of the contemporary world and the theatre in its assertive desire to provide 'room to play' for the spectators' imagination, engaging it to contemplate the possibilities of reconstructing the collapsed world (see Connelly 2012, pp. 2, 12, and Chap. 1).

On the other hand, we have seen that the impact of Ridley's grotesque does not quite result in the rejuvenation of the world that Mikhail Bakhtin has tried to assert in his discussion of the concept (see Chap. 1). Although the emancipatory potential of the grotesque in plays such as *The Fastest Clock in the Universe* or *Leaves of Glass* is apparent in the forceful moral points that these works make, the characters still remain stuck in their depraved world. *Ghost from a Perfect Place* and *Mercury Fur* do go a step further in that they open a door out of the lies and corruption but the characters are left in a quandary and the renewal of their moral selves is only alluded to as one of the options.

Finally, Ridley's pyrotechnics also intimate certain limits concerning the measure in which the grotesque may be useful in a work of art that strives to involve the audience in ethical dilemmas or in a critique of noxious human relations or nefarious politics: while the playwright's propensity for exuberance and outrage has resulted in a unique body of work, it has undeniably discouraged many spectators from coming to see it. Moreover, Ridley's plays have rarely failed due to excess, but when it has happened—as in the case of *Piranha Heights*—it became apparent that an overabundant mixing of the incongruous and unrestrained shock tactics may result not only in the side-lining of the issues that are being addressed but ultimately also in a dismissal of the work as merely ludicrous and, in effect, tiresome.

Notes

1. For a discussion on the recurrence of the Minotaur in Picasso's work and the development from *Minotauromachia* to *Guernica*, see Ries (1972).
2. Lilly evidently refers to the 2005 terrorist attacks on the London public transport and claims that there were seventy people dead at Bethnal Green station (pp. 319–20). However, the total number of casualties of the terrorist attack was in fact fifty-six (including the four bombers), while the Bethnal Green station was unaffected. Her account may moreover conflate the 2005 events with a disaster that occurred at the tube station in 1943, when 173 people were killed in a crush as they were seeking shelter from a threatening air raid. I am grateful to Linda Turner for pointing out the 1943 tragedy to me.

Works Cited

Billington, M. (2005, March 3). Review of *Mercury Fur*, by Philip Ridley. *Guardian*. Retrieved July 13, 2015, from http://www.theguardian.com/stage/2005/mar/03/theatre

Connelly, F. S. (2012). *The Grotesque in Western Art and Culture: The Image at Play*. Cambridge: Cambridge University Press.

Gardner, L. (2005, February 9). The Devil Inside. *Guardian*. Retrieved July 12, 2015, from http://www.theguardian.com/stage/2005/feb/09/theatre3

Gardner, L. (2007, May 12). Review of *Leaves of Glass*, by Philip Ridley. *Guardian*. Retrieved July 12, 2015, from http://www.theguardian.com/stage/2007/may/12/theatre2

Gardner, L. (2008, May 27). Review of *Piranha Heights*, by Philip Ridley. *Guardian*. Retrieved July 12, 2015, from http://www.theguardian.com/stage/2008/may/27/theatre
Harpin, A. (2011). Intolerable Acts. *Performance Research, 16* (1), 102–111.
Marlowe, S. (2007, May 10). Review of *Leaves of Glass*, by Philip Ridley. *Times*, p. 22.
Rebellato, D. (2011). Philip Ridley. In M. Middeke, P. P. Schnierer, & A. Sierz (Eds.), *The Methuen Drama Guide to Contemporary British Playwrights* (pp. 425–444). London: Methuen.
Ridley, P. (2005, March 4). Interview by Rachel Haliburton. Retrieved July 13, 2015, from http://www.theatrevoice.com/audio/interview-philip-ridley-the-controversial-writers-latest/
Ridley, P. (2009). *Plays: 2*. London: Methuen.
Ridley, P. (2012). *Plays: 1*. London: Bloomsbury.
Ridley, P., & Sierz, A. (2009). "Putting a New Lens on the World": The Art of Theatrical Alchemy. *New Theatre Quarterly, 25* (2), 109–117.
Ries, M. (1972). Picasso and the Myth of the Minotaur. *Art Journal, 32* (2), Winter 1972/1973, pp. 142–145. Retrieved July 11, 2015, from http://www.martinries.com/article1972-73PP.htm
Sierz, A. (2000). *In-Yer-Face Theatre: British Drama Today*. London: Faber and Faber.
Sierz, A. (2011). *Rewriting the Nation: British Theatre Today*. London: Methuen.
Sierz, A. (2012). *Modern British Playwriting: The 1990s. Voices, Documents, New Interpretations*. London: Methuen.
Sweet, M. (2005, March 3). Welcome to Dystopia, review of *Mercury Fur*, by Philip Ridley. *Evening Standard*. Retrieved July 13, 2015, from http://www.standard.co.uk/goingout/theatre/welcome-to-dystopia-7384045.html
Taylor, P. (2005, March 9). Review of *Mercury Fur*, by Philip Ridley. *Independent*. Retrieved July 12, 2015, from http://www.independent.co.uk/arts-entertainment/theatre-dance/reviews/mercury-fur-menier-chocolate-factory-london-6150742.html
Urban, K. (2007). Ghosts from an Imperfect Place: Philip Ridley's Nostalgia. *Modern Drama, 50* (3), 325–345.
Wise, L. (2008, June 8). Review of *Piranha Heights*, by Philip Ridley. *Sunday Times*, p. 19.
Wyllie, A. (2013). Philip Ridley and Memory. *Studies in Theatre and Performance, 33* (1), 65–75.

CHAPTER 3

Wild Justice: Mark O'Rowe

I

Mark O'Rowe's reputation as one of the most distinctive voices in contemporary Irish theatre has its origins in the impressive first production of his third full-length play, *Howie the Rookie* at the Bush Theatre in London (1999). Directed by Mike Bradwell and starring Aidan Kelly and Karl Shiels, the visceral tale delivered in two stylized monologues transferred to Dublin and Edinburgh; eight years later, O'Rowe mesmerized critics and audiences alike with another puzzling and extremely brutal monologue drama entitled *Terminus*, first performed on the Peacock stage of the Abbey Theatre in Dublin, directed by the author. Both plays were swiftly taken up by theatres throughout Europe and in the United States and given a number of accomplished productions there.

Howie the Rookie and *Terminus* are emblematic of O'Rowe's oeuvre in their graphic depiction of violence and ferocious violation of the human body. Both dramas revolve around what Brian Singleton has termed 'toxic masculinity' (Singleton 2006, p. 277); they also demonstrate O'Rowe's keen interest in revenge and the notion of retributive justice. These three central themes permeate all of O'Rowe's work for the stage (and for the screen) and, as a rule, are presented in the context of the grotesque. His first full length play, formally a conventional naturalist drama entitled *The Aspidistra Code*, was performed as a rehearsed reading on the Peacock stage of the Abbey in 1995. It explicitly discusses the concepts of a moral code and justice as a working-class couple who are unable to pay off a loan are facing the imminent

© The Editor(s) (if applicable) and The Author(s) 2016
O. Pilný, *The Grotesque in Contemporary Anglophone Drama*,
DOI 10.1057/978-1-137-51318-2_3

57

visit of a vicious extortionist and hire a self-styled noble criminal to protect them. Their thinking is that since the 'loan-shark' (O'Rowe 2011, p. 62) who calls himself Drongo is intent on harming them, it is only right that they ask their 'friend' Crazy Horse to harm him instead. The planned retribution gets complicated when Drongo and Crazy Horse meet and discover that in the past and under different names, they used to be close friends. The subsequent discussion of what is right and what is wrong, which also features a next-door neighbour, eventually involves gambling and is ultimately resolved through a slapstick gag.

The title of the play seems to indicate that the protracted debate concerning ethics should be viewed as social satire, with the aspidistra being a plant customarily associated with middle-class Victorian values. However, the relevance of the latter to these impoverished working-class Dubliners is not elaborated upon, while the involvement of semi-lunatic hoodlums (with their very names being indicative of this) in a slapstick context dismisses the serious aspects of the moral debate. *The Aspidistra Code* thus comes across as proffering the kind of grotesque entertainment found in Tracy Letts's *Killer Joe* or Martin McDonagh's *The Lieutenant of Inishmore*, and again points towards inspiration from the cinematic precedents in the form of early works by Quentin Tarantino and Danny Boyle, among others.

O'Rowe characterized *The Aspidistra Code* as 'kitchen-sink-crime-comedy-drama' (O'Rowe 2011, p. vii) and also applied the label to his next play, *From Both Hips* (1997, Fishamble Theatre Company, Dublin), although the latter features considerably less humour. Its plot concerns Paul, a working-class man who was accidentally shot in the hip by police officer Willie during a raid on a council estate and who is now seeking retribution. The play shows its protagonists firmly in the grip of a stereotype of masculinity whose origins are linked through numerous allusions to cinematic representations of male heroes in westerns and in TV crime series such as *Miami Vice*. Both Paul and Willie are possessed by what they perceive as their loss of manliness: Paul because of the temporary physical handicap due to his injury, and Willie because he had wet himself in reaction to the shock of shooting another human being and Paul now threatens to publically expose him. The dark absurdity of the solution that the two men settle on demonstrates the extent to which their idea of masculinity is bound with the notion of revenge as the fundamental law: Willy proposes to Paul to shoot him in the hip, too. '[D]o it and solve all our problems. I'm sick of this inaction', he argues, adding: "Cos if we do this, we're quits. You shooting me cancels out you telling on me' (O'Rowe 2011, pp. 163, 164). It hardly comes as a surprise that this idea of 'manliness' makes the men treat women as sexual objects (Paul) or simply ignore them (Willie).

From Both Hips is perhaps the only one of O'Rowe's works to contradict his insistence that his work was not intended as 'social commentary' (qtd in Haughton 2011, p. 154): social critique comes to the fore particularly since the gender stereotypes are linked to models taken from brands of popular culture avidly consumed by the men. Moreover, as the characters—male and female alike—tend to use a local rag, the *Echo*, as their principal source of information and opinion on everything, their beliefs are also associated with the impact of tabloid journalism. Nevertheless, the critique is somewhat blunted by the social status of the characters, which is bound to function as a distancing device, together with the ludicrously extreme conclusion at which the men arrive.

Retributive violence among males is also the central focus of O'Rowe's gangster comedy *Made in China* (Schauspielhaus Bochum, January 2001; the Peacock stage of the Abbey Theatre, Dublin, April 2001). Here, two violent criminals struggle over the loyalty of an impressionable third; their strife culminates in a fight involving all three, martial arts techniques, a prosthetic leg, and an umbrella. The characters' idea of manliness is again determined by Hollywood, this time chiefly martial arts movies and crime dramas starring Al Pacino, and their machismo is compounded by their excessive emphasis on what a real man is supposed to wear. Although, unlike in *From Both Hips*, the macho values are not subject to direct critique, the vicious gangsters are placed in the context of slapstick and depicted as ridiculous, which might be regarded as a form of condemnation. The ambivalent attitude to the physical prowess and fighting skills of the men stands in the way of critique, however; the martial arts gimmicks and attire used by small-time gangsters in working-class suburbia may be depicted as imitative of Hollywood and pretentious, but it is still combat skills and brutal violence that are decisive in defeating the "bad guy" Kilby at the end of the play.

Similarly, the grotesque foregrounding of the bodily aspects throughout the play—such as protracted defecation and a discussion thereof, Paddy's penis repeatedly sticking out of his underwear, and even the brandishing of the artificial limb—might indicate an affinity with Bakhtin's notion of the carnivalesque and a gesture towards hope for a renewed social order. Yet the parading of such corporeal aspects does not go beyond base humour. Indeed, a reviewer of the German première of *Made in China* was moved by the author's use of defecation and by the vulgarity of the language to coin the term 'faecal theatre' ((dpa) 2001)[1] rather than to ponder a potential critique of macho attitudes.

In the present chapter, I would like to focus on the much more intricate use of the grotesque in Mark O'Rowe's three remarkable monologue dramas, *Howie the Rookie*, *Crestfall* (2003), and *Terminus*. As noted, O'Rowe's monologues continue to advance the playwright's central themes of extreme violence, revenge, and a crisis of masculinity, and as such present a particularly dark world. Nevertheless, the stories delivered by the narrators are at the same time distinctly aestheticized. In contrast to the plays of Philip Ridley, in which any aestheticization of their dark and violent world occurs through lush images or the use of exuberant costume, O'Rowe uses dramatic structure, mythical or supernatural motifs, and, above all, highly stylized language, which develops—to use Karen Fricker's term—from the 'staccato near-poetry' (Fricker 2003) of the first two plays to an original take on rhymed verse drama in *Terminus*. My main concern will be with what happens to justice and the moral code in the context of O'Rowe's aesthetically alluring version of a very grim grotesque.

II

Howie the Rookie was Mark O'Rowe's first full-length monologue drama. As the author recently stated, he drew his inspiration for the format of the play from a 1995 drama *This Lime Tree Bower* by the most famous Irish contemporary author of monologues, Conor McPherson; this is where O'Rowe discovered the possibility of an entire play consisting of single actors on stage simply delivering their lines to the audience. Another source of inspiration was Samuel Beckett's novel *Molloy*, which allowed O'Rowe to see the potential of using two seemingly disconnected protagonists (O'Rowe 2011, p. viii). The play follows the actions of two young men from a Dublin council estate over the course of two days. First it is the Howie Lee who delivers his story in the first person, to be succeeded by the Rookie Lee, who has featured in the Howie's story and now delivers what gradually turns out to be its continuation, this time from his own perspective. The characters are connected by a shared surname (although they are not related) and by their mutual admiration for another namesake, the famous 1960s martial arts actor Bruce Lee; their identities are literally intertwined in the title of the play.

The Howie Lee narrates a story about looking for the Rookie Lee as part of a group intending to beat him up in retribution for infecting the Howie's friend Ollie's mattress with scabies. When their mission is accomplished, the Howie returns home, only to learn that his five-year-old brother has been run over by a lorry. The Howie feels guilty for the accident as he had refused to babysit his brother and gone out instead. In the second monologue, the Rookie mentions his beating but it is something else that worries him more than his bruises: he is due to pay an exorbitant sum for a couple of fighting fish belonging to a notorious thug called Ladyboy, which he has accidentally spilled. He tries to get a young woman of his acquaintance, Bernie, to lend him some money; however, he ends up being attacked by her mentally handicapped son. This is where the Howie appears, having decided to help the Rookie as a form of atonement for his brother's death. He saves the Rookie from the fight, provides him with some ointment for scabies, and accompanies him to a party where the Rookie is to hand over the money to Ladyboy. Mortal combat ensues between the Howie and Ladyboy, during which Ladyboy bites off part of the Howie's face and numerous other ruptures of the body are inflicted. The Howie eventually wins but is immediately attacked by his friends Ollie and the Peaches because he had rejected the Peaches' sister, Avalanche. He is thrown out of the window and ends up impaled on a railing. Shortly afterwards, he is crushed to death by Flann Dingle's van with a youngster nicknamed Ginger Boy surfing on the roof. The Rookie decides to convey the news to the Howie's parents; once he arrives at their flat, he is confronted with video footage of the Howie's dead brother, which is the final image of the play.

O'Rowe's central themes are clearly in evidence in this gruesome tale. The characters' idea of manliness is again shaped not only by the patriarchal context of their world but also by Hollywood cinema: as Brian Singleton has observed, the young men suffer under its influence from 'a drive to construct the self as a wounded hero' and relish in telling 'tales of survival from violent scrapes' (Singleton 2006, p. 263). Women are again conceived of as sexual objects only, and while the male characters are not as rampantly homophobic as in *From Both Hips* or *Made in China* (they do not mind Ollie being gay), their masculinity is still characterized by 'compulsory heterosexuality' (Singleton 2006, p. 263). Outspoken racism is very much part of their assertion of identity, despite the fact that their Hollywood action heroes Bruce Lee and John Woo are of Asian descent.

Violence serves as the only means of establishing justice, which is purely of a retributive nature. It is governed by the principle of an eye for an eye, where even the adequacy of the revenge taken is often not an issue, as in beating up the Rookie for unintentionally spreading a contagious disease or the Howie's friends' decision to throw him out of the window for offending one of theirs sister. The vindictive world of *Howie the Rookie* truly testifies to Francis Bacon's dictum that 'Revenge is a kind of wild justice; which the more man's nature runs to, the more ought law to weed it out' (Bacon 1912, p. 19). However, this is a lawless world and the characters lack the ability to see any alternatives. As a result, their lives are lived in 'a world of pain', as the Rookie acknowledges (O'Rowe 1999, p. 37). Their toxic masculinity (to return to Singleton's phrase) stands in the way of love, and revenge obliterates any friendship. Even the Howie's seemingly redemptive gesture of fighting the Ladyboy is really an act of self-destruction, rather than a sacrifice for the sake of another, as Eamonn Jordan has noted (Jordan 2010, p. 174): both combatants have tears of existential despair in their eyes, confirming Francis Bacon's conclusion that vengefulness leads to unfortunate ends (Bacon 1912, p. 21). Individual identity is ultimately abolished in this desperate world, which applies in particular to the main protagonists, as indicated by their shared surname and the merging of their names in the play's title.

Since the action is unmistakably set in Dublin and the characters use an appropriate slang, it may be tempting to interpret *Howie the Rookie* as an idiosyncratic form of commentary on the contemporary issues of that city, and perhaps even of Ireland. Given that the drama was written and first produced at the height of the unprecedented boom of the Irish economy, customarily referred to as the Celtic Tiger, the temptation may be all the stronger. Numerous social and cultural commentators repeatedly pointed out during that period that the sudden prosperity experienced by most Irish people had bypassed the lowest stratum of society, leading to the total neglect of entire areas and to an enormous widening of the gap between the poor and the rest of Ireland's population. Consequently, many critics and reviewers from Ireland have explored the relation between the dystopian world of the play and the reality of the rough parts of Dublin. For instance, Cathy Leeney has described O'Rowe's plays as an 'attempt to dramatize the imagined lives' of 'people on the margins of the recent bonanza' who subsist in depleted urban areas (Leeney 2007, p. 109). Brian Singleton has spoken of the author's 'infatuation with the criminal underbelly of Dublin's sprawling working-class suburbia' (Singleton 2006, p. 262). Nevertheless, as Eamonn Jordan has pointed out, the references to parts of West Dublin in *Howie the Rookie* are deliberately blurred and often misplaced, which is in line with the characters' disorientation in the world and results in the impression of the setting as a 'non-place' in Mark Augé's sense of the term (Jordan 2010, p. 8). Jordan's observation thus demonstrates that while O'Rowe's plays may reference locations and milieus associated with the negative aspects of Celtic Tiger prosperity, they are not really *about* them (see also Haughton 2011, p. 154).

The grotesque is present in multiple forms in *Howie the Rookie*. First of all, the vivid and ubiquitous images of the body often take the form of the Rabelaisian carnivalesque, such as in the erotic scenes involving Avalanche who is overweight and intersperses the action with loud belching, or in the Howie's and Ladyboy's fight, with the individual rounds punctuated by the sound of the Rookie's farts. Yet, as in the work of Sarah Kane, Mark Ravenhill, or Philip Ridley, the liberating potential of the laughter at the carnivalesque propounded by Bakhtin is quenched by the human body being principally the target of violation in the play, as the overwhelming imagery is that of lacerations, wounds, and bruises inflicted in savage fights. The cruelty and darkness of O'Rowe's alienated world is consequently akin to the bleakest versions of the Romantic grotesque. Scabies, a disease associated with insanitary living conditions and neglect, is present in *Howie the Rookie* literally but bears a figurative meaning as well: this is a truly scabrous world.

The most fascinating grotesque feature of the play is the contrast between the dystopian content and the language through which the dystopia is conveyed. While the narrators use a slang that is in tune with their social milieu, their monologues are also heavily aestheticized: speech is orchestrated in punchy rhythm, abounds in alliteration, and often twists the syntax to a poetic effect. To give just one prime example, the Ladyboy's dying moment is depicted as follows: 'Til Ladyboy, knackered, his bein' the weaker flesh, spent, spent like seed, like spunk, sinks to the floor, sits, then lies down' (p. 49). This peculiar aestheticization of the language is complemented by O'Rowe's attempt to involve enigmatic mythical forces in the plot. The fateful HiAce van driven by Flann Dingle, with Ginger Boy surfing on the roof, thus races through the events of the two days and appears at strategic points to the Howie and to the Rookie, and is interpreted by the latter as an incarnation of the Mayans' God of Death (see pp. 31, 44, 50–1). The precise significance of the Rookie's observation is impossible to unravel, however.

The discrepancy between the harshness of the reality and the formalized language and partially mythologized content induces an effect that is typical of the grotesque: the world of the characters is dangerous, frightening, and repulsive, but the impact of the strange poeticization of the language and the hint at a mysterious supernatural intervention allures the spectator to it. Nonetheless, the nature of the audience engagement produced has become the object of some justified criticism: O'Rowe has been accused of glorifying the criminal underworld (Singleton 2006, p. 262) or even fetishizing it (Jordan 2010, p. 167).

III

Quite untypically, Mark O'Rowe wrote his next monologue drama *Crestfall* for an all-female cast. The play was first staged at Dublin's Gate Theatre in 2003, and despite the accomplished performance by Aisling O'Sullivan, Marie Mullen, and Eileen Walsh and the able directorial hand of Garry Hynes, the event was regarded as a failure. This was partly to do with the choice of venue, since the Gate's audience is rather conservative—as a result, the play was ill attended and there were mass walkouts every night. Reviewers almost universally panned the play, many wondering like Karen Fricker why 'a woman as smart as Hynes' decided to direct a play that was so gratuitous, humourless, and empty (Fricker 2003). *Crestfall* fared better in its first London production four years later (Theatre503, 2007, dir. Róisín McBrinn) but the reviews were still mixed. The text remained unpublished until 2011, when it appeared in the first volume of O'Rowe's collected plays. The author decided to rewrite the play substantially for publication; apart from some cuts, O'Rowe's alterations were predominantly to the rhythm and the flow of the language (see O'Rowe 2011, pp. ix–x). Most significantly, the frequency of rhyming was increased to a degree that brought the play closer to its successor, *Terminus*, rather than the largely non-rhyming lines of *Howie the Rookie*.

Crestfall consists of three successive monologues that outline the events of a single day in a small Irish town. The narrative is even more savage than *Howie the Rookie*, featuring as it does not only brutal fights but also rape, women being beaten, a massacre with a shotgun, drug abuse, and the torture of a horse as a public spectacle. The first speaker is Olive Day, a young incest victim who asserts her identity by sexual voraciousness, arguing that 'The woman's better/ the match of the men, / a kind of queen of this fucking hole' (O'Rowe 2011, p. 328). At the same time,

Olive is trying to turn her loving husband into an aggressive macho by ostentatiously sleeping around, so that he would behave like all the other men in town. Ultimately, she succeeds but with the most tragic consequences, as her husband ends up brutally beating her first, and then shooting her together with the father of her child (whom he thought was his) and two other people before blowing his own head off.

The second monologue is delivered by Alison Ellis, who is also the mother of a young boy. Her son Philip had been kicked in the head by a horse in an accident, and was mentally handicapped as a result. The local people decide to take revenge on the animal, horrendously torturing it in a communal scene that is reminiscent of a carnival gone berserk, and they have Philip brought in to finish the poor horse off with an axe. Alison and her husband manage to save their son at the last minute and bring him back home, where Alison says a prayer to God for them to 'be taken care of' in 'this savage quarter' (p. 353).

The final speaker is Tilly McQuarrie, a drug addict who has been making ends meet as a prostitute. Tilly had been forced to have an abortion by her pimp Inchy, who was the father of this child and also of Olive's son. Out of envy, and as she has had a fight with Olive earlier in the day, Tilly informs Olive's husband about the real paternity of "their" son. This triggers the concluding massacre, before which Tilly is brutally hammered by Inchy's mates. In a final scene that returns to the idyllic opening image of the play with children bathing in a river in sunshine, she enters the water with Olive's infant son and washes away the gore he was splattered with during the shooting.

As in O'Rowe's previous work, the 'wild justice' of revenge plays a central role in *Crestfall*, and its tragic results are blatantly evident, as is the fact that vengefulness stands in the way of community. A vendetta is even effected on an animal, as if this horse had caused the accident out of malevolent free will. O'Rowe indeed depicts 'a society calcified by violence' (Fricker 2003), while it is doubtful whether 'society' is in fact the appropriate term here. We have noted that the play is supposed to be set in a rural Irish town. Yet in contrast to *Howie the Rookie*, there are no specific geographical references and the monologues feature very few elements of dialect or slang. The connection of the play's world with specific reality is therefore even looser: O'Rowe presents a self-contained realm of crestfallen individuals whose only remaining reaction to their condition is to lash out against one another. The place they inhabit is truly a grotesque pit of hell, as fierce as that painted by Hieronymus Bosch; as in the early plays of Sarah Kane, the only difference consists in the bodily harm being inflicted solely by humans.

What is remarkable here is that *Crestfall* is O'Rowe's first drama that involves God. However, the attitude to faith of most of the town's inhabitants is iconically embodied in the mutilated statue of Christ whose hands had been broken off and then used as ashtrays by Inchy and his associates in a bar. Alison seems to be the only person to have retained faith but her desperate prayer is left unanswered, beyond the fact that her family suffers no more harm for the rest of the day. The closing baptismal image of Tilly and the baby provides a mere moment of hope, as the child is inevitably to be taken away from its temporary surrogate mother, while the cataclysm that the boy had just undergone is not likely to leave him unscathed. All in all, the indication is that this 'hole' is Godforsaken.

The grotesque contrast between the content and the stylized language observed in *Howie the Rookie* is maintained in *Crestfall*. An accurate assessment of its details and impact is complicated by the fact that the text of the play as it was originally performed is unavailable and, at the same time, the text published in *Plays: One* remains hitherto unproduced. The discussion of the Dublin and London productions by reviewers and critics shows that the original version of the play was rhythmically close to *Howie* and featured flamboyant alliteration. The published text has added rhyme—as noted earlier—and further sound patterning including consonance and assonance. There is no doubt that from a formal point of view, this has made *Crestfall* a significantly more interesting play. Nevertheless, the increased aestheticization makes the author all the more susceptible to accusations of glorifying and fetishizing violence and the lurid, regardless of the fact that the prominence of horror may perhaps be motivated by what one of Philip Ridley's characters refers to as humanity's 'need for the shivers' (Ridley 2012, p. 67; see Chap. 2), a compulsion that has been consistently catered for by modern writing at least since the era of the early gothic stories.

Moreover, O'Rowe's aestheticizing tendency is again complemented by the involvement of a mysterious supernatural presence: this time, it is a three-eyed dog seen running at the head of a pack several times in the course of the events, ultimately chasing the carcass of the victimized horse that is floating in the river. The accusations come across all the more strongly due to O'Rowe's replacement of rampant machos as speakers by a trio of women whose stories revolve around motherhood. In Eamonn Jordan's view, *Crestfall* thus appears as an instance of 'a brutal search for extremes that seems to be validated by the authenticity of a female voice' (Jordan 2010, p. 226). The effect of the mixture of repulsion and attraction produced by the play's grotesque is similar to *Howie the Rookie* yet even more intense, having been described by one reviewer as producing a 'terrible fascination' that feels like 'watching a deep root-canal filling being conducted without anaesthetic' (Gardner 2007).

IV

Terminus is Mark O'Rowe's most accomplished work to date by universal consent. It consists of three interlocking monologues by two women and a man, delivered in a static theatrical situation similar to *Howie the Rookie* and *Crestfall*. Of the three monologue dramas, *Terminus* uses the most specific references to the Dublin of the Celtic Tiger era. Apart from featuring an accurate topography of the city and its surroundings, it reflects the recent construction boom and depicts Dublin as a pulsating metropolis. The play uses its setting as a backdrop for a true human inferno, where almost everyone is intent on doing harm to others. The city is again characterized largely by its underbelly; while the protagonists are distinctly middle class, their self-destructive excesses and spiritual emptiness are consistent with O'Rowe's previous work.

The author's interest in popular cinema had been imprinted in his early plays chiefly in a range of allusions, as mentioned earlier. *Terminus* fully demonstrates that at least since *Howie the Rookie*, O'Rowe's work for the stage has become increasingly cinematic, both in its imagery and in its construction, reflecting his experience as a screen writer. The sequence of individual scenes within the plot of *Terminus*, and the individual shots, so to speak, within the scenes, are closely reminiscent of the conventions of a Hollywood thriller or action movie. In fact, were it not for the place names, Dublin could be mistaken for any American industrial city serving as a location for such a film, featuring as it does street gangs, brutal assaults on public transport, swishing knife blades, and martial arts feats. There is also a spectacular car chase, an extract from which will document the generic affinity; it is narrated from the perspective of speaker C who is fleeing from the Gardaí in a stolen lorry:

> It's been a dead straight run so far, but, approaching Dublin, that run is marred by an escalation of cars and shit, necessitating split-second steering, which, I fear, my recurring exhaustion is queering up and causing a couple of wrong decisions resulting in a collision or two.

Like at The Red Cow, when I plough into a car and tear off two of its doors, or in Inchicore, when, avoiding a bus, I annihilate, or just about, some traffic lights, and, heart in mouth and knuckles white on the wheel, I peel ahead in a fever, totally juiced, toward Heuston Station, where another collision sends a taxi crashing off the bridge and into the Liffey, the driver still steering as if he can prevent his descent—a splash—he can't—then a dash up the quays, squeezing through gaps in traffic, nudging cars aside when the space isn't wide enough, some of them crashing badly—tough. (O'Rowe 2007, p. 45)

Spectators are accustomed to such scenes from action movies; the exuberance in the play is provided by the fact that it is set in Dublin, and by the stylized language and tone of cynical detachment typical of O'Rowe's monologists in *Terminus*, particularly when describing violence.

Terminus interestingly compares with another drama by an author who had provided inspiration for *Howie the Rookie*, Conor McPherson's *Port Authority* (2001). McPherson's play also uses the form of interlocking monologues and is likewise set in Celtic Tiger Dublin. In both works, Dublin provides the scenery for the unfolding of the characters' lives and their crises; what *Port Authority* shares with *Terminus* in this respect in particular are the unfulfilled desires, frustrated love relationships, and the alienation experienced by all and sundry. For all that, McPherson's is essentially a nostalgic play, characterized by its lyricism and by the compassion that it lavishes on its troubled protagonists. Moreover, its outline of Dublin is much more diverse, both in terms of locations and the social milieu of different generations: ultimately, *Port Authority* comes across as a fairly realistic map of the city with its inhabitants.

In contrast to McPherson, O'Rowe is not concerned with any extensive mapping of the city or even the vaguest form of social realism. Rather, the use of the Dublin setting for ubiquitous brutal acts of violence makes it worthwhile to resuscitate the term 'neo-Jacobean', which I have already referred to in relation to the work of Philip Ridley (see Chap. 2). Neo-Jacobeanism was a category used in the late 1990s to describe some of the early works of 'in-yer-face theatre', highlighting the unrelenting controversial focus on blood and guts in these works, which made them akin to the Jacobean tragedies of John Webster and Thomas Middleton, and their precedents such as Shakespeare's *Titus Andronicus* or Christopher Marlowe's *Massacre at Paris*. It is indeed the aestheticization of brutality and carnage that comes across as a chief characteristic of *Terminus*, a feature that we have already observed in *Howie the Rookie* and *Crestfall*.

However, unlike most of in-yer-face theatre—and, as a matter of fact, also the Jacobean tragedies—O'Rowe's play prominently involves supernatural elements and mythical creatures. What appeared merely as an enigmatic motif in his earlier monologue dramas becomes a central element in *Terminus*. Not only does the play feature a Faustian selling of C's soul to the devil, but outstandingly, the protagonist B (a woman in her twenties) is rescued when falling to her death from a crane by a dragon-like demon with hooves, horns, and a face composed of worms, who turns out to be the soul of the serial killer C come to reclaim him. The woman ends up having passionate sex with the demon; together they are chased by seven angels, with faces also made of worms. Part of their journey takes them underground in imitation of the epic *katabasis*; the underworld they reach is an empty cavernous space, which becomes the setting of a battle between the demon and the angels over the young woman, and eventually the site of her peaceful drowning in a river, during which her memory is erased and she is reborn as a child presented to her own mother. The demon in turn locates C, his 'other half' (p. 46), prizes him out of a speeding Mercedes, and on top of the arm of a crane, effects the final revenge for his murderous deeds.

Terminus can be recognized as a grotesque play due to the seamless but at the same time puzzling mixture of the natural world with assorted supernatural motifs and characters, ranging from Christian mythology to the Faust legend, Greek epic and myth, Oriental tales, the myth of metempsychosis, and the fantasy creatures and fighting featured in computer games. The incongruity of these elements corresponds to the principles of the early grotesque ornamentation that gave rise to the concept (see Chap. 1). Moreover, the shock and terror experienced watching the play results from the realization 'that the familiar and apparently harmonious world is alienated under the impact of abysmal forces, which break it up and shatter its coherence', to return to Wolfgang Kayser's pertinent observation (Kayser 1966, p. 37). According to Kayser, the fear of the mysterious abysmal—or perhaps rather abyssal—forces appears first with the Romantic grotesque, following from the absence of God. O'Rowe's play may be regarded as a curious development in this tradition, as it substantially engages with the concepts of universal justice and divine judgment. For one, the violent actions of the protagonists A and C, of the demon, the angels, and others are repeatedly considered to be at least partially fair ways of retaliation for some injustice committed either on them, or—in the case of the demon and the angels—against universal order.

Nevertheless, the notion of what might be fair is profoundly complicated in the play, as becomes apparent from the stories of the three speakers. A, a woman in her forties, is guilty of wilfully destroying her daughter's relationship; she eventually regrets this profusely and starts working as a counselling specialist on a crisis hotline. She decides to save a pregnant ex-pupil of hers, Helen, from the monstrous Celine who has come to dominate Helen's life; A ends up brutally murdering Celine who is about to impale Helen's unborn baby (following two fierce assaults on A)—only to learn that Helen actually wanted the child to die, since it had been diagnosed with an incurable debilitating disease. Helen jumps under C's lorry, and dies after giving birth to a baby girl, who provides A with a moment of union with her own lost daughter (we are to learn that the baby actually *is* her daughter, reincarnated). A is finally left sitting waiting on her adult daughter's doorstep, and the indication is that she is eventually going to be imprisoned for the murder of Celine.

The story of B represents another negotiation of the concept of justice, which is perhaps less disorienting but still peculiar: B is a largely innocent young woman who has a relationship destroyed by her mother (speaker A), lives a frustrated single life, and dies in an accident following a set-up by her best friend; she is "rewarded" by being given, temporarily, a demon lover, and then being reborn as a terminally ill child.

Finally, the serial killer C, a man in his thirties, turns out to be committing all his heinous deeds because of having been tricked by Satan. C barters his soul to the devil for the gift of singing, so that he would feel more at ease with women; or, in the cynical wording of his soul, in order 'to become through song some kind of stud' (p. 25). At any rate, it turns out that although the gift is given, it does not work in public: C becomes a divine singer in private but is possessed by crippling stage fright in front of people. Regardless of the question of the adequacy and the form of C's revenge, it is Satan who first plays foul. The presence of the devil, angels, and demons indicates the existence of a transcendent moral order; yet God appears to be as silent as in *Crestfall,* and the events in the lives of the three protagonists make the audience wonder about the exact nature of the moral code, creating a sense of confusion that is so distinctive of the grotesque.

The principal means used by O'Rowe to seduce the audience into his savage world again consists in the aestheticization of language. This device is used to the greatest extent in *Terminus,* a play that comes across as an idiosyncratic version of verse drama. O'Rowe's chosen verse form is hardly conventional. The basic iambic rhythm of the speech is strong, and metrical irregularities often correspond to emphases or pauses required by the meaning. The most conspicuous poetic feature is the ostentatious use of rhyme. O'Rowe's rhyming is perfect at times but almost as frequently, it unabashedly descends into rough half-rhymes. Furthermore, the positioning of the rhymes is mostly eccentric. Rhyme would customarily appear at the end of lines of the same length when used in a verse play; any attempt to divide O'Rowe's text into such standard lines would reveal that the rhyming pattern is mostly a wild combination of end rhymes with internal rhymes, which are often intended to deliver a specific effect, be it that of comedy or of shock. This bespeaks both the author's exuberant sense of mischief and his propensity for excess, as does the embellishment of the speeches with ad hoc patterns of assonance, alliteration, and consonance. In the following extract, the iambics spring merrily forward and are combined with the repetition of consonant and vowel sounds and an excess of rhyming in a comic rendering of a scene; we are still in the car chase, at a point where C has picked up a hitchhiker and an announcement comes on the radio concerning the search for a savage murderer on the run:

> [...] I make a gesture, stutter, "Hey, man. That's not me." His answer: a wee. You can see the spreading blotch across his crotch, the smell of which is rich with dread and fear, so I say, "Is what I said not clear? It's someone else they're talking about!" But no. The stupid fuck lets out a shout and grabs my throat and squeezes and squeals.
> Then, that's all she wrote because, Jesus, the wheels just turn of their own volition: we're out of control, then there's a collision. A pole. And, one second he's there, the next: thin air. He wasn't wearing his seat belt, see, and so was catapulted through the windscreen. This has-been, or once-was, so-called because he's no more. [...] (p. 31)

Apart from the obvious incompatibility of the subject matter, it is O'Rowe's parodic imitation of an elevated form that produces the effect of a casual "coolness" of depiction, one that corresponds so well with the hard-boiled and often plainly cynical attitude of a speaker such as C. Audiences have become used to this cool swagger from numerous gangland films since the early 1990s, including recent Irish features such as O'Rowe's own *Intermission* (2003). It has been subsequently manifest in some of the dark comedies seen on stage, including those of Martin McDonagh, and has of course been ubiquitous in early hip hop music and rap in general, to which the rhythms of O'Rowe's language have sometimes been likened.

O'Rowe's monologue dramas—and *Terminus* in particular—add a new dimension through the formal linking of their grotesque world with that of the gory Jacobean verse tragedies.

A central trope in the plot of *Terminus* is the desire to sing. The venerable precedent in this respect is clearly Tom Murphy's celebrated *The Gigli Concert* (1983). In both plays, the wish for a perfect singing voice serves as a metonym of transcendence, which is eventually achieved, with some unexpected twists. In *The Gigli Concert*, it is, ironically, not the Irishman but JPW King who sings like Beniamino Gigli in the end. There is the distinct possibility that the final experience of transcendence may be a hallucination triggered by excessive frustration and the use of alcohol and prescription drugs; but regardless of that, the singing comes across as a sublime moment for the audience (see Murphy 1988, pp. 38–9). *Terminus*, on the other hand, treats the image in a parodic manner, as it does the conventions of verse drama: not only are Gigli's arias replaced with a song by Bette Midler, but the singing takes place when the protagonist is hanging by his intestines from the arm of a crane, while the moment of transcendence has been preceded by a series of brutal, premeditated murders committed by the singer.

Christopher Murray has argued that of all the plays of that decade, *The Gigli Concert* 'best encapsulates the frustrated aspirations' in Ireland in the 1980s. According to Murray, Murphy's 'frightening portrait of a soul in torment' is illustrative of the contemporaneous concern among playwrights with the 'redefinition of self and aims in a society where old structures are disintegrating'. Viewed in such light, JPW King's final aria represents a 'triumph over tragic circumstance', which elicits empathy from the audience and bases its relation to experience in 'a combination of compassion and an ethic derived from music' (Murray 1997, pp. 225–6). While a certain degree of empathy with the tortured singer in *Terminus* may be reasonably predicted, his situation and its framing is more complicated than in Murphy's play. What is of particular significance is that whereas the singing in *The Gigli Concert* is witnessed only by the actual audience in the theatre, O'Rowe also describes the reaction of a crowd of spectators in his play. C speaking:

> So, filled with exhilaration at the gift of the weight that's been lifted this late, after waiting so fucking long, I launch into song and the crowd all start to sway, I swear, this way then that, all unaware of anything but the

disembowelled man who swings, the song he sings, Bette Midler's "Wind Beneath My Wings". And, they're mesmerised—man, look at their eyes!— enraptured, captured, enchanted, transplanted by my voice to a better place, and rejoice at the hour of my death that I'm getting to show them what I've got. (p. 48)

There is no doubt that the scene is blatantly grotesque; nonetheless, the reaction of the audience within the play is, curiously enough, depicted as a typical response to an encounter with the *sublime*. Ever since antiquity, the concept of the sublime has been defined through its effect on the recipient, who is entranced and transported by the incommensurable or the unimaginable (Hrbata and Procházka 2005, pp. 120–21). While the grotesque and the sublime have more often than not been regarded as opposites, at least since the late eighteenth century—particularly Immanuel Kant's discussion in *The Critique of Judgment*—the two concepts have also been closely juxtaposed because of the important features that they share. Both have been characterized as eliciting a strong emotional reaction, one that is conflicting and often involves terror of the unknown, both have been associated with excess, and also with the transgression of an accepted aesthetic norm.[2] Indeed, one of the most insightful recent commentators on the grotesque, Geoffrey Galt Harpham, has ultimately gone so far as to argue that 'what is commonly conceived of as an opposition between the sublime and the grotesque is often a mere difference of point of view' (Harpham 2006, p. 22).

In light of these observations, the final scene of O'Rowe's grotesque drama presents us with a rather disturbing version of the sublime for the contemporary era, which is quite in tune with O'Rowe's brazenly playful use of poeticized language in a ghastly thriller. While JPW's singing like the great Italian tenor in *The Gigli Concert*, despite its carefully highlighted ambiguity, still follows the tradition of associating the sublime and transcendence with high art, *Terminus*, a drama obsessed with death, gives us a terminal, parodic version of the same, in which a serial killer flawlessly sings a trite love song by a pop diva[3] and solicits from his audience a 'combination of adoration and wonder' (p. 48). The rendering of the Gigli aria by a 'soul in torment' aims for the audience's empathy and inspires a feeling of awe. The same applies to *Terminus*, but only as regards the audience *depicted in the play*; the actual audience in the theatre is much more likely to experience a much broader variety of emotions, possibly including uneasy chuckles of laughter.

Such a conflicting reaction would indeed be typical of many other scenes in this grotesque play, which implies that Harpham's observation needs to be somewhat qualified here. It is true that Harpham plausibly cancels the radical opposition between the sublime and the grotesque but an important difference must still be borne in mind. This consists in the fact that the sublime never elicits amusement; the reaction to the grotesque, on the other hand, frequently alleviates terror with laughter. As outlined in my introductory chapter, Ralf Remshardt has described such laughter as always 'inappropriate': it counteracts the horrific but simultaneously is aware of its own 'callousness' (Remshardt 2004, pp. 81, 85); in other words, we are aware that we should not be laughing at something but we somehow cannot help doing so. Frances Connelly has also pointed out that while the grotesque closely 'cleaves to the sublime', it 'reaches down deep into visceral experience. It counters the disembodied abstraction of the sublime with a power that is felt and expressed through the body' (Connelly 2012, p. 154). By depicting a crowd of admirers as enraptured by sublime experience when what they are watching is in fact a grotesque spectacle that involves disembowelment, O'Rowe's play metatheatrically reflects the problematic glorification of the violent and the lurid noted earlier in this chapter, and makes an uncomfortable statement concerning contemporary tastes. It is of note that the statement obviously includes the preferences of the author of the image, too.

Reading *The Gigli Concert* in the context of Irish drama, Christopher Murray noted the shift of the setting in the 1980s from the heretofore typical house or a home to that of the more ambivalent, 'decentred' shabby office as a space that more credibly reflected the fundamental negotiations of individual identity, which he regards as characteristic of the period. Despite the torturous internal conflicts that both protagonists, the Irish Man and JPW King suffer from, the play ultimately sees the human being, in Murray's words, as 'capable of growth in a crumbling world of brute force and material ambition' (Murray 1997, p. 225). Moreover, JPW King is conceived as a 'Faust/Houdini figure', which serves as 'an image of transcendence, of an alternative to the new Irish culture of success' (p. 226).

Terminus, like *Port Authority* and several other of Conor McPherson's plays, then moves the setting in another significant spatial shift from any indication of an indoor space to an empty stage. From this space, the stories of the protagonists are unravelled to the audience; these narratives feature domestic settings only for scenes of frustration and loneliness, while in *Terminus*, much of their action is set in a version of the Dublin cityscape shaped by the convention of the thriller and the action movie. In their landmark study of space and place in Irish theatre, Chris Morash and Shaun Richards have observed that Dublin place names in O'Rowe's play 'take on the aura of film sets or videogame scenarios'; they have argued that this in effect deprives them of specific reference in the offstage world and O'Rowe thereby creates a space where 'all is free and all is terrifying' (Morash and Richards 2013, pp. 120–1). At the same time however, the spaces featured in *Terminus* can be related together with their dwellers to the spiritual void of the contemporary era. In this context, Murray's 'Faust/Houdini' figure of *The Gigli Concert* may be seen to have turned into that of Faust/Jack the Ripper, as the ruthless killer C is hardly capable of any spiritual growth.

Moreover, the possibility of an 'ethic derived from music', to refer to another phrase by Murray (p. 226), is plainly travestied by the nature of the song that is sung, and by the way the audience in the narrative are awestruck by it, regarding it as sublime. The ethical flux and arbitrariness of justice, in which revenge plays a role that is perhaps not so central as in *Howie the Rookie* or *Crestfall* but certainly not negligible, remains unresolved, and the implicit desire for a metaphysical arbiter is frustrated. It may be true that C is going to roast in hell. Nevertheless, O'Rowe endows him with the 'bliss-inducing memory' of his ultimate vocal achievement, which is going to 'ease whatever suffering is in store' for him (p. 48). The play's coda—'I've heard tell that even the Devil remembered Heaven after he fell' (p. 49)—thus serves only as a final confirmation of the blurred contours of any potential transcendental moral order.

The hopefulness embodied in the final cathartic scene of *The Gigli Concert* clearly has no counterpart in *Terminus*, notwithstanding any sense of catharsis that may be created by the final punishment of the protagonist that is so ardently qualified. What O'Rowe's *pièce de résistance* and Murphy's modern classic share is that they present the audience with a tantalizing theatrical event. Yet in the case of *Terminus*, that event remains, at heart, fundamentally puzzling—in line with the entire tradition of the grotesque.

V

The emergence of monologue drama as a major strand of Anglophone theatre since the mid-1990s has been generally acknowledged, notwithstanding the recurrent complaints about a lack of theatricality allegedly implied by the absence of dialogue and multiple characters. The editor of the first essay collection in English on the subject of contemporary monologue, Clare Wallace, has pointed out the scope of the dramatic context in which monologue has been used, ranging from 'radically anti-narrative theatre of the fragmented subject' to 'a much more conventional drama of storytelling, testimony, confession and so on' (Wallace 2006, pp. 13–14). Wallace has also noted '[t]he use of persona as a means of social critique, the undermining of gender stereotypes through role-play, blurring the outlines of the autobiographical, "authentic" subject' in numerous monodramas and solo performances (p. 13). When the position of Mark O'Rowe's monologue dramas is considered within this context, it becomes clear that despite their linguistic aestheticization, they clearly foreground conventional storytelling and the confessional mode. In that, they join the work of prominent Irish contemporaries such as—again—Conor McPherson, Owen McCafferty, and the earlier monologue dramas by Brian Friel, all of whose focus has been on 'issues of male inadequacy, both sexual and social' and which have also been theatrically conservative (Lonergan 2009, p. 177; see also Singleton 2006, pp. 260–1). As indicated in my discussion of *Howie the Rookie*, *Crestfall*, and *Terminus*, there is virtually no social critique, undermining of macho masculinity, or questioning of the authenticity of narrative in O'Rowe's work. The ultimate reason for this absence is the lack of alternatives in the world of these dark dramas: what O'Rowe offers the audience are only mesmerising insights into grotesque, infernal worlds.

The self-enclosed nature of O'Rowe's dramas has mostly been underlined by the manner in which the plays have been staged. This applies in particular to the first productions of all three monologue works discussed in this chapter. First of all, the actors delivered their speeches mostly from a static position in space. Moreover, as Cathy Leeney has outlined, the stage design of the Dublin productions of both *Howie the Rookie* and *Crestfall* confirmed the lack of an outside to the worlds presented: Es Devlin's dark grey angular design for *Howie the Rookie* absconded from commenting on the content of the narrative and enhanced the sense of anomie, while Francis O'Connor's set and costumes for *Crestfall* 'framed the narratives of the three women as coming from hell', suspending them 'in an unreachable space, beyond history, beyond change' (Leeney 2007, pp. 111–12). Jon Bausor's design for the Peacock *Terminus* in turn placed the performers on raised podiums on a grey stage, surrounded by broken mirrors used to reflect their gestures (see Haughton 2011, p. 156), emphasizing the containment of the space inhabited by the characters.

Artistically striking in their own right and appropriate given the nature of the play texts, these designs also brought out a fundamental likeness of all of O'Rowe's protagonists that is determined both by their surroundings and by the fact that the formalization of their language does not deviate according to the speaker. As Harvey O'Brien has put it, O'Rowe's writing is distinctive by an 'inevitable collapse of characterization in the face of a consistent authorial vision. Though each of the performers is distinctive, their speech does not vary' (O'Brien 2003). Some of the international productions of the plays have sought to employ intensive physicality and have often used stage space in a much more active manner. Such was the case with the first German performance of *Howie the Rookie* by Patrick Schlösser at the Düsseldorf Municipal Theatre (1999), for instance. Schlösser staged the play in an underground garage, using an elevator, and had the space dominated by the physical action of the performers. A Prague production of *Terminus* directed by Marek Němec (Divadlo v Celetné 2013) also utilized elements of physical theatre but excelled particularly in the creative approach to stage space, featuring a revolving platform centre stage used, among other things, to facilitate a degree of physical interaction between the actors. Yet despite the amazing theatricality of these productions, the sense of the circumscribed nature of the characters' world still remained overwhelming.

The harrowing content of O'Rowe's work combined with imaginative aestheticization of language and a gradually increasing involvement of supernatural or mythical elements in the plot certainly confirms Frances Connelly's observation that the grotesque 'creates meaning by prying open a gap, pulling us into unfamiliar, contested terrain' (Connelly 2012, p. 2). Even more so, O'Rowe's drama testifies to Ralf Remshardt's assertion that the grotesque is 'by nature aggressive, unbending, anarchic, disruptive, and unregulated' (Remshardt 2004, p. 75). However, O'Rowe's brand of the grotesque is assuredly not emancipatory, since the audience's gaze into its abyss is essentially voyeuristic, and when read against the backdrop of contemporary reality, these plays may 'signal a crisis in the articulation of resistance to normalized violence, and the patriarchal structures that support it, where conservative theatrical forms [...] frame that violence as inevitable, fateful and immutable', as Leeney has argued (Leeney 2007, p. 115). As mentioned, O'Rowe has been repeatedly charged not just with presenting violence as inevitable, but also with glorifying it. It is difficult to contest this accusation, despite the author's artful metatheatrical reflection of the issue in *Terminus*, which spotlights the role of audience tastes.[4]

NOTES

1. In German translation, the play comes across as more scatological than in the original due to the customary translation of the English f-word as 'Scheiße' in many contexts; the reviewer of the Bochum production complained that '[t]he word "Scheiße" was heard at least 100 times before one gave up counting' ((dpa) 2001; my translation).
2. An excellent critical introduction in English to the history of the concept is provided by Costelloe (2012). For a comprehensive survey on the sublime and the grotesque in the seminal area of Romantic fiction, poetry, and drama, see Hrbata and Procházka 120–66. Elżbieta Baraniecka has recently put forward the philosophically challenging proposition to regard 'in-yer-face drama' through the prism of the sublime (Baraniecka 2013).
3. Notwithstanding her earlier engagement with multifarious music genres and with the stage, it seems justified to characterize Bette Midler in 1988 (which is when she recorded 'Wind Beneath My Wings') as a pop diva. The song appears in the soundtrack to the film *Beaches*, which the female monologists of *Terminus* are depicted as watching in a rare moment of happiness.
4. It will be curious to see whether O'Rowe's recent flawed attempt at a psychological family drama, *Our Few and Evil Days* (Abbey Theatre, Dublin, 2014), indicates more than a temporary change of direction.

WORKS CITED

(dpa). (2001, February 25). O'Rowe's "Made in China" uraufgeführt [The Premiere of O'Rowe's *Made in China*]. *Schwäbische Zeitung*. Retrieved January 19, 2015, from http://www.schwaebische.de/home_artikel,-_arid,108841.html
Bacon, F. (1912). *Bacon's Essays* (Sydney Humphries, Ed.). London: Adam & Charles Black.

Baraniecka, E. (2013). *Sublime Drama: British Theatre of the 1990s.* Berlin: de Gruyter.
Connelly, F. S. (2012). *The Grotesque in Western Art and Culture: The Image at Play.* Cambridge: Cambridge University Press.
Costelloe, T. M. (Ed.). (2012). *The Sublime: From Antiquity to the Present.* Cambridge: Cambridge University Press.
Fricker, K. (2003, May 24). Review of *Crestfall*, by Mark O'Rowe. *Guardian.* Retrieved January 15, 2015, from http://www.theguardian.com/stage/2003/may/24/theatre.artsfeatures1
Gardner, L. (2007, December 1). Review of *Crestfall*, by Mark O'Rowe. *Guardian.* Retrieved January 15, 2015, from http://www.theguardian.com/stage/2007/dec/01/theatre1
Harpham, G. G. (2006). *On the Grotesque. Strategies of Contradiction in Art and Literature* (2nd ed.). Aurora, CO: Davies Group.
Haughton, M. (2011). Performing Power: Violence as Fantasy and Spectacle in Mark O'Rowe's *Made in China* and *Terminus*. *New Theatre Quarterly, 27* (2), 153–166.
Hrbata, Z., & Procházka M. (2005). *Romantismus a romantismy* [Romanticism and Romanticisms]. Prague: Karolinum Press.
Jordan, E. (2010). *Dissident Dramaturgies: Contemporary Irish Theatre.* Dublin: Irish Academic Press.
Kayser, W. (1966). *The Grotesque in Art and Literature* (1957) (Ulrich Weisstein, Trans.). New York: McGraw-Hill.
Leeney, C. (2007). Men in No-Man's Land: Performing Urban Liminal Spaces in Two Plays by Mark O'Rowe. *The Irish Review, 35*, 108–116.
Lonergan, P. (2009). *Theatre and Globalization: Irish Drama in the Celtic Tiger Era.* Houndmills: Palgrave Macmillan.
Morash, C., & Richards, S. (2013). *Mapping Irish Theatre: Theories of Space and Place.* Cambridge: Cambridge University Press.
Murphy, T. (1988). The Gigli Concert. In *After Tragedy: Three Irish Plays by Tom Murphy* (pp. 1–39). London: Methuen.
Murray, C. (1997). *Twentieth-Century Irish Drama: Mirror up to Nation.* Manchester: Manchester University Press.
O'Brien, H. (2003, May 5). Review of *Crestfall*, by Mark O'Rowe. *CultureVulture.* Retrieved January 15, 2015, from http://culturevulture.net/theater/crestfall-mark-orowe/
O'Rowe, M. (1999). *Howie the Rookie.* London: Nick Hern.
O'Rowe, M. (2007). *Terminus.* London: Nick Hern.
O'Rowe, M. (2011). *Plays: One.* London: Nick Hern.
Remshardt, R. E. (2004). *Staging the Savage God: The Grotesque in Performance.* Carbondale: Southern Illinois University Press.

Ridley, P. (2012). *Plays: 1*. London: Bloomsbury.
Singleton, B. (2006). Am I Talking to Myself? Men, Masculinities and the Monologue in Contemporary Irish Theatre. In C. Wallace (Ed.), *Monologues: Theatre, Performance, Subjectivity* (pp. 260–277). Prague: Litteraria Pragensia.
Wallace, C. (2006). Monologue Theatre, Solo Performance and Self as Spectacle. In C. Wallace (Ed.), *Monologues: Theatre, Performance, Subjectivity* (pp. 1–16). Prague: Litteraria Pragensia.

CHAPTER 4

Life in a Box: Enda Walsh

I

Enda Walsh achieved a measure of success in his native Ireland with his third play, *Disco Pigs* (Corcadorca Theatre Company, 1996), which launched the career of star actor Cillian Murphy; the play became a hit at the Dublin Theatre Festival, and was highly acclaimed at the 1997 Edinburgh Festival. The production subsequently transferred to the Bush Theatre in London and toured internationally. *Disco Pigs* was simultaneously picked up by German dramaturges in Edinburgh and made Walsh one of the most celebrated playwrights of the late 1990s in German-speaking countries, with an astonishing forty-two productions of the play between 1998 and 2001 alone, and its production statistics were apparently rivalled only by Patrick Marber's *Closer* (Huber 2012, p. 84). But it was not until the sparkling Druid Theatre staging of *The Walworth Farce* in Galway (2006) that this outstanding playwright was really granted a place in the canon of Irish drama, alongside more famous contemporaries such as Martin McDonagh, Marina Carr, and Conor McPherson.

The reception of Walsh's recent major dramas—*The New Electric Ballroom* (2004), *The Walworth Farce* (2006), *Penelope* (2010), and *Ballyturk* (2014) has been overwhelmingly enthusiastic in Ireland, the UK and the United States alike. However, scholarly attention has been surprisingly minimal,[1] and reviewers have on the whole remarkably eschewed any attempts at consistent interpretation of the plays. While almost unanimously agreeing that Walsh's work provides a heady celebration of the theatre as a

© The Editor(s) (if applicable) and The Author(s) 2016
O. Pilný, *The Grotesque in Contemporary Anglophone Drama*,
DOI 10.1057/978-1-137-51318-2_4

vibrant medium and that Walsh has an exuberant way with words, reviews have mostly resorted to name-dropping: Walsh's drama has been frequently likened to plays by Samuel Beckett and Harold Pinter, and, somewhat less plausibly, to themes or motifs present in the works of a chaotic mixture of authors ranging from Dylan Thomas to William Golding or Tom Stoppard. The more honest theatre critics admitted that Walsh left them not just enthralled but also baffled. It is my contention that the bewilderment of both reviewers and audiences has been due to the fundamentally grotesque nature of Walsh's drama. This chapter will discuss Walsh's major works, outlining his consistent and elaborate use of the grotesque and examining how it may be related to contemporary reality.

II

As noted in Chap. 1 of this book, the grotesque is defined by blending together incongruous elements and confounding the recipient. Furthermore, as Wolfgang Kayser has observed, the familiar world is unhinged in the grotesque, inspiring insecurity and terror in the beholder: 'The grotesque world is—and is not—our own world' and we are strongly affected since we recognize that our world has ceased to be reliable and has become a terrifying place to live in (Kayser 1966, pp. 37, 185). This summarizes some of the principal effects of Enda Walsh's work, which, especially more recently, abounds in an eclectic mixing of genre elements and seamless blending of reality with wild figments of the imagination, and presents a radically alienated world. The characters in the plays are subjected to insecurity and terror, which are also likely to be felt by audiences at important moments, demonstrating a confluence between Kayser's concept of the grotesque as 'a comprehensive structural principle of works of art' and his notion of the phenomenon as being 'experienced only in the act of reception' (Kayser 1966, pp. 180–1).

In the introductory chapter, I have also shown that citationality has been a recurrent feature of the grotesque in drama at least since Alfred Jarry's Ubu plays. While this technique may be regarded as typical of much of recent Irish and British theatre (see Wallace 2006), and Western theatre in general, it has always played a special role in enhancing the effects of the grotesque. Enda Walsh's drama is a case in point, as citationality has been a vibrant structural and semantic component, particularly as regards allusions to the work of Samuel Beckett, whose name has so often been listed by reviewers. A consistent engagement with Beckett's work is remarkable particularly in the plays Walsh has written since the early 2000s, despite his recent denial of Beckett as a conscious influence (see Billington 2014). Nonetheless, the extent of this engagement varies significantly, ranging from drawing superficial parallels to elaborating a similar basic situation, using an identical device, or quoting Beckett directly. It is specifically the compulsion of the characters to narrate stories about their past that comes to the fore in *bedbound* (2000), while the accuracy of these reminiscences is largely impossible to judge. For instance, the father tells a realistic, gruesome story of how he murdered a manager in one of his shops in plain view of a crowd of people and reporters but implies that he was never arrested or imprisoned; apparently, the truth about the event cannot be discovered. A comparable unreliability of compulsive narrators had been, of course, one of the standard features in Beckett's prose at least since *The Trilogy* and *First Love*, and in most of his drama. Moreover, Walsh adopts a typically Beckettian device in *bedbound* to punctuate the play, having the daughter switch the narrative sequence on and off, ultimately in a neverending cycle, a fact that is indicated in her closing speech: 'I'm in the bed. The panic is gone and all that's left is ta start over. I get that tiredness turn to calm ... and I give in to sleep. I let go. Go' (Walsh 2011, p. 126).

In contrast to the mere use of Beckettian themes and devices, the entire short play *How These Desperate Men Talk* (2004) may be seen as an idiosyncratic version of Beckett's *Ohio Impromptu*: two men seated at a table trying to find out 'how it was' by narrating a story from the past and commenting on it. But it is more than little that is left to tell in Walsh's sketch, as the story recounted is one of murder and revenge, and one of the men forces the other to go on by holding a gun to his head. In true Beckettian fashion, the protagonists are not certain what exactly it is that they are trying to find out by narrating the story ('The *exact* truth hardly matters'. Walsh 2011, p. 134) but they are compelled to continue in their search incessantly.[2]

Elaborate engagement with Beckett is also apparent in *The Small Things* (2005), a play commissioned by Paines Plough together with Philip Ridley's *Mercury Fur* for its project 'This Other England' (Sierz 2012, p. 39, n. 2). In *The Small Things*, an old couple are involved in another repetitive storytelling routine, which features some of Beckett's seminal themes: the compulsion to speak that is accompanied by pain, the need for another person to listen, and the sense that once narration ceases, the end finally and mercifully ensues ('Can I leave the words and find a proper sleep?' Walsh 2011, p. 179). Moreover, the play is divided into equal segments by the roll of a timpani drum, and punctuated by the mechanical intervention of the characters' personal alarm clocks; like all of Beckett's drama, the play involves a precise rhythm and a strategic use of silence.[3] There are also numerous specific allusions to Beckett's plays in *The Small Things*, reinforcing the overall Beckettian atmosphere: analogous to Clov in *Endgame*, the Man asserts: 'Finished. I'm finished' (p. 171) at a moment that is hardly final; his shoes are remarkably out of tune with the rest of his costume, a tape recorder with a recorded memory of the past is used, and the couple's story includes a central silent love scene (pp. 165–6) as in *Krapp's Last Tape*. The most vital intertext in many ways is Beckett's *That Time*, however: not only does Walsh use similar devices and motifs (such as dividing the speeches into equal segments, or the memory of a remarkable scene of wordless love, of which there are several in *That Time*) but, most importantly, *The Small Things* eventually comes across as a lyrical play about old age, love, and memory, quite similar to Beckett's play. The Woman asserts: 'What time do you think it is? [...] That time' (p. 160), and by the end of the play, regardless of the violent revelations featured in the narrative, the overwhelming sense is that of a life drawing to a close; in the words of Beckett's protagonist, 'was there ever any other time but that time?' (Beckett 1990, p. 395).[4]

Significant nods in Beckett's direction continue in the recent major works by Enda Walsh that are the principal focus of the present chapter. In *The New Electric Ballroom*, *The Walworth Farce*, *Penelope*, and *Ballyturk*, the action again consists in an endless repetition of the same with minor variations, and language—despite its incessant flow—is insufficient to convey the most important aspects of human interaction and existence. To borrow a phrase from one of Walsh's characters, Breda, language amounts merely to 'People talking just for the act of it. Words spinning to nothing. For no definable reason. Like a little puppy, a hungry puppy yapping for his supper, yap-yap-yap-yap ... that's people with words' (Walsh 2008b, p. 6). The most significant analogy with Beckett goes hand in hand with this scepticism towards the expressive power of language: like many of Beckett's plays and prose texts, Walsh's dramas present stories of entrapment, and characters entrapped in stories. This applies to the private world of Pig and Runt in the early *Disco Pigs* as well as, most remarkably, to the obsessive re-enactment of stories in *The New Electric Ballroom*, *The Walworth Farce*, and *Ballyturk*, and to the peculiar assortment of males stuck in the swimming pool in *Penelope*.

Yet the conditions of this entrapment and the nature of the stories are only some of the many aspects of Walsh's work to highlight how it fundamentally differs from that of Beckett: not only do Walsh's stories involve a high level of verbal and physical violence and often include characters who intend to harm one another by their narration, but the later plays in particular feature multifaceted verbal fireworks within outrageously vivid settings. The Beckettian elements thus always serve as a mere substratum, to which Walsh adds vibrant colour and an often manic physicality. While this inclination towards the lush, loud, and physical may have been partially inspired by Walsh's first-hand experience with the frequently excessive German director's theatre, it has certainly been encouraged by his collaboration and friendship with Mikel Murfi, an exuberant comic actor and director trained at the Jacques Lecoq school of physical theatre in Paris, who directed *The Walworth Farce* and *Penelope* for Druid Theatre, and acted both in the Druid production of *The New Electric Ballroom* and in the first production of *Ballyturk* (presented by Landmark Productions in Galway).

III

The Walworth Farce and *The New Electric Ballroom* were conceived as companion pieces, characterized by their author somewhat later as 'very Irish', meaning that these are 'plays about a shared family story where a person visiting will somehow force the truth out of that uncertain history' (Walsh 2014b, p. vii). There has been some confusion as to the genesis of the respective plays, supported by the order in which they were first produced. *The New Electric Ballroom* was commissioned by the Münchner Kammerspiele theatre and amply assisted in its development by the theatre's dramaturge at the time, Tilman Raabke (see 'Not Looking for Irishness' 2015, pp. 126–8, 135–6); the play was consequently first staged in Munich in 2004, almost four years before its first English-language production by Druid (2008). *The Walworth Farce* was commissioned by Druid in 2003 and given its world première in Galway in 2006, the production subsequently toured over four years to venues in the UK, North America, Australia, and New Zealand.

Reviewers in Ireland and the UK have understandably considered *The New Electric Ballroom* as a sequel of a kind to *The Walworth Farce*, which would have made little sense to audiences in Continental Europe. However, the author revealed in a recent statement that *The Walworth Farce* was really written first and the initial idea for *The New Electric Ballroom* occurred to him as he was finishing it (Walsh 2014b, p. vii).[5] Although *The*

Walworth Farce features a more detailed treatment of themes that are only outlined in *The New Electric Ballroom*, and is the more elaborate of the two in terms of structure (see Pilný 2013, p. 218), the order in which the original manuscripts of the two dramas were completed will be honoured in what follows.

Both plays show their characters engaged in a constant re-enactment of a version of their past. *The Walworth Farce* focuses on a tyrannical Irish father and his two sons locked up in a council flat on Walworth Road in South London, replaying the story that preceded their departure from Cork almost fifteen years earlier. *The New Electric Ballroom* is set in a small rural Irish town and features two spinster sisters in their sixties, Clara and Breda (whose names echo those of Declan Hughes's 1991 play *Digging for Fire*). Clara and Breda keep on revisiting the frustrating story of trying to have their first sexual experience in their late teens with a showband frontman named Roller Royle. The re-enactment also includes their younger sister Ada, now aged forty, and eventually Patsy, a local fishmonger.

The patterns of interaction among the characters in both plays are clearly pathological in the sense of the Palo Alto communication theory (see Watzlawick et al. 1967): they are stuck in an endless repetition of the same routine, many of them face several double-bind situations, and unhindered communication about the nature of their relationship is impossible. Moreover, the sudden shocking outbursts of violence are indicative of the characters' frustrated desire to break free from the oppressive patterns. Walsh aims at more than simply depicting unbearable family relations or pathological interaction among people sharing an enclosed space, however, since metatheatricality is a seminal structural element of the plays. In fact, what the spectators are watching are mostly elaborate plays-within-a-play enacted by the dramatis personae. Their productions are characterized by ostentatious theatricality that is melodramatic or farcical in turn and features role doubling and cross-dressing that is accompanied by ample use of wigs, lipsticks, fake moustaches, and gaudy costumes. To complicate matters further, the spectators are often not sure whether what they are watching is a "real" interaction between the characters, or rather part of a play that the protagonists are enacting for themselves.

As outlined in the introductory chapter of this book, the confusion created by metatheatricality is an effect included by Wolfgang Kayser among the typical features of the modern grotesque in drama, and it was first introduced by Luigi Pirandello and other playwrights of the Italian *teatro del grottesco*. Walsh's grotesque—like that of Martin McDonagh's *The*

Pillowman—may thus be seen as linked to an influential type of avant-garde theatre where multiple levels of illusion result in the audience 'losing its foothold on reality' (Kayser 1966, p. 137). Nevertheless, Walsh's use of macabre, violence, and excesses of all kinds makes this dramatist a very peculiar successor to the much more sombre Pirandellian tradition. Walsh moreover combines the device of the play-within-a-play with a similar strategy in both dramas in order to provide the central conflict in the plot, whereby the re-enacted pattern is upset by an intrusion from the outside. The ludicrous play enacted in *The Walworth Farce* is completely derailed by Sean having accidentally picked up the wrong bag of shopping at the local Tesco, and by the subsequent arrival of Hayley, a black cashier who has come to rectify the error; the accident ultimately generates the most tragic consequences. In *The New Electric Ballroom*, the story replayed by the three sisters seems to be disrupted by the arrival of Patsy and the revelation of him being the son of Roller Royle by Clara and Breda's rival; the nature of the disruption is qualified though, since it eventually becomes clear that it had been craftily devised by Clara and Breda in order to gain full control over their younger sister's fate.

The ubiquitous manipulation of the "actors" in the plays-within-a-play by their "directors" points to another feature that is distinctive of the grotesque in drama according to Kayser (pp. 44, 91–2): the degeneration of characters into puppets. Walsh's plays clearly differ from the theatrical epitome of the Romantic grotesque, Georg Büchner's *Woyzeck*, in which characters seem to be operated by an incomprehensible force that has replaced God. At the same time, the coherence of narrative distinguishes Walsh's work from the fragmentary, puppet-like world of the more recent archetypal classic, Jarry's *Ubu Roi*. Yet the element of mechanical manipulation is seminal in Walsh's drama, and this comes most clearly to the fore in *The Walworth Farce* and *The New Electric Ballroom*. Instead of some mysterious force behind the scenes pulling the strings of everyone on the stage, however, the manipulation is performed by individual characters in these plays. In *The Walworth Farce*, the father manipulates his sons in order to conceal a double murder, and when Blake makes sure in the end that even after the father's and his own death, Sean will remain inescapably trapped in an incessant replay of their doctored past, his reiteration of their mother's 'Now leave, love', complete with kissing Sean on the lips, appears genuinely horrific (Walsh 2007, p. 84). In *The New Electric Ballroom*, Ada and Patsy are manipulated by Breda and Clara out of sheer spite, and when Ada accepts her role in the re-enactment orchestrated by her sisters, she evidently agrees to life-long imprisonment. Consequently, the endings of the two plays involve an ethical judgment, which makes them also much more comprehensible; in this, *The Walworth Farce* and *The New Electric Ballroom* considerably differ from McDonagh's *The Pillowman* where the manipulation of the characters by the puppeteer serves as an entertainment device (see Chap. 1)—Walsh's plays, fantastic as they are, designate manipulation as evil.

The moral judgment in *The Walworth Farce* and *The New Electric Ballroom* is closely associated with the role of stories in the pathological patterns of interaction. It is a widely held belief that identity, be it individual or collective, is based on narrative. To put it simply, what makes you who you are is your story. Should an individual not be able to order the events of his or her existence into a coherent narrative, he or she is likely to succumb to utter disorientation and consequently be unable to make sense of his or her life. This view has been the basis of therapy from Freud up to the narrative therapy focused on the management of trauma; its general validity had also been relentlessly and painfully scrutinized by Beckett ever since the *Trilogy*. In the closing scene of *The Walworth Farce*, Dinny asks: 'For what are we, Maureen, if we're not our stories?' (p. 82). This memorable moment seems to confirm the notion of identity being founded on narrative; but one must remember the nature of Dinny's story of the family's past, which is both fantastic and mendacious. Narrative and identity are closely juxtaposed in *The New Electric Ballroom*, too, where people are depicted as being dressed with words, perhaps in reference to the old cliché that clothes make the man. Most remarkably, Patsy is stripped and literally scrubbed clean of his previous story by Clara in preparation for his new identity as the glorious descendant of Roller Royle. Despite the elder sisters' effort, Patsy eventually rejects his new identity and leaves.

In his discussion of *The Walworth Farce*, Eamonn Jordan saw as quite problematic the fact that the story forming the foundation of identity, be it individual or collective, is supposed to possess authenticity even in contexts where verification is impossible. In his view, this amounts to dismantling the whole concept (Jordan 2010b, p. 350). Contrary to Jordan's assertion, however, Walsh's plays do not necessarily question the narrative basis of identity per se. As regards *The Walworth Farce*, a narrative therapist might argue that the reason why independent selfhood is denied to Dinny's sons is that their life story remains static and is only mechanically reproduced, rather than because it is a constructed story that lacks any means of verification. Patsy's rejection of his new identity is not due to it being grounded in a story that cannot be verified either: he walks out on the sisters since he regards the story as inappropriate and because it has been put in his mouth by Clara and Breda. What *The Walworth Farce* and *The New Electric Ballroom* thus primarily indicate about narratives of identity is that it is the *purpose* of the stories that matters, particularly as any such story is shown to be inextricably linked with the distribution of power. The re-enactment of the stories of the past is ostentatiously presented to Sean and Blake, and to Ada, respectively, as protection from the hostile world outside. Nonetheless, the father in *The Walworth Farce* uses the fabricated story in order to keep his terrible secret hidden and to maintain dominance over his sons. For their part, the elderly sisters in *The New Electric Ballroom* do not so much wish to protect Ada from the dangers of the world outside as for her to remain a virgin spinster like themselves. Their plan is for Patsy's delivery of his new story to first open up the possibility of love for Ada, and then to crush her emotionally for good after he has rejected the story. Thus, narratives of identity—and stories and words in general—are ultimately shown in both plays to be instruments of oppression connected with entrapment, and it is also in this light that the prominent Beckettian allusion to the child being better off staying in the womb and not entering this world (Walsh 2008b, pp. 5–6) needs to be perceived.

While the central position of stories in the characters' world has an early precedent in Beckett's work, as we have observed, it parallels a similar concern of numerous contemporary playwrights; of those discussed in this book, the most interesting comparison is with Philip Ridley. As outlined in Chap. 2, prominent characters in all of Ridley's plays tell a wide variety of stories in order to gain a basic sense of the world around them. Moreover, in early works such as *The Pitchfork Disney* the stories are narrated in the context of perpetual entrapment that is not unlike that of *The Walworth Farce* or *The New Electric Ballroom*. In *Ghost from a Perfect Place*, some of the stories are even re-enacted, albeit only once. Finally, *Mercury Fur* foregrounds storytelling as an essential activity that makes us human, a point that is evidently implied throughout Walsh's work as well. However, Ridley's concern is primarily with the veracity of the stories, in the sense that his plays from *The Pitchfork Disney* up to *Piranha Heights* continue to iterate a powerful argument against basing one's identity in a fictionalized past or in a fantasy. Judging by Walsh's recent commentary on his own work provided in the form of a brief two-hander entitled *My Friend Duplicity* (Traverse Theatre, Edinburgh 2010), imaginary narratives are conceived as a weapon against a dull or, alternately, a threatening reality, similarly to how they are often employed by Ridley's characters. The fundamental difference is that whereas in Ridley's world, fiction is ultimately rejected, the issue of truthfulness is of secondary importance in Walsh as he turns the focus on the use of stories for manipulating and maintaining control over others; after all, even in *My Friend Duplicity*, it is by force that the creator of the stories, Fergal, makes his auditor and collaborator, Jean, stay part of the process.

IV

Walsh's next play, *Penelope*, was commissioned by the municipal theatre in Oberhausen, Germany as part of the *Odyssey Europa* project created by six theatres in the Ruhr Valley in 2010 for the region's season as a Capital of Culture. At the invitation of Tilman Raabke, chief dramaturge at Oberhausen, Walsh joined five other European playwrights (Grzegorz Jarzyna, Péter Nádas, Emine Sevgi Özdamar, Christoph Ransmayr, and Roland Schimmelpfennig) in adapting stories from Homer's *The Odyssey*. His part focused on the suitors who strive to ingratiate themselves with Penelope in the absence of Odysseus. The play premièred in February 2010, directed by Tilman Knabe. Although Walsh was working on commission from Oberhausen, he indicated that he was writing with a specific Irish cast in mind (the actors being Niall Buggy, Karl Shiels, Denis Conway, and Tadhg Murphy; McBride 2010) who all appeared in the first English-language production by Druid in Galway five months later, directed by Mikel Murfi.

Penelope is a truly madcap rewrite of Homer in which four remaining suitors desperately strive to win Penelope's love from the bottom of a disused swimming pool on a Greek island in the boiling summer heat. Lounging in front of a CCTV screen, Odysseus's wife—who has the looks of a young supermodel—watches the effort of these desperate wrecks in their swimwear. They know they are doomed, since a shared dream showing their barbecue on fire has revealed to them that Odysseus is going to arrive today and hack them all to pieces. Consequently, they employ a whole arsenal of persuasive speeches and eventually even a wordless cabaret number with rapid costume changes in order to seduce Penelope, which may possibly save them.

The men in *Penelope* are locked in the endless routine of courting, in the same way that the characters in *The Walworth Farce* and *The New*

Electric Ballroom are stuck in their re-enactments; nevertheless, a question creeps in concerning their entrapment: why do they come back to the pool every morning? They act as if they were firmly in the hands of inexorable fate—but they clearly have the option to leave. No dominating presence forces them to stay. Hence, they may be perceived as puppets that allow themselves to be operated in a scenario of their own making and who finally accept the divination in their dream. Despite that, they do not intend to give in: on the contrary, they are ready to do their utmost to achieve their goal. This places them in the paradoxical situation where they know that they must collaborate in order to strengthen their chances of winning but, at the same time, only one of them can gain Penelope's hand. Not surprisingly, then, the patterns of their interaction are as pathological as in the two preceding plays and, due to the lethal nature of the competition, involve a high degree of vengefulness and spite.

The role of stories in *Penelope* is as crucial as in *The Walworth Farce* and *The New Electric Ballroom*. All the suitors end up delivering confessional and often poetic monologues about themselves; unlike in the previous plays though, these narratives do not so much advance a version of their past as unravel the speakers' deepest emotions and fantasies of love. Much as their confessions may come across as honest, the audience have no means of establishing whether they are really truthful accounts. Regardless of that, it is again the reason for telling these stories that is of ultimate importance: whatever the basis of the suitors' outpouring of their hearts may be, their stories are intended as an instrument for usurping the place of the husband of a beautiful young woman. The moral judgment concerning the suitors' action is thus evident. Their amorous attempts are eventually presented by Burns as an effort to save love as an authentic emotion despite the suitors' inevitable doom; but his statement is forcefully undermined by the fact that he and his accomplices are all covered in blood, as they have just stabbed Quinn—who is wearing a winged, angel-like costume of Eros—to death. This intricate coda indicates that at the end of the day, positive values and true emotions require bloody violence, which supports the overall moral verdict.

The features of the grotesque in *Penelope* remain principally identical to Walsh's earlier work, consisting of the blending of the incongruous, presenting an alienated world, and having the characters replay, puppet-like, the same scenario over and over again. There is one notable embellishment, nevertheless: as Walsh has the decrepit male bodies of the suitors stripped into trendy swimwear, aspects of the body such as protruding bellies are emphasized. This calls to mind the Rabelaisian grotesque as outlined by Mikhail Bakhtin, in which 'Images of the body are offered [...] in an extremely exaggerated form' (Bakhtin 1984, p. 18).

Penelope is also a play that foregrounds the playwright's growing preoccupation with mortality and death, which became a central concern in his subsequent work. Asked by the Bush Theatre in London to contribute to its 2011 project entitled 'Sixty-Six Books: 21st-Century Writers Speak to the King James Bible', Walsh produced a brief monodrama, *Room 303*. In it, an ageing man who used to spread 'the good word' to strangers from door to door (Walsh 2014b, p. 211) is placed in a situation very much reminiscent of Beckett's protagonists in the *Trilogy*: alone in a room, prostrate in bed, he is determined to 'finish things' (p. 211). Unlike Molloy, Malone, or the Unnamable, however, his urge to speak incessantly is motivated by his fear of death rather than any desire to finally perish, and is clearly related to his loss of faith, which has left him dying in anguish. Together with *My Friend Duplicity*, which, as noted earlier, discusses the relative value of constructing fantasy worlds, *Room 303* prepared the ground for Walsh's next major play, *Ballyturk*.

Premièred at the Galway International Arts Festival in July 2014 with Cillian Murphy, Mikel Murfi, and Stephen Rea, and directed by Walsh himself, *Ballyturk* subsequently toured to Dublin, Cork, and the London National Theatre. Its writing was apparently triggered by the image of an actor and a production manager engrossed in their individual tasks while sharing the same space in rehearsal; the image was combined with a question posed by the author's small daughter about death and whether people think about it all the time (Billington 2014). *Ballyturk* concerns two men—one in his mid-thirties and the other in his mid-forties and simply labelled 1 and 2—sharing a box-like room and spending their days creating the world of a fictitious village called Ballyturk through a re-enactment of the stories of its invented inhabitants. Their only contact with the outside world consists in occasionally overhearing voices that might belong to neighbours, until the moment when they receive an unexpected visitor, in his sixties, who has arrived to take one of them away. Despite an air of mystery that surrounds his identity and action, the visitor is evidently an embodiment of death.

Walsh's technique, language, and the use of the grotesque in the play seamlessly follow on from his preceding major dramas. The principal developments in *Ballyturk* concern further emphasis on physicality and a consistent and ubiquitous use of slapstick gags and clowning routines:

Walsh was clearly intent on exploiting both the skills of Mikel Murfi as a clown and the love of slapstick that he, Murfi, and Murphy share. Moreover, the playwright has also considerably enhanced and embellished his use of music: *The Walworth Farce* and *The New Electric Ballroom* utilized sentimental Irish songs at strategic points and *Penelope* was introduced by and interspersed with a Herb Alpert tune in order to support the multiple ironies in the plays. *Ballyturk* is steeped to the same effect in early eighties pop music, combined with an original soundtrack by the celebrated Italian author of film scores, Teho Teardo. The effect the play has had on its audiences is clearly apparent from the description provided in Fintan O'Toole's review:

> So Jean-Paul Sartre, Samuel Beckett and Flann O'Brien are jointly commissioned to write a sketch for *The Morecambe & Wise Show*. Over a bottle of absinthe they concoct something like Enda Walsh's *Ballyturk*. It has elements of Sartre's *No Exit*, Beckett's *Waiting for Godot* and O'Brien's *The Third Policeman*. But it's also pure Eric and Ernie: two weirdly innocent men who share a bed but are not lovers, trapped in an endless knockabout farce, putting on "a play what I wrote". The result is strange and funny and manic and very, very dark. (O'Toole 2014)

Ballyturk has caused the same bafflement on the part of reviewers as Walsh's earlier work, together with the same range of references to other authors. The affinity of the play to *Waiting for Godot* has been noted universally, however, and it is true that *Godot* forms an important intertext to the play. We are essentially watching two men engaged in a variety of routines devised to pass the time (here in the course of almost three days rather than Beckett's two) and it becomes apparent that the bond between the men and the company and help they provide each other with are of crucial importance. The symbiotic relationship between the characters puts the play in contrast with *The Walworth Farce*, *The New Electric Ballroom*, and *Penelope* where relations are by and large poisonous and malevolent. As so often in Walsh, the engagement with Beckett is not only sombre but also playful, since he has the small boy in *Godot* (and, for that matter, also in *Endgame*) replaced in a surreal final moment with an *Alice in Wonderland*-like girl who enters to replace the departed man through a small door in the wall. Moreover, the citational range in *Ballyturk* is much broader than in any of the previous plays, referencing mostly cinema, such as Buster Keaton's films, Daphne du Maurier/Alfred Hitchcock's *The Birds*, and possibly also the Wallace & Gromit animated feature *The Curse of the Were-Rabbit*.

The world presented in *Ballyturk* is again a radically alienated version of the everyday, and it is in turn frightening and funny. And again, the characters live in self-imposed isolation from the outside world. Yet this time, the entrapment must give way to the superior force of death. Walsh highlights the inevitability through the use of stage technology and corresponding sound effects: in order to indicate that it is time for one of the men to follow their visitor, the entire back wall opens up to the surrounding world with 'a huge hydraulic noise' and 'the sound of cracking' (Walsh 2014a, p. 35), literally ripping the room apart like a shoe box. This moment rather dramatically unravels the symbolic dimension of what had looked like a realistic stage space, despite its somewhat idiosyncratic furnishings; in fact, the realism of the set is simultaneously put in doubt by it being linked with the inside of a mind, in another echo of Beckett's *Endgame* (as a high-pitched tone grows louder in preparation for the dismantling of the space, 2 asserts: 'The mind is a thunderous place—with all manner of dreams and wants and half-notions and clouded thoughts'; p. 35). The symbolism of the space ultimately solicits an allegorical interpretation, and much more strongly than in any of Walsh's previous works: the story of the two nameless men depicts humankind's futile struggle with mortality, and scenes like the frantic work-out room routine (p. 47) speak volumes. All the activities of the two characters, and the spinning of the stories of an invented place called Ballyturk in particular, are thus revealed to be not only pastimes, or ways of staving off a dangerous world outside, but also strategies for keeping death at a distance. As these ritual actions merely emphasize their lack of impact, *Ballyturk* comes across as remarkably different from Philip Ridley's 1992 play concerned with mortality and transience, *The Fastest Clock in the Universe*, in which the futile rituals engendered by the refusal to age ultimately lead to brutal violence (see Chap. 2).

When the mysterious stranger appears and lets the two men choose who will follow him outside, the radical ambiguity so typical of the grotesque reaches its climax: initially, 2 is prepared to go and sacrifice himself for the sake of his younger friend. Nonetheless, the twelve seconds that it takes to walk towards death (p. 54) are then conjured up in 1's final monologue as a moment of absolute freedom. Consequently, 2 orders 1 to go, and it is 1 who ends up leaving. Whichever of the characters is deemed by the spectator to be better off as a result, the juxtaposition of life and death is perhaps as radical as in Beckett's late works, while being positively more enigmatic. Fintan O'Toole's perception of the play as emphatically bleak compared to that of other reviewers, no doubt also because of the final arrival of the little girl entering what seems like a life-long entrapment with an older man. Nevertheless, the empathy between the male friends and their desire of the best for the other allow for a slightly more optimistic reading of this drama of inevitability, as does the perception of the girl as someone to whom 2 will provide sustenance and company.

V

Enda Walsh has asserted in a number of recent statements and interviews both his unwillingness and his inability to write drama that would overtly relate to contemporary reality. For instance, in the foreword to his second volume of collected plays he stated: 'I'm always surprised how my British contemporaries often write plays directly about the world around them— like theatre is there to dramatise what we see in the news or talk about at dinner parties' (Walsh 2014b, p. viii). As apparent from the discussion of his work in the present chapter, Walsh's strategy of relating his drama to the world has consistently been oblique and/or hyperbolical. However, we have also noted that Walsh has referred to *The Walworth Farce* and *The New Electric Ballroom* as 'Irish' plays, and has in fact recently presented himself more often as an Irish playwright, as opposed to, simply, a playwright. Given Walsh's disinclination to any form of topicality or specificity, the nature of his engagement with Ireland and Irish drama in the last decade calls for some scrutiny.

It is certainly true that the characters in *The Walworth Farce* and *The New Electric Ballroom* are (mostly) Irish, and they speak with Irish accents and often use dialectal expressions. Both plays also reflect prominent aspects of Irish culture and history. *The Walworth Farce* seems to tell a typical story of the diasporic experience of Irish migrant workers in London who feel uprooted in the foreign city and are engrossed in nostalgic memories of the Emerald Isle. Similarly, *The New Electric Ballroom* seems to outline an emblematic story of small-town life in Ireland, such as that depicted in Brian Friel's *Dancing at Lughnasa* (1990), a play that also focuses on the life of unmarried sisters in a gossipy provincial town and features dance as a central motif.

Yet these narratives are far from being simple reiterations, and in many ways significantly qualify what seems to be a typically Irish dimension of the plays. In *The Walworth Farce*, the enacted memories of Ireland indicate a parodic treatment. For one, the play caricatures the stereotypical notion of the Irish as a nation of storytellers in that it involves one of the most improbable yarns ever told: the story of a speedboat hitting a sea lion, careering through the air onto the mainland where it kills a horse, whose carcass is then sent flying over the hedge where it kills the boys' grandmother who is gathering gooseberries for the illicit production of alcohol. Furthermore, the protagonists' situation is not really that of Irish migrant workers in England: neither the father nor the sons actually ever work in London and apart from Sean's periodic trips to Tesco for food, they enter into no contact with their surroundings. As Eamonn Jordan has observed, Dinny denies his sons 'diasporic identity' by keeping them at home 'and only grants them the substantial identities as children or as performers' (Jordan 2010b, p. 351). The play may recall a whole series of Irish literary texts and documentaries concerned with the migrant experience in England, which include a prominent dramatic antecedent, Tom Murphy's *A Whistle in the Dark* (1961) whose scenario involving a dominant father, oppressed sons, and a trophy is echoed in the *Farce*. Nevertheless, Walsh's intention is to 'explode that kind of play and bring it somewhere else' (Walsh qtd in Jordan 2010a, p. 244). The images of Irish small town life in *The New Electric Ballroom* likewise verge on parody, particularly when vented through the talkative simpleton Patsy. Moreover, *The New Electric Ballroom* is akin to the absurdities of Martin McDonagh's *The Beauty Queen of Leenane* (1996) in its depiction of the locals quibbling over trivial details and the spitefulness of older women who are trying to deprive a younger one of any chance to gain freedom and an independent life.

The stories of the inhabitants of the village of Ballyturk in the eponymous play follow on from Walsh's use of (stereo)typical narratives of Irish identity in *The Walworth Farce* and *The New Electric Ballroom* in that together they form a picture of oppressive, economically backward rural Ireland where time has more or less stood still. This has in fact been listed among the few reservations that Fintan O'Toole has had about the play: he complained that Walsh's fictional town was 'locked away from any sense of what has happened in Ireland in the past 20 or even 30 years' (O'Toole 2014). O'Toole's remark gives away the firm rootedness of Irish drama criticism in the idea of theatre as a 'mirror up to nation' (to quote Christopher Murray's influential phrase; Murray 1997), and fails to see the irony present in such an embodiment of Ireland. While the tendency to parody iconic images of Ireland is less pronounced in *Ballyturk*, being overshadowed by elements of the crime story and the neo-gothic (consider the use of the malevolent birds), the rural clichés still come across as such, and are enhanced by direct reference to Martin McDonagh's caricatured country shop in *The Cripple of Inishmaan* and its shelves filled with an excess of canned peas (Walsh 2014a, pp. 21, 32). Furthermore, the creation of Ballyturk is ultimately just a game and its actual content has little impact on the lives of the characters: their situation would hardly change were their imaginary world filled with stories of inhabitants of an English industrial town or, for that matter, an Egyptian village.

Chris Morash and Shaun Richards have argued that Walsh's plays document how 'the social formations that once grounded Irish drama in a cultural network extending beyond the world realised on stage are now only retained in "stories"' (Morash and Richards 2013, p. 120). This is certainly a pertinent observation on Irish drama, and Morash and Richards may be right in that the work of Enda Walsh—together with Mark O'Rowe's *Terminus*—thus signifies the end of a long era of Irish theatre. Still, to return to an earlier point, I would add that Walsh's tendency to employ caricature and parody not only demolishes 'a dramatically viable Irish sense of place' (Morash and Richards 2013, p. 118) but also forcefully turns our attention to the way in which such 'stories' pertaining to dated 'social formations' may function as instruments of manipulation and oppression or, at best, create escapist fantasy worlds.

Curiously enough, Walsh has singled out *Penelope* as an exception in his oeuvre: he described the play as 'My one attempt to talk specifically about "something that was actually happening"' (Walsh 2014b, p. viii), referring to the collapse of Ireland's economy in 2008. *Penelope* may indeed be seen to reflect prominent aspects of post–Celtic Tiger Ireland, since the protagonists are ex-businessmen surrounded by the debris of former prosperity, and are supposed to speak with gentrified provincial accents from across the country (Walsh 2010, p. 5). Moreover, their names are based on those of prominent Irish business moguls, bankers, and developers who had been directly involved in the downfall of the Irish economy.[6] The play also includes a satirical interpretation of the fairy tale about the Magic Porridge Pot with an obvious relevance for Ireland; in this, an entire town is seen as having 'ground to a standstill when it became awash with porridge' since its inhabitants 'took with no notion of responsibility or future'. Consequently, the affected country is viewed in a Yeatsian allusion as having 'a heart fed on a diet of sweet stodgy oats'. 'What the pot needed was regulation', one of Walsh's businessmen facing ruin asserts; 'It needed that little girl to stay at home with the sole purpose of saying, "Cook-pot-cook" and "Stop-pot-stop"' (p. 9). As Clare Wallace has recently argued, these elements, together with the fact that the failed businessmen are stripped to their Speedos, live in a swimming pool that has lost its liquidity, and there is the blood on the wall of those who have perished in the crisis, provides enough for the play to be read as an allegory of Ireland at that particular point in its history (Wallace 2015).

However, audiences of the play by and large failed to interpret *Penelope* as related to Ireland at all. This is testified by the reviews of the Druid Theatre production: none of the reviewers even mentioned the crash of the Irish economy in their discussion of the play, and the origin of the characters' names was briefly noted only by Lorraine Courtney in the *Sunday Tribune* (Courtney 2010). The lack of recognition of what seems to have been an intended interpretative framework may have been partly because the play was produced in Ireland and in the UK almost two years after the actual demise of the Celtic Tiger. What is certain, however, is that the grotesque pyrotechnics involved in the piece discourage its interpretation as an image of specific reality: *Penelope* is a drama that combines elements of the theatre of the absurd, melodrama, conversation comedy, in-yer-face theatre, and the TV reality show, in which references to contemporary Ireland are a relatively minor component. Moreover, the Greek setting results in marginalizing the Irish references further, together with the mythical framework of *The Odyssey* that invites another form of allegorization which concerns European civilization as a whole and reaches beyond geographical specificity altogether.

Just like it does not propound any direct social or political observations concerning other societies or cultures, Walsh's recent work can hardly be viewed as a commentary on Ireland. Instead, Irish linguistic and cultural references serve in plays such as *The Walworth Farce*, *The New Electric Ballroom*, *Penelope*, or *Ballyturk* as a backdrop for more general reflections on the contemporary era. As I have attempted to suggest, these pertain chiefly to the ethics of human interaction in *The Walworth Farce* and in *The New Electric Ballroom*, and in *Ballyturk* life is presented as a futile struggle with mortality in which empathy and company are vital. *Penelope* continues Walsh's examination of pathological human interaction, specifying its focus in terms of the abnegation of basic human values in global capitalism and the concurrent loss of true emotions. In wearing their local references lightly—to paraphrase Dan Rebellato (see Rebellato 2011, p. 426)—Walsh's plays are similar both to Philip Ridley's treatment of his East End settings and to Mark O'Rowe's use of Dublin or the Irish countryside: as discussed in Chaps. 2 and 3 of the present volume, neither Ridley nor O'Rowe are particularly interested in providing straightforward links to specific reality either.

Walsh's vision of the world has certainly not been idyllic and, accordingly, he has spoken of humans as being 'only accidents away from becoming monsters' (Walsh 2008a) and of theatre as 'a bin lid', rather than a mirror (Crawley 2014). However, his plays have at the same time been consistently very funny. The nature of the laughter engendered by his work is typical of the grotesque in that it is always 'inappropriate', and reflects the generic fundament of modern grotesque drama in a blend of tragedy with farce, as detailed by Ralf Remshardt (Remshardt 2004, pp. 81, 92). Indeed, all of Walsh's major works provide spectacular examples of the farcical rooted in the tragic. Some of their humour has been conveyed through the use of slapstick gags, which have gradually become a seminal part of Walsh's drama, as noted particularly with *Ballyturk*. Here we may recall Václav Havel's essay on 'The Anatomy of the Gag' discussed in the introductory chapter of this book: Havel has described the gag as 'deliberate nonsensification' of a faulty reality, intended to result in purifying laughter, and asserted that the estrangement caused by 'absurd humour' is probably the most adequate manner in which 'the contemporary man achieves catharsis' (Havel 1963, p. 8). There is no doubt that Walsh's brand of the grotesque follows on from its comfortless and puzzling versions created in the Romantic period, and that it hardly permits the radical liberating power associated with the concept by Mikhail Bakhtin, particularly as the entrapment of Walsh's characters tends to be terminal in all senses of the word. Still, the cathartic potential of Walsh's humour offers a measure of deliverance.

Like Philip Ridley or Mark O'Rowe, Walsh is among the contemporary dramatists whose ample and original use of the grotesque has held his audiences not just bewildered, but also riveted. His plays have offered veritable feasts of theatricality in which—to quote Eamonn Jordan—'The assuredness, exuberance and the commitment of the performers win out despite the chaos' (Jordan 2010b, p. 354). The nature of audience engagement solicited by Walsh's work is more plausibly described in emotional or even existential terms rather than socio-political ones; whether it can 'open up new passages towards new forms of subjectivation', as Jacques Rancière would wish (Rancière 2011, p. 82), is not easy to judge. But the surge of energy emanated from the stage is certainly a major reinforcement for theatre as an art form.

Notes

1. The long awaited first collection of essays on the theatre of Enda Walsh, edited by Mary Caulfield and Ian Walsh, finally appeared from Carysfort Press in early 2016.
2. The static noise that opens and closes the play, rendering the words of the characters incomprehensible, has an interesting parallel in the technological noises of a commencing film projection that Anthony Minghella used in his film adaptation of Beckett's *Play* for the *Beckett on Film* series (2001).
3. A feature highlighted by Walsh in his 2010 introduction to *Plays: One* (Walsh 2011, p. ix).
4. Of all of Walsh's shorter plays, *The Small Things* is most intensely characterized by citationality: besides the Beckettian allusions, it makes obvious references to *The Glass Menagerie*, featuring a woman who talks to 'knick-knacks' in her room, and its combination of the unfixed identity of protagonists and characters mentioned within the narrative (the woman's father and the chip shop man) with reconstructions of the stories of the past resembles Harold Pinter's treatment of character identity in plays such as *Old Times*.
5. *The New Electric Ballroom* was premièred at the Münchner Kammerspiele theatre in Munich on 30 September 2004, directed by Stephan Kimmig. The first English-language production was by Druid Theatre in Galway (14–16 July 2008 in Galway and 3–24 August 2008 at the Traverse Theatre in Edinburgh), directed by Enda Walsh himself. *The Walworth Farce* was premièred by Druid Theatre in Galway on 20 March 2006, directed by Mikel Murfi. The extent of any alterations that may have been made between the manuscript of *The New Electric Ballroom* that served as the basis for the German translation presented in Munich and the version later produced by Druid remains to be established, as does the extent of any rewrites of the original manuscript of *The Walworth Farce* subsequent to the first production of *The New Electric Ballroom*.
6. See Pilný 2012, p. 172: Quinn comes from Sean Quinn, a major shareholder in the Anglo-Irish Bank whose business was destroyed by its collapse; Fitz's name is that of Sean Fitzpatrick, the corrupt head of the same bank; Dunne is eponymous with Sean Dunne, a notorious property mogul; and the name of Burns was most likely inspired by Johnny Burns of the Burns Construction company. I am grateful to Eamonn Jordan for bringing this point to my attention, complete with details concerning Quinn, Fitz, and Dunne. The attempted identification of Burns is my own.

Works Cited

Bakhtin, M. (1984). *Rabelais and His World* (1965) (Hélène Iswolsky, Trans.). Bloomington: Indiana University Press.
Beckett, S. (1990). *The Complete Dramatic Works*. London: Faber and Faber.
Billington, M. (2014, September 18). Enda Walsh: "Pure Theatre Animal" Explores Solitude and the Void Below. *Guardian*. Retrieved December 28, 2014, from http://www.theguardian.com/stage/2014/sep/18/enda-walsh-playwright-screenwriter-theatre-animal-solitude-roles-void-physical-comedy
Courtney, L. (2010, July 18). The Penelope Pit Stop, review of *Penelope*, by Enda Walsh. *Sunday Tribune*. Retrieved May 18, 2011, from http://www.tribune.ie/arts/article/2010/jul/18/theatre-penelope/
Crawley, P. (2014, June 21). Enda Walsh's *Ballyturk*: Dabbling with Mortality in Our Own Private Universes. *Irish Times*. Retrieved December 28, 2014, from http://ballyturk.com/2014/06/21/enda-walshs-ballyturk-dabbling-with-mortality-in-our-own-private-universes-the-irish-times/
Havel, V. (1963). Anatomie gagu [The Anatomy of the Gag]. *The Václav Havel Library Online Archive*. Retrieved November 7, 2012, from http://archive.vaclavhavel-library.org/Functions/show_html.php?id=156819
Huber, W. (2012). Contemporary Irish Theatre in German-Speaking Countries. In N. Grene & P. Lonergan (Eds.), *Irish Drama: Local and Global Perspectives* (pp. 81–91). Dublin: Carysfort Press.
Jordan, E. (2010a). *Dissident Dramaturgies: Contemporary Irish Theatre*. Dublin: Irish Academic Press.
Jordan, E. (2010b). 'Stuff from back home': Enda Walsh's *The Walworth Farce*. *Ilha do Desterro*, 58, 333–356.
Kayser, W. (1966). *The Grotesque in Art and Literature* (1957) (Ulrich Weisstein, Trans.). New York: McGraw-Hill.
McBride, C. (2010, June 10). Enda Walsh—From the Odyssey to Penelope. *Galway Advertiser*. Retrieved May 18, 2011, from http://www.advertiser.ie/galway/article/27155
Morash, C., & Richards, S. (2013). *Mapping Irish Theatre: Theories of Space and Place*. Cambridge: Cambridge University Press.
Murray, C. (1997). *Twentieth-Century Irish Drama. Mirror up to Nation*. Manchester: Manchester University Press.
Not Looking for Irishness: Tilman Raabke and László Upor in Conversation with Ondřej Pilný (2015), *Irish Theatre and Central Europe*, ed. Ondřej Pilný, special issue of *Litteraria Pragensia*, 25 (50), 120–136.
O'Toole, F. (2014, August 16). Review of *Ballyturk*, by Enda Walsh. *Irish Times*. Retrieved December 28, 2014, from http://ballyturk.com/2014/08/18/review-fintan-otoole-irish-times/

Pilný, O. (2012). Whose Ethics? Which Genre?—Irish Drama and the Terminal Days of the Celtic Tiger. In M. Berninger & B. Reitz (Eds.), *Ethical Debates in Contemporary Theatre and Drama* (pp. 195–210). Trier: Wissenschaftlicher Verlag Trier.
Pilný, O. (2013). The Grotesque in the Plays of Enda Walsh. *Irish Studies Review, 21* (2), 217–225.
Rancière, J. (2011). *The Emancipated Spectator* (2008) (Gregory Elliott, Trans.). London and New York: Verso.
Rebellato, D. (2011). Philip Ridley. In M. Middeke, P. P. Schnierer, & A. Sierz (Eds.), *The Methuen Drama Guide to Contemporary British Playwrights* (pp. 425–444). London: Methuen.
Remshardt, R. E. (2004). *Staging the Savage God: The Grotesque in Performance.* Carbondale: Southern Illinois University Press.
Sierz, A. (2012). *Modern British Playwriting: The 1990s. Voices, Documents, New Interpretations.* London: Methuen.
Wallace, C. (2006). *Suspect Cultures: Narrative, Identity and Citation in 1990s New Drama.* Prague: Litteraria Pragensia.
Wallace, C. (2015). In a Precarious Space: Enda Walsh and the Performance of Vulnerability. Paper delivered at the IASIL 2015 conference at The University of York, 24 July. Unpublished.
Walsh, E. (2007). *The Walworth Farce.* London: Nick Hern.
Walsh, E. (2008a, November 3). Interview by Aleks Sierz. Retrieved June 3, 2012, from http://www.theatrevoice.com/listen_now/player/?audioID=627
Walsh, E. (2008b). *The New Electric Ballroom.* London: Nick Hern.
Walsh, E. (2010). *Penelope.* London: Nick Hern.
Walsh, E. (2011). *Plays: One.* London: Nick Hern.
Walsh, E. (2014a). *Ballyturk.* London: Nick Hern.
Walsh, E. (2014b). *Plays: Two.* London: Nick Hern.
Watzlawick, P., Bavelas, J. B., & Jackson, D. D. (1967). *Pragmatics of Human Communication: A Study of Interactional Patterns, Pathologies, and Paradoxes.* New York: Norton.

CHAPTER 5

Mutabilities: Suzan-Lori Parks

I

Suzan-Lori Parks ranks among the most original and versatile playwrights working in the United States today. She first began writing drama in the early 1980s, prompted by her creative writing teacher, novelist James Baldwin. To date, she has been the recipient of three Obie Awards, the Pulitzer Prize for Drama for the two-hander *Topdog/Underdog* (2001), and numerous other awards and nominations. Although Parks won her first Obie for the experimental drama *Imperceptible Mutabilities in the Third Kingdom* back in 1990, when she was still in her mid-twenties, her work did not begin to receive significant critical attention until the production of the controversial pseudo-historical play *Venus* (1996).

Throughout her career, Parks's principal concern has been with American history and the erasure of the African-American experience. Central tropes in her work are related to remembering and dismembering; they involve the digging up of the dead and their resurrection, or alternately the dismantling of cultural and political icons and concepts (see Geis 2008, p. 11). Parks typically mines the African-American oral tradition, including minstrelsy and popular music, in order to recover the unrecorded experience of African Americans. As a number of critics have argued, Parks uses this heritage to 'signify' on the dominant discourse in the sense discussed by Henry Louis Gates, Jr.; in other words, like many other African-American authors, Parks mimics the discourse of white, patriarchal America with subversive difference (see Geis 2008, pp. 14–15).

© The Editor(s) (if applicable) and The Author(s) 2016
O. Pilný, *The Grotesque in Contemporary Anglophone Drama*,
DOI 10.1057/978-1-137-51318-2_5

This technique makes her essentially a postcolonial dramatist with a strong moral purpose since, as S. E. Wilmer has asserted, she positions African Americans as a people whose bodies were colonized by slave traders who deprived them of their land, families, language, and culture (Wilmer 2000, p. 443). However, Parks has also been drawing extensively on the inheritance of European and American modernism, which has been as important for her style as the African-American tradition. Writers as diverse as William Faulkner, Gertrude Stein, Virginia Woolf, James Joyce, and Samuel Beckett all provided inspiration for Parks, particularly as regards her experimentation with language and the disruption of the linear level of time (see Geis 2008, pp. 6, 13–14; Innes 1999, p. 96). Furthermore, she has used almost the entire palette of Western theatre including, in particular, Greek tragedy, melodrama, naturalism, expressionism, Brechtian epic theatre, and absurdism, as required by the particular subject of each of her plays.

Parks's use of the grotesque has been so abundant and multifaceted that a single book chapter can barely do justice to it. My discussion will therefore be limited to a selection of her most significant works. First, I would like to examine how Parks restages the conceptualization of African Americans, and more specifically the black female body, as grotesque in *Venus*. Subsequently, my focus will be on Parks's grotesque re-enactment of the assassination of Abraham Lincoln by black impersonators in two formally very different dramas, *The America Play* (1994) and *Topdog/Underdog*. The chapter will be concluded by a brief analysis of Parks's most recent work, *Father Comes Home from the Wars (Parts 1, 2 & 3)* (2014), which grafts the journey of African Americans from slavery to emancipation onto Homer's *The Odyssey*.

II

Venus was first produced by the Joseph Papp Public Theater in New York City in conjunction with Yale Repertory Theatre in 1996, directed by Richard Foreman. The play tells the story of Sara 'Saartje' Baartman, a Khoisan woman who was taken from South Africa in 1810 and exhibited in London as 'The Hottentot Venus'. Crowds of spectators ranging from the working class to royalty came flocking in to stare at Baartman as a specimen of an inferior race, admiring particularly the black woman's large buttocks. This notorious freak show travelled across England, and in 1814, Baartman was exhibited in Paris, where she died a year later.

Parks's play is written fundamentally as a tragedy of a human being whose body was perceived as grotesque. Apart from the abject misery of Baartman's life, Parks also stages the reactions of the spectators to her as a grotesque freak. The 'Venus' is viewed in the play by numerous members of the general public with 'horror and fascination': many are dumbstruck with amazement but a spectator is also seen to scream with terror; the show triggers protests, but a crowd is also observed to erupt in laughter (Parks 1998, pp. 46, 47, 54–6). Christopher Innes has suggested that the spectacle 'correspond[s] exactly to Bakhtin's image of the excessive body displayed in carnival' (Innes 1999, p. 102). This may be true in terms of the virtually naked posterior that the unfortunate woman exhibits. Nevertheless, instead of indicating the eventual rejuvenation of order described by Bakhtin, the reaction of the spectators repeatedly develops into mob hysteria and violence that has to be quelled by force (see Parks 1998, pp. 71, 77, 148). The ethical stance taken by Parks is unwavering here: no rejuvenation can be triggered by the denigration of others. Moreover, her play reflects a long, infamous history of racial objectification whereby non-whites have been perceived as simultaneously human and non-human, as grotesque creatures who served to reinforce the identity of Europeans and white Americans as superior, and often became the object of their fetishistic attention (see Cassuto 1997, pp. xv, 179). The desire was particularly strong for black women, who were widely considered to be over-sexed and sexually available (see Anderson 2008, p. 58). Regardless of Parks's powerful indictment against racism and the preposterous stereotyping of black women, *Venus* has met with considerable controversy. While it was widely hailed as a theatrical tour de force, many people walked out during the first production, and the play was soon attacked for taking liberty with the facts and for the 're-objectification and re-commodification' of Sara Baartman (see Young 1997).

The facts of Baartman's life, as established mostly from third-party accounts, are outlined in Sara Warner's excellent article entitled 'Suzan-Lori Parks's Drama of Disinterment: A Transnational Exploration of *Venus*', together with the considerable grey areas in what we know about the ill-fated woman (Warner 2008, pp. 183–5). Sara Baartman was an orphan whose husband was killed in an armed conflict with the Dutch colonizers. She was taken into custody by Pieter Cesars, a free black hunter and trader who was in the business of supplying European scientists with specimens, including humans. Pieter gave Baartman to his brother Hendrick as a maid and wet nurse. Hendrick worked as manservant to Alexander Dunlop, a British military doctor; together they decided to smuggle Baartman—aged twenty-one at the time—to London and use her as a source of income by exhibiting her in public. The operation was part-funded by Pieter Cesars. Hendrick assumed the role of a ringmaster for 'The Hottentot Venus', ordering her to exit her cage, perform tricks and music for the audience, and threatening her with a stick if she disobeyed. The extreme popularity of the show not only generated a proliferation of cartoons and articles in the press but also drew the attention of local abolitionists, who took Dunlop and Cesars to court over the violation of the 1807 Act for the Abolition of the Slave Trade. Baartman was questioned with the help of Dutch interpreters for more than three hours and based on her testimony, the judge found that she entered willingly into a contractual agreement with her employers, exhibited herself of her own free will, and had no desire to return to South Africa.

When Dunlop died in 1812, Cesars disappeared with Baartman for about two years, causing speculation about pregnancy or marriage. In 1814, the two emerged in Paris, where the show was resuscitated. Yet, as Baartman was ailing, Cesars sold her to an animal trainer named Réaux who then rented Baartman to Georges Cuvier, Napoleon's surgeon general, naturalist, and founder of comparative anatomy. In his effort to prove that Africans were the missing link between apes and white humans, Cuvier assembled a team of scientists and artists who examined Baartman and produced sketches of her body. Very shortly afterwards, Baartman died; scholars are still debating whether the main cause of her death was an untreated respiratory disease or alcoholism. Cuvier secured permission from the French government to perform an autopsy on her body, producing a plaster cast, a model of her buttocks, and preserving her skeleton, genitals, and brain (the latter two in jars, which he allegedly displayed outside the door of his flat). Baartman's remains were eventually placed on public display in the Parisian National Museum of Natural History, where they could be viewed up until 1976. They were rediscovered in the museum's archive in the 1980s by paleontologist Stephen Jay Gould.

The most controversial aspect of Parks's account of 'The Hottentot Venus' is that she made Baartman a willing accomplice in her predicament, acting almost like an entrepreneur at times (see Innes 1999, p. 102). First, the Venus agrees to leaving South Africa with her master in a business deal; while there is not enough evidence to prove that this would not have been impossible, some scholars have argued that Baartman was a slave and as such, she would not have had the liberty of choice (see Anderson 2008, p. 57). On the Venus's arrival in London, Parks has her sold to 'The

Mother-Showman', who becomes her impresario-cum-ringmaster in a curiously gendered twist of the facts. The Venus repeatedly asserts her willingness to perform and even suggests improvements to the show (p. 60), as she is intent on making a fortune and finding love. This is also why she refuses to return to South Africa, regarding her life there as hopeless, although—unlike the real Sara Baartman—she is said to have a family there (p. 109). Furthermore, the Venus talks about having sex with some of the spectators after the show and there is no evidence of this in Baartman's life. Parks merges Réux and Cuvier into the figure of 'The Baron Docteur', with whom the Venus has a prolonged love affair, leading to two pregnancies and at least one abortion, which is performed by her lover. She also contracts gonorrhoea from the Baron Docteur. Ultimately, the Venus is imprisoned for indecency and dies in jail. None of this is evidenced in reality.

Although the play has never been presented as an accurate reconstruction of history, the amount of historical information encourages the audience to perceive it as such. *Venus*—like several other of Parks's dramas—features significant period detail and even involves the presentation of information by way of 'footnotes', delivered as monologues by a character called 'The Negro Resurrectionist' who acts as the master of ceremonies in the play. He quotes extracts from contemporaneous newspapers, sings slightly doctored verses from two broadsides about 'The Hottentot Venus' from the early 1810s, and most importantly, reads out passages from Cuvier's report on the autopsy of Sara Baartman. It is only natural that audience members unfamiliar with the details of Baartman's life would tend to view Parks's version of it as historically correct, despite the fact that *Venus* is clearly not a realist drama.

However, the accusations of misrepresenting history that were raised when the play first opened were also strongly related to the symbolic status that Sara Baartman had acquired for black South Africans in particular. Warner reminds us that shortly after the end of apartheid in South Africa, Nelson Mandela used his first state visit to France as president in 1994 as an opportunity to formally request President Mitterand to facilitate the repatriation of Sara Baartman's remains. A lengthy process ensued, in which France was initially reluctant to oblige as it feared that it would set a precedent for the return of artefacts acquired in the colonial era. Baartman's remains were eventually returned in 2002 and buried during ceremonies lasting several months (Warner 2008, pp. 185–6). When *Venus* was staged in New York in 1996, the negotiations were still very much in progress and Baartman was already perceived globally as a symbol of colonialism, racism, and the sexual and economic exploitation of women. The attack on the playwright should then be understood primarily in this context, which caused Parks's drama to be viewed not so much as a harrowing story of an abject individual but rather as a cavalier treatment of the life of a collective icon.

Provocatively, Parks frames the tragedy of Sara Baartman as a show, utilizing elements of the circus and of vaudeville. At the same time, she uses a number of Brechtian devices: she has the Negro Resurrectionist introduce the individual scenes (see Geis 2008, p. 79) and the manner in which he disseminates information in order for the audience to engage with political and moral issues is likewise much in the spirit of Brecht's epic theatre.[1] The use of role doubling and cross-dressing also foregrounds the theatrical nature of the representation in accordance with Brecht's stipulations, as Deborah Geis has argued, and is analogous to major neo-Brechtian political dramas of the postmodern era, such as Caryl Churchill's *Cloud Nine* or Tony Kushner's *Angels in America* (Geis 2008, p. 88). Moreover, the nature of the characters in *Venus* requires Brechtian distancing from the role in terms of acting, which is palpable particularly in the final commentary delivered by the Venus on her fate (see Geis 2008, p. 96).

Notwithstanding all the elements that discourage the perception of the play as naturalist, Parks maintains a linear plot line that follows the Venus from her time as a servant in South Africa up to her premature death in Paris. Although the scenes are numbered in reverse order, their announcement resonates as an inexorable countdown towards death (Innes 1999, p. 98); this countdown is also aligned with the counting of money, which is the focus of several scenes (Miller 2002, p. 135), emphasizing the role of poverty in the tragic fate of the Venus. Last but not least, the reversed numbers indicate that this is a world that is upside down, a trope that has frequently been associated with the grotesque and linked to its unravelling of social vices.

The play's structure explicitly comments on the issue of representing Sara Baartman's life. A number of critics have emphasized that Parks takes its impossibility as a premise, having the Negro Resurrectionist open the drama by announcing: 'I regret to inform you that The Venus Hottentot iz dead. [...] There wont b inny show tonite.' The statement is repeated in what is almost a ritual chant several times during the first scene (pp. 11, 13, 16). In a situation where the closest one can get to Sara Baartman's voice is in her testimony at the London court, the recovery of her story is simply not feasible: the one statement that we appear to have from Baartman is merely an official record produced by an institution that—despite Baartman's knowledge of some English and the presence of interpreters—seemed to have had some difficulty understanding what she was saying (see Worthen 2010, p. 180, n. 23). In fact, the erasure of the real woman by the forces of colonialism is already inscribed in the name under which she has become known to us, since Sara (or, for that matter, the diminutive Saartje/Saartjie used in condescension by her masters) Baartman is a name attributed to the Khoisan woman by the Dutch administration, presumably in place of her—unknown—original one (see Geis 2008, p. 77). The absurdity of attempting an accurate rendering of Baartman's life is further underlined by Parks in adopting a circular structure for her play, which not only starts but also ends with the death of the Venus.

What Parks does instead of delivering a strictly biographical play is to focus the spectacle of 'The Hottentot Venus' on the issue of the gaze. As Greg Miller has asserted, *Venus* 'posits an additional subject beyond Baartman, and this subject is that of the spectator in all its guises, onstage and off' (Miller 2002, p. 128). Indeed, the play consists largely of scenes in which the Venus is watched by paying customers and/or the Negro Resurrectionist, who also looks in on the action of numerous others (see Warner 2008, p. 194). Furthermore, Parks intersperses the story of the Venus with extracts loosely adapted from an 1814 popular play *The Hottentot Venus or the Hatred of French Women* (see Worthen 2010, p. 183). This performance is watched onstage by the Baron Docteur and later the Negro Resurrectionist. By having the audience constantly watch somebody watching, Parks transforms the spectator into 'a culpable participant, a voyeur' (Worthen 2010, p. 179). The fact that the Venus frequently returns the gaze of the audience (see Saal 2005, p. 60) implicates the spectator even further and creates a discomfort similar to that engendered in Samuel Beckett's later dramas such as *Play* or *Not I*, where the audience are made aware of their prying on the suffering of others. It is in this context that the initial line 'Exposure iz what killed her', which is repeated at the end of the play (pp. 11, 161), receives its full, uncanny resonance.

As much as scholar and artist Jean Young may be unjust in condemning the fact, she is right to point out that the Venus is not only objectified in this way but commodified, too (Young 1997, p. 706), as we are constantly reminded that the show is being presented for a paying audience—

including us. The commodification is conclusively underscored by the Venus delivering what she introduces as 'A Brief History of Chocolate' in Scene 3, that is, two scenes from the drama's finale. Throughout Act II, the Venus is witnessed to be a compulsive chocolate eater, an addiction that replaces Sara Baartman's apparent alcoholism in the play. As a number of commentators have noted, the 'History of Chocolate' is firmly linked with the manner in which both the on- and offstage audiences have been devouring the woman with their eyes. Moreover, we are reminded that chocolate has been traditionally regarded as an aphrodisiac, whereby the sexual nature of voyeurism comes to the fore (see Miller 2002, p. 134; Geis 2008, p. 93; Worthen 2010, p. 187). The irony pertaining to the juxtaposition within the plot of the play is scathing: the Venus, a woman who craves to be loved, receives her chocolates in a heart-shaped box from the Baron Docteur, a lover who ends up betraying her and ultimately purchasing her body through 'The Grade-School Chum' in order to further his scientific career. The appellation given to the young woman by her handlers—'The Venus'—thus continues to signify only the desire of others for sexual gratification.

Coming back to the matter of implicating the audience, it is noteworthy that the 'History of Chocolate' features some of the many anachronisms in the play (other instances include, for example, a prominent reference to jet lag; see Miller 2002, p. 128): the Venus asserts that 'Chocolate was soon mixed with milk and sugar and formed into lozenges which one could eat on the run', and refers to the tendency of 'some persons, especially women', to go on 'chocolate binges' when dealing with 'emotionally upsetting incidents' (p. 157). However, she is supposed to be speaking in 1815 and chocolate confectionery was not available anywhere but within royal courts up to the late 1840s, becoming affordable to ordinary members of the public even later. Such anachronisms serve to highlight the topicality of the play as regards the exploitation of the black female body; as Arlene Keizer has asserted, similar exploitation currently pertains, for instance, to the 'obsession' with stereotyped images of black female physicality and sexuality in hip hop and related popular culture (Keizer 2011, p. 209).

The actual shape of the Venus's body presents a difficult decision for any producer of the play to make in terms of casting and costuming, as Deborah Geis has pointed out. 'What about the famous rump for which she was exhibited?' Geis asks. 'To what extent is she sexualized?' (Geis 2008, p. 83). Geis discusses the first production of *Venus* in which the actress wore a padded costume and shows that while some critics regarded this as appropriate because, in their view, the play itself stages Baartman as a prosthesis, the decision runs the risk of making the character look ridiculous. On the other hand, productions that do not involve an artificial enhancement of the buttocks indicate that the Venus's body is a projection of the audience's view of it; according to Geis, this solution will benefit from portraying the character as sexually provocative, since the hope is that the self-awareness of the audience as voyeurs will thereby be stressed (pp. 83–4).

Be that as it may, voyeurism is rather blatantly accentuated in the play by two scenes featuring masturbation triggered by the Venus's body, first by the Baron Docteur and then by 'The Chorus of the 8 Anatomists'. These explicit scenes very likely contributed to the number of walkouts that occurred during the first production in the United States. Furthermore, any audience's endurance is bound to be tested by the autopsy report, which involves not only graphic details of the woman's private parts but also comparisons to primates that indicate the speaker's purpose of proving Africans to be an inferior race or even species. The predominant part of the report is delivered in the form of a lecture by the Baron Docteur during the intermission. He tells the audience that 'if you need *relief*, please take yourselves uh breather in thuh lobby. My voice will surely carry beyond these walls and if not, my finds are published' (pp. 95–6; emphasis in the original). As Harry Elam and Alice Rainer have observed, this puts the audience in an ethical quandary because leaving means ignoring the reality of what is being presented, while staying amounts to having to listen to flagrantly racist discourse (qtd in Saal 2005, p. 61). Although the reactions of individual audience members have varied along a fairly broad scale, as instantiated in Geis's discussion on the subject (Geis 2008, p. 89), the uneasy nature of the situation may again have played a role in the negative response of some of the spectators to the first staging of the play.

Most commentators have regarded *Venus* as open-ended, and this is certainly true in the sense that the final scene replays the opening one and the play refuses to deliver an unequivocal interpretation of the central character. However, as noted, Parks's drama simultaneously features a coherent tragic narrative of a woman who puts herself on show in the hope that this might bring her a better future. Her choice is certainly extreme but as Adina Porter, who played the Venus in the first production, has asserted, the fact that the Venus is seeking financial independence and love essentially equates her with most contemporary women (qtd in Geis 2008,

p. 95). The suffering of a fellow human being, her constant mistreatment, and ultimate betrayal clearly invite sympathy, which is in fact only one of several prominent features that aligns the play with classical tragedy. The audience are aware from the onset of the protagonist's death at the end, and learn what her fateful mistake was: leaving Africa for England, which the Venus also comes to realize. Dying in jail, she confesses: 'I always dream of home, in every spare minute. It was a shitty shitty life but oh I miss it' (p. 158). In accord with the conventions of the genre, the audience are likely to experience pity and horror at the end. Nevertheless, we have seen that there are as many devices that alienate *Venus* from Greek tragedy, which problematizes the delivery of catharsis (see Warner 2008, p. 196; Geis 2008, p. 96). The spectators are provided in its stead with a laconic summary by the Venus:

> Tail end of the tale for there must be uh end.
> Is that Venus, Black Goddess was shameless, she sinned, or else
> Completely unknowing thuh Godfearin ways, she stood
> Showing her ass off in her iron cage.
> When Death met Love Death deathd Love
> and left Love tuh rot
> *Au naturel* end for Thuh Miss Hottentot.
> Loves soul, which was tidy, hides in heaven, yes, that's it
> Loves corpse stands on show in museum. Please visit.
> (p. 162)

Blatant indeed. There may be a tiny measure of justice in that the Venus positions her soul in heaven, in what constitutes a reversal of the passage originally spoken by the Negro Resurrectionist at the beginning of the play. Yet, the uncertainty in the following 'yes, that's it' undercuts even that small solace. The subsequent invitation by the Venus for the audience to kiss her right at the end of the play is 'viciously sardonic, bitter and profoundly disconcerting', to quote Arlene Keizer's apt words (Keizer 2011, p. 212). Catharsis in a Greek tragedy would typically result in the renewal of the social bond on the part of the spectators; in Parks's *Venus*, they are provoked to 'moral outrage' (Miller 2002, p. 126). The tragedy of 'The Hottentot Venus' appropriately ends with her death, but her story is not laid to rest, as also indicated by the master of ceremonies being called the Negro Resurrectionist, an appellation that is racist while at the same time referring as an integral pun both to stealing corpses and the belief in resurrection.

Venus by Suzan-Lori Parks powerfully testifies to Frances Connelly's assertion that the grotesque may function as a weapon against social, racial, and sexual oppression (Connelly 2012, pp. 18, 144). Yet, paradoxically perhaps, the subversion of racist and sexist discourse is not achieved so much by Parks's play as a grotesque work of art but rather by her implication of the audience in watching the denigration of a person conceptualized as grotesque by her oppressors. The onstage spectators' laughter at the "grotesque" Venus may conceal a sense of unease but it is the experience of watching them laugh that produces true revulsion; and as Sara Warner has asserted, when the Venus laughs back at the most absurd moments, her laughter is 'as invasive as any scalpel' (Warner 2008, p. 196). Despite the forceful nature of the indictment, Parks still refuses to deliver it in the form of a hagiographic narrative which would meet the expectations of contemporary activists: she pulls back from casting the Venus as a conventional tragic heroine, replacing catharsis with re-exposure (see Warner 2008, p. 199).

III

The grotesque re-enactment of President Lincoln's assassination by John Wilkes Booth with a black man posing as Lincoln is a central trope in *The America Play* and *Topdog/Underdog*. Parks uses this mischievous synecdoche to indicate that there is something fundamentally amiss with the grand narrative of American history. Divided as the plays are by approximately a decade, however, the replay of shooting the Great Emancipator has a somewhat different role in each of the dramas, each with distinct implications.

The America Play was written over the period between 1990 and 1993; following workshop productions at Arena Stage and Dallas Theater Center in 1993, the play officially opened at the Joseph Papp Public Theater in New York City in February 1994 as a co-production with Yale Repertory Theatre, directed by Liz Diamond. The play's setting is delineated as follows: 'A great hole. In the middle of nowhere. The hole is an exact replica of The Great Hole of History' (Parks 1995b, p. 158). Act I consists largely of a monologue by a character named 'The Foundling Father', a grave-digger who tells of his life as a Lincoln impersonator: having visited a historical theme park that he describes as 'A Big Hole' on his honeymoon (p. 162), he decided to replicate the colonization of America by going West and digging his own Hole there. He eventually performed in the West as Abraham Lincoln on the fateful night at Ford's Theatre, following the realization that audiences were not interested in him reciting the President's speeches but rather in being allowed to shoot their own Lincoln. A number of such re-enactments are presented on stage by way of demonstration, with different customers in the role of Lincoln's assassin, Booth. Act II follows the Foundling Father's son, Brazil, and his widow Lucy as they are attempting to dig him up from his replica of The Great Hole of History. This part of the play is structured as a series of scenes interspersed with 'Echoes', which are brief sequences featuring the Foundling Father; the play concludes with the Foundling Father's body placed in a museum of historical artefacts, poised as the body of Abraham Lincoln.

Parks's preoccupation in *The America Play* with unattainable historical accuracy is foregrounded, as in *Venus*, by the use of mock-academic footnotes in the text of the play, although in contrast to the later drama, none of the footnotes are actually spoken on stage. Some of Parks's annotations authenticate lines used in the staged assassination as words really uttered by Booth or by Lincoln's wife, Mary Todd. Other lines spoken in the re-enactment are identified as those of the Confederate General Lee or the Secretary of War, Edwin Stanton, originally uttered in a different context, while several sentences are described as what Booth or Mary Todd Lincoln *may* have said in Ford's Theatre. To complete the mix, a citation in the Foundling Father's monologue is footnoted as coming from an unpublished poem written by the character. In turn scholarly and ironic, Parks's use of annotations is thus aligned with that employed in postmodernist fiction concerned with the constructed nature of history, from Jorge Louis Borges's stories up to more recent masterpieces such as Alasdair Gray's novel *Lanark*. Moreover, the first three footnotes—which appear on the first page of the text—focus on the rhetorical figure of chiasmus and so underscore the play's concern with the antithetical.

Indeed, Parks's negotiation of contrasts stands at the oxymoronic heart of the pun involved in setting the play in the Great W/Hole of History: as Parks stated in the programme for The Public Theater's production of the play, 'You think of h-o-l-e and then w-h-o-l-e and then black hole ...'

(qtd. in Innes 1999, p. 106). The Foundling Father thus repeatedly announces, 'He digged the hole and the whole held him' (Parks 1995b, pp. 159, 164), and his statement simultaneously testifies to an obsession with history that results in perennial entrapment and the erasure of the experience of African Americans in the grand narrative of US history, which has swallowed them like a black hole. Apart from these polar opposites, the Hole accumulates a number of other meanings, poignantly summarized by Soyica Diggs Colbert: it refers to the bullet hole in Lincoln's head, the hole created by the trans-Atlantic slave trade, 'to graves and women's genitals', and, simultaneously, it 'undermines a teleological view of history, functions as a locale for improvisation and creation, and recalls the trauma enacted when the Foundling Father leaves Brazil and Lucy' (Colbert 2011, pp. 1–2).

As in *Venus*, Parks takes the elusiveness of historical truth in its entirety as a premise but at the same time insists on a recuperative probing of the past. Here, she uses a combination of 'digging' and 'faking', that is, the recovery of any available fragments of history and their creative re-presentation, which according to Colbert stand out as prominent examples of the 'reparative modes central to the black theatre throughout the twentieth century', a theatre that has sought redress and social justice (p. 2). 'Digging' and 'faking' in *The America Play* specifically concern the conflicting legacy of Lincoln. While for most white citizens Lincoln became the emancipator and the architect of contemporary US democracy who was martyred for his ideas, many African Americans would regard him instead as a white supremacist moderate whose abolition of slavery fell dramatically short of bringing about racial equality (see Geis 2008, p. 98; Colbert 2011, p. 238). *The America Play* reflects this clash of perspectives by giving an opportunity to the individuals acting as Booth to have their say about the Liberator. Some replay the scene in its canonical version; however, there are numerous dissident voices, the most powerful of them belonging to a woman—quite likely African-American, although this is not explicitly stated—who shoots Lincoln and exclaims: 'LIES! (*Rest*) LIIIIIIIIIIIIIIIES! (*Rest*) LIIIIIIIIIIIIIIARRRRRRRRRRRRS! (*Rest*) Lies' (p. 167).

Underscoring the concerns of black Americans, Parks builds in a playful manner on the fact that the occupation of the African-American 'digger' conspicuously rhymes with the common racist insult. Indeed, she revealed in a 1994 interview that 'the relationship between "nigger" and "digger" was the whole play' for her, also because it allowed her to let humour in

(Parks 1994). Chuckling at the juxtaposition might seem inappropriate but Parks has endowed *The America Play* with moments of positive hilarity, such as having the Foundling Father ponder which fake beard to wear for which particular occasion of the re-enactment, including a blond one (pp. 168–9). In scenes like this, laughter at the grotesque clearly serves to liberate, highlighting the emancipatory intent of postcolonial mimicry (see Saal 2005, p. 64).

Nevertheless, the idea of liberation by laughter is simultaneously complicated by the fact that Lincoln gets shot when he is roaring with laughter. The fateful last laugh pertains not only to Abraham Lincoln the president but, of course, also to the black man enacting the role of the victim (as Christopher Innes has observed, the moment bears an uncanny resonance with 'the long history of violence against Blacks in America and the shooting of Martin Luther King'; Innes 1999, p. 97). Moreover, since the scene is repeated eight times over Act I, and replayed one last time as a monologue in Act II, the reaction of the spectators is bound to develop: much depends on the director's decisions and on the acting of the protagonist but a probable trajectory would be moving from laughter that is typical of the grotesque and involves a chill in the spine towards ponderous detachment. The complex function of humour in *The America Play* reflects the unfinished business of the past which is its subject, as well as the difficulties entailed in charting a path towards successful liberation. The comedy of Parks's diggers may then really be perceived, as Elinor Fuchs has suggested, as descendant from 'the gravedigger-clowns' in Shakespeare's *Hamlet*, commenting as it does on sombre matters through an 'onstage *clownerie*' (Fuchs 2001, p. 341).

Emancipation in *The America Play* is conditional upon successfully coming to terms with the inheritance of the past, and Parks characteristically explores the issue both at the collective and at the family level. These levels are inextricably linked, as the Foundling Father, an African American orphaned by history, attempts to dig up his heritage by impersonating Lincoln, and is in turn being dug up from the past by his son. Both are grave-diggers who—like the Negro Resurrectionist in *Venus*—are engaged in disinterment. But while the figurative aspect of their digging may be reminiscent of the poet's excavation in the bottomless marshes of the past that was central to the work of another great literary explorer of conflicting history, Seamus Heaney, Parks is interested in more than the exposure of and confrontation with the past. In the context of the African-American experience, the past must be re-performed, mourned, and laid to rest.

At the same time, since history features critical lacunae, its re-enactment must inevitably involve 'faking', which is duly highlighted by Parks's foregrounding of theatricality. The Foundling Father speaks of turning his search for Lincoln into a comprehensive performance of the assassination that would eventually involve his son as a professional mourner and his wife as a whisperer of the confidences of the dead. Together they would present history as a 'theme park' (Parks 1995b, p. 162) for a paying audience of customers craving sensation and nostalgically yearning for the great moments of the past. As Innes has argued, this form of reliving past events 'plays on the popular American pastime of taking part in historical pageants, re-enacting battles from the Civil War' (Innes 1999, p. 102); its nature as simulation is further highlighted by the Foundling Father presenting his story to the audience with constant nods and winks to a pasteboard cutout and bust of Abraham Lincoln that are placed on the stage. The ceaseless replay of history in *The America Play* obliterates the original event and transforms its world into a realm of Baudrillardian simulacra crafted from iconic images and (pseudo)historical debris. As a number of commentators have emphasized, the very setting of Parks's "archaeological dig", the Great Hole of History, is a replica in itself. The process is completed by Lucy and Brazil unearthing a television that plays a loop of the Foundling Father's performance, from which he re-enters the stage in order to be present at his own funeral (see Wilmer 2000, pp. 446–8).

However, we have also seen that the emotional investment of some of the participants in the re-enacted assassination is considerable and they actively rewrite it; similarly, when Brazil unearths trivia belonging to his father, his loud weeping is, in the words of Deborah Geis, 'both a real act of mourning' and 'a demonstration of his ability […] to perform grief' (Geis 2008, p. 110). All this indicates that the fabrication of history involves a powerful enabling potential and is expressive of a different kind of nostalgia than that attached to iconic moments of the grand narrative of history: as Fuchs has put it, 'Behind Parks's Baudrillardian America of the theme park, side show, and carnival concession is an ideal "real" America, preserved in a space-off of the imagination that neither Disney nor racism can invade' (Fuchs 2001, p. 351). Nonetheless, this nostalgia can never be satisfied and the process of remaking history is marked out as ongoing: instead of being laid to rest, Lincoln ends up sitting upright in his grave at the end of the play.

The multiple paradoxes of *The America Play* are amply reflected in its structure. Using the method of repetition and revision borrowed from jazz music—or 'Rep & Rev', as she tends to call it (see Parks 1995a, pp. 8–10)— Parks transforms linear time into a cumulative series of repetitions with variation. As S. E. Wilmer has observed, 'The narrative therefore continually echoes itself' (Wilmer 2000, p. 447). Time thus paradoxically flows simultaneously backwards and forwards (see Worthen 2010, p. 177). The backward direction is demarcated as absurd and mistaken through the Foundling Father who speaks about 'trying somehow to follow in the Great Mans [i.e. Lincoln's] footsteps footsteps that were of course behind him. […] trying somehow to catch up to the Great Man all this while and maybe running too fast in the wrong direction' (p. 171). However, the ceaseless nature of the repetition together with the open ending of the play show that the magnetic pull of the past is inevitable.

The sense of repetition being ubiquitous is enhanced by the multiplicity of theatrical levels that feature in *The America Play* and in the historical event it revolves around. Not only do significant parts of the drama present the spectators with performers re-enacting a performance, but as commentators have almost universally remarked, the killing of Abraham Lincoln itself took place in the theatre and was effected by the hand of John Wilkes Booth who, apart from being a Confederate sympathizer, was also an accomplished actor. Moreover, Parks's play includes staged extracts from the popular comedy that was in progress when the president was shot, *Our American Cousin* by English playwright Tom Taylor; these scenes are introduced by the Foundling Father, who eventually steps into one of the principal roles. In contrast to most other self-reflexive dramas that strategically employ the grotesque, such as Pirandello's *Six Characters in Search of an Author* or *The Walworth Farce* by Enda Walsh, Parks's complex use of metatheatricality does not really produce any sense of disorientation: its ultimate aim is to demonstrate that reality past and present is a product of performance.

IV

Topdog/Underdog is a considerably darker drama. As a naturalist two-hander, it is also formally very different from Parks's preceding Lincoln play. *Topdog/Underdog* opened at The Joseph Papp Public Theater in July 2001, directed by George C. Wolfe and starring the acclaimed actors Don Cheadle and Jeffrey Wright. The play transferred to Broadway in April of the following year, with the rapper Mos Def replacing Don Cheadle in the role of Booth. As it is a more accessible work than most of Parks's preceding plays, its Broadway staging drew a wide audience, including a high number of young African Americans (many of whom, one would imagine, were fans of Mos Def as a famous hip hop performer). The production garnered enthusiastic reviews, with Ben Brantley calling it 'the most exciting new home-grown play to hit Broadway [...] since *Angels in America*' (see Geis 2008, pp. 112–13).

Topdog/Underdog is set in the present in a one-room apartment with no running water or toilet. It depicts the events of a single week and focuses on the relationship between two brothers, Lincoln and Booth, named by their father as a morbid joke. Having been abandoned by their parents when Lincoln was sixteen and Booth eleven, the brothers were forced to scrape together an existence from an early age. Lincoln used to hustle cards for a living and now earns a miserable salary acting as Abraham Lincoln in a penny arcade. Booth is unemployed and spends his time daydreaming about affluence and social status; although he seems to own the flat, he lives off his brother's income and obtains more expensive items by stealing in shops. Throughout the play, we see him trying to learn to hustle three-card monte as expertly as his brother so he can have an easy source of revenue.

As the title of the play indicates, the brothers' relationship involves rivalry and struggle for the upper hand. The younger Booth periodically attempts to assert himself as the dominant one, using a variety of threats including eviction, and humiliating his brother particularly by throwing his impotence in his face: 'You a limp dick jealous whiteface motherfucker whose wife dumped him cause he couldn't get it up' (Parks 2002, p. 45). At the same time, Booth readily assumes the role of the 'underdog' whenever he is pleading with his brother to teach him the secrets of the card hustle. As the older brother and the breadwinner, Lincoln naturally occupies the role of the 'topdog' and tends to ward off Booth's attacks with silence or by changing the subject; he rarely lashes back.

The relationship between Lincoln and Booth is also a fond one, however, as Booth helps Lincoln to improve his performance in the re-enacted assassination, and Lincoln in turn provides advice and a sympathetic ear as regards his brother's attachment to Grace, an attractive lover whom the audience never see and who—as Patrick Maley has suggested— might even be a fantasy, 'no more real than George and Martha's son is in Edward Albee's *Who's Afraid of Virginia Woolf?*' (Maley 2013, p. 193).

Together, the brothers bond over their childhood memories, which they gradually share, often attempting to ameliorate their harsh nature because their father was a drunk and a womaniser who used to take Lincoln with him on his sexual exploits and their mother had a regular 'backdoor man' (Parks 2002, p. 100) she eventually ran away with after he made her pregnant. The 'inheritance' (p. 63) of 500 dollars, which the mother secretly gave to Booth when she was leaving plus the same amount that the father slipped to Lincoln when he walked out on the children, were their way of trying to buy forgiveness. The favouritism involved in each of the parents' lame gestures implied that they believed the other child was less worthy and thus encouraged the two boys' sense of superiority over the other. Recapitulating these grim matters together is the only way the brothers are able to face their trauma.

As multiple commentators have asserted, by focusing on a fraught fraternal relationship, Parks follows a strong line of literary precedents that begins with the stories of Cain and Abel and Jacob and Esau, and, in terms of canonical American drama, culminates in Sam Shepard's *True West* (see, for instance, Colbert 2011, p. 239; Maley 2013, p. 188; LeMahieu 2012, p. 40). In an alternative genealogy, *Topdog/Underdog* may be placed in the lineage of modern American dramas focusing on neglected sons from Arthur Miller's *Death of a Salesman* to August Wilson's *Fences* (Maley 2013, p. 188). What is notable in the context of the present study is that as regards both themes, Parks's play has strong parallels in the darkly grotesque work of Philip Ridley, with the sets of brothers in *Mercury Fur*, *Leaves of Glass*, and *Piranha Heights* on the one hand and the Stray siblings in *The Pitchfork Disney* on the other (see Chap. 2). In contrast to Ridley's plays, however, the relationship between the brothers in *Topdog/Underdog* and their situation as abandoned children has universally been allegorized by commentators. This reflects the strong tradition of the family play, which stands at the heart of the American dramatic canon and presents the family as a synecdochic image of society. Despite her strong spotlight on the individual in *Topdog/Underdog*, Parks encourages the allegorical interpretation by involving Abraham Lincoln in the play.

The presence of the grotesque in *Topdog/Underdog* is more subdued than in *The America Play* and consists in the infiltration of the "Lincoln act" into the story of the two brothers. This is prefigured in the opening scene, in which the audience observe a black man hustling cards and being silently watched behind his back by the figure of Abraham Lincoln, impersonated by an African American wearing whiteface. Unlike in *The America*

Play, however, the assassination of The Great Emancipator as replayed in the penny arcade is never enacted on stage, and is merely narrated to the audience. Moreover, as Geis has outlined, while the Foundling Father 'seems to create a self out of his act', Lincoln in *Topdog/Underdog* refuses to accept the idea that clothes make the man, 'claiming an identity that comes from within rather than from the figure he is playing' (Geis 2008, p. 118). The unproductive nature of the mechanical re-enactment of history in a theme park is further underscored by the fact that Lincoln's employers ultimately replace him with a wax dummy in a move to save on costs.

In his effort to make Lincoln teach him how to throw the cards, Booth criticizes his brother's impersonation of the president in a similar manner and equates it with the three-card monte: 'dressing up like some crackerass white man, some dead president and letting people shoot at you sounds like a hustle to me' (p. 22). Lincoln argues that there is a fundamental difference, since when people participate in the re-enactment, they know the 'real deal', and 'When people know the real deal it aint a hustle' (p. 22). It is true that his spectators prefer an approved version of the grand narrative: in Lincoln's words, they 'like they historical shit in a certain way. They like it to unfold the way they folded it up. Neatly like a book. Not raggedy and bloody and screaming' (p. 52). Consequently, the re-enactment must not look too realistic: an excessive thrashing of the president on the ground, for instance, would scare the customers away. Nevertheless, according to Lincoln, it is still an honest commercial transaction in which both parties get what they want—the customers are able to replay a sanitized version of history, and he gets his money. Hustling cards, on the other hand, amounts to 'cheating some idiot out of his paycheck or his life savings' (p. 55).

The most important difference—which, significantly, Lincoln never mentions—is that in a hustle, the customer can never win. This is a lesson that Lincoln gradually decides to teach Booth the hard way: when Booth ridicules his sexual deficiency and adds insult to injury by mentioning that he has slept with his brother's wife, Lincoln succumbs to the attraction of the cards (which he has been eyeing 'like an alcoholic would study a drink'; p. 56) and becomes intent on showing Booth, once and for all, who is the topdog. However, Parks withholds his intention from the audience: up until the final scene in which Booth gambles away his 'inheritance' of 500 dollars, Lincoln continues to appear to be a supportive older brother who eventually gives in and proceeds to teach Booth the skill that he desires the most and thus help him obtain a source of income and be able to marry

Grace. It is only in the final round of the game the brothers play against each other that Lincoln is unravelled as the expert hustler he is, who has been pretending all along and is now laughing at his brother's gullibility and at him losing all his money.[2]

It has been repeatedly argued that Parks's strategy in *Topdog/Underdog* amounts to a hustle played on the audience, whereby an apparently naturalist play is ultimately exposed as not naturalist at all (see, for instance, Maley 2013, p. 187; LeMahieu 2012, pp. 34, 44–5). I would argue that, formally speaking, this observation is misleading: rather than subverting naturalism, Parks adheres to its conventions remarkably closely, particularly as regards the presentation of the story and creating characters whose behaviour is determined by heredity and environment. The trick she plays on the audience consists in making her characters unreliable; but this is quite in accord both with the noxious effect of their parents' betrayal and with their social abjection. The unreliability of what is told by the characters gradually comes to the fore in the play, from the improbable twists in the development of Booth's relationship with Grace to the grey areas in the brothers' childhood memories. Eventually, even the fact that Lincoln and Booth are brothers is called into question ('I know we *brothers*, but is we really brothers, you know, blood brothers or not, you and me, whatduhyathink?' p. 103). The ultimate deception concerns the true nature of the older brother, Lincoln, of course, whom the audience are bound to sympathize with rather than with his impulsive and violent sibling but who is eventually unmasked as a conman.

The predetermination of the characters by heredity is blatantly asserted on a further level, in that Lincoln indeed gets shot by Booth. This is what the characters' names suggest from the start, and as Parks has mentioned in an interview, in this sense her play operates in the 'Greek tragedy mode' (qtd in LeMahieu 2012, p. 44); moreover, the fatal outcome for Lincoln is heralded in the opening scene by Booth pulling a gun on him and threatening to shoot him. Nevertheless, one of Parks's greatest achievements in the play is that she makes the spectators forget all this, not only by diminishing the significance of the names, which are presented as a father's silly joke, but primarily through her persuasive revelation of the brotherly love that exists between them alongside the rivalry. As a result, the final killing of Lincoln involves a considerable element of shock.

Parks demonstrates in the dénouement that the hustler's game ultimately catches up with him, expert as he may be. Moreover, she lets him die in his Abraham Lincoln costume, complete with whiteface, slumping forward like the president he used to imitate, which turns his commercial re-enactment into 'an eerie rehearsal for his own real death' (Geis 2008, pp. 123–4). Lincoln's earlier insistence that his identity has nothing to do with his costume is thus belied; this happens with a robust dose of irony, which is already prefigured, as observed by Ilka Saal, by the way in which Lincoln progressively takes to wearing his costume at home and even sleeping in it (Saal 2014, p. 253). What is implied here by Parks is that Booth's earlier criticism of his brother for dressing up as a white man for money is justified: to mechanically re-enact an iconic moment in the history of white America is not just senseless, but also wrong, and is bound to exact its price.

Shooting Lincoln is the only solution that the hot-headed and ambitious Booth can see that allows him to remove himself from the position of the underdog; yet, within a few moments, he realizes that he has just killed the closest person he has ever had. He wails helplessly over his dead brother, hugging his body. The ending in which one of the brothers is left dead and the other destitute may be perceived as 'fatalistic' (Saal 2014, p. 254) but, at the same time, Parks invests it with a powerful condemnation of social injustice: the focus of *Topdog/Underdog* on African-American men subsisting on the margins of society reveals that, as Maley has asserted, their alleged access to upward social mobility in the present-day United States is 'a scam' and that 'any notion of racial or familial unity' is illusional (Maley 2013, p. 192). While Parks's use of heredity and the environment as determining the behaviour of the characters follows the tradition of nineteenth-century naturalism, the dénouement of *Topdog/Underdog* in this context amounts to what Geis has referred to as a 'heavily ironic playing out' of inevitability (Geis 2008, p. 125). It is in the final moments of the play that the grotesque has moved centre stage. The dead Lincoln held by Booth is at one and the same time his dead brother and a life-size puppet of Honest Abe, a strikingly grotesque image that serves as a principal means of Parks's indictment of the wrongs of American society.

V

Father Comes Home from the Wars (Parts 1, 2 & 3) is Parks's latest work to date. This sequence of three one-hour long dramas represents the first instalment of a nine-part cycle tracing the lives of African Americans from the onset of the Civil War up until the present day. The project may be viewed as revisiting the terrain of August Wilson's monumental *Pittsburgh Cycle* (1982–2005) and extending its historical scope back to the times of slavery. Seedlings, so to speak, of the nine plays already appeared as part of Parks's 2002 venture in which she set herself the task of writing a play a day for the entire year; the plays were subsequently produced under the umbrella title of *365 Days/365 Plays* in the 2006–2007 season in more than 700 theatres across the United States.

The first three parts of *Father Comes Home from the Wars* premièred together at The Public Theater in New York in October 2014, directed by Jo Bonney, and transferred in January 2015 to the American Repertory Theatre in Cambridge, Massachusetts. The production was acclaimed by audiences and reviewers alike; Charles Isherwood described it as 'three endlessly stimulating hours, reimagining a turbulent turning point in American history through a cockeyed contemporary lens' and applauded it as the best new work he has seen all year (Isherwood 2014). The play went on to win the Edward M. Kennedy Prize for a theatrical work inspired by American history, won an Obie Award for Playwriting and was a finalist for the Pulitzer Prize for Drama in 2015.

Following a group of slaves on their uneasy path to emancipation, *Father Comes Home from the Wars (Parts 1, 2 & 3)* is presented by Parks as a grotesque version of *The Odyssey*. Parks's treatment of Homer's epic is similar to James Joyce's in that it mythologizes the mundane while simultaneously desacralizing the mythical. Like Joyce, Parks adds numerous ironic twists, such as having her Penelope character, called Penny, get pregnant while waiting for her husband to return, and there are also significant non-correspondences, the most striking of which is perhaps the absence of Telemachus in the story. As a three-part sequence that is mapped onto the entire plot of *The Odyssey*, its engagement with Homer is understandably more extensive than was the case with Enda Walsh's grotesque elaboration of Homeric material in *Penelope*, the commission of which limited the focus on a single episode of the epic (see Chap. 4). Compared to Joyce, Parks playfully expands her frame of reference to include both the author of *The Odyssey* and its title as names of characters in her drama: hilariously, 'Odd-See' is the appellation of Odysseus's dog which—as Jeffrey Gantz reminds us—greets his master in *The Odyssey* on his return by giving 'a wag of his tail before giving up the ghost' (Gantz 2015). Homer is in turn a slave who had been punished for his attempted escape by having his foot cut off, and who has been taught to read and write by a group of runaways. He is the only one who knows the geography of the surrounding territory well; or, in the words of one of the runaway slaves, he is 'the man who's got tha land written down in his mind' (Parks 2015, p. 109).

The Odysseus character is called simply Hero at the beginning of his journey: in Part 1, entitled 'A Measure of a Man' and set in 'Far West Texas' in early 1862, we see him pondering whether to accompany his master to the Civil War and fight on the Confederate side in exchange for 'Boss-Master's' promise of granting him freedom after the war. As another of Parks's African-American foundlings, he discusses the issue with his foster father, or 'fake-father' (p. 20), 'The Oldest Old Man', and with his partner, Penny. In a forceful reflection of the extent to which slavery deprives humans of free will, Parks has him consider self-mutilation in place of making a decision, only for the dilemma to be abruptly resolved by the terrible revelation that it was Hero who gave away Homer's hiding place and thus caused his punitive mutilation, which he was forced to perform himself. Disgraced, Hero has no other option but to leave for the war; like the Negro Resurrectionist in *Venus*, who sells the Venus's body to the Grade-School Chum for a gold coin (see Parks 1998, p. 154), he is marked as a Judas.

In Part 2, 'A Battle in the Wilderness', Hero discusses the value of freedom with Smith, a Union soldier captured by Boss-Master and now held in a cage. It turns out that Smith is a freed black slave who has joined a Colored battalion; however, his appearance allows him to pass for white, a feature he has been using to his advantage with his white captor so as not to be killed immediately. When Smith suggests that freedom is 'like living in Glory' (p. 95) and encourages Hero to escape his master, Hero is torn by doubt, as the only way he seems to be able to measure his own worth is in terms of his price as someone else's property. Hero muses: 'Seems like the worth of a Colored man, once he's made Free, is less than his worth when he's a slave. [...] me running off would be like stealing' (p. 96). The urgent need to create an identity for oneself is foregrounded by the emphasis that Parks places on costume in this part of the play, revisiting the central theme of "clothes making the man" discussed earlier in the context of *The America Play* and *Topdog/Underdog*. First, Boss-Master is depicted as a ridiculous 'Peacock' in his Colonel's uniform, who is too embarrassed to wear the ostentatious white plume on his hat in public, as it makes him look all too theatrical. Furthermore and more significantly for the main protagonist, Smith passes on his Union coat to Hero, who starts wearing it under his own Confederate one; this is how he arrives home in Part 3, which is aptly entitled 'The Union of My Confederate Parts'.

Hero's return is announced by the Odyssey Dog (who is the 'Odd-See' of Part 1). The Dog acts not only as a messenger: he also possesses a gift of vision, immediately recognizing Penny's pregnancy despite the fact that she is not showing yet, and acts as Hero's conscience. For the large part, he assumes the role of a clown. Embodied by an adult male actor, the effect of his performance in the American Repertory Theater production was described by Gantz as follows: 'Sporting an oversize shaggy sweater and sneakers, panting and slavering and rolling onto his back to have his tummy rubbed, he's not just faithful, he's a hoot' (Gantz 2015). Apart from the incongruity of the character's multiple functions with its role as the only animal in the play, it is also its appearance and demeanour that makes it grotesque: while at home in theatre for children or in dramatized fables, for instance, the bouncing, leaping, and talking Dog appears here in the framework of a largely sombre drama that heavily references Greek theatre by its use of the chorus in Parts 1 and 3 and by its frequently heightened language. Moreover, the ongoing preoccupation with fathers and sons against the backdrop of reconfigured myth gestures towards symbolic dramas by W. B. Yeats, such as *On Baile's Strand* or *Purgatory*, while the presence of a musician on stage throughout the action is reminiscent of some of Yeats's 'Plays for Dancers'. The interference of the Dog serves as a counterpoise that alleviates the potential burden of such references, injecting them with comedy and maintaining the focus on the ordinary life of the characters, which is indeed the fundamental concern of Parks's Odyssey.

In Part 3, which takes place in the autumn of 1863, approximately nine months after the release of Lincoln's Emancipation Proclamation and still a year and a half before the end of the Civil War, it is the initial effect of freedom that becomes the principal focus. Hero returns with a new name, which is Ulysses, '[l]ike the Union General' (Parks 2015, p. 138) and future US president, Ulysses S. Grant; we are thus ironically reminded that Hero has gained his name by fighting for the wrong cause. Ulysses's elation over his freedom takes him home as a true macho, bringing another woman with him and proposing to Penny that they live in a ménage à trois. Ulysses also bears a set of memorable gifts: he presents Homer with a foot of white alabaster and Penny with a silver-tipped gardening spade. Glaringly, he does not realize that both objects are patently useless to their recipients and may even be perceived as offensive. He also bears a copy of the Emancipation Proclamation, which is presented in the play—in accordance with its lack of actual impact on the lives of many African Americans at the time—as a mere piece of paper. When Penny leaves him for Homer, Ulysses is stunned; the play closes with the "hero" crushed, wearing the two uniforms on top of one another and holding the silver-tipped spade. As Gantz has poignantly summarized, 'understanding how much his life and his soul have truly been changed by his experience will take some time. With his newly free hands, his first act will be to bury the man he still refers to, even in death, as his "boss-master"' (Gantz 2015). If *The America Play* is anything to go by, Hero/Ulysses will join Parks's line of 'diggers'.

Parks's blending of Homer, events of the Civil War, and the story of a group of displaced African Americans in Parts 1 to 3 of *Father Comes Home from the Wars* continues her exploration of the grand narrative of American history vis-à-vis the unrecorded experience of ordinary African Americans, with the grotesque playing a fundamental role in ripping open the contours of accepted interpretations and enabling a creative refiguring of the past and its impact on the present. Parks's entire dramatic oeuvre, from the earliest experimental plays up to more immediately accessible works such as *Topdog/Underdog* and the first instalment of her current dramatic cycle, is deeply couched in an understanding of history as a constructed discourse, as proposed by Michel Foucault or Hayden White (see Wilmer 2000, p. 450). While challenging the hegemonic "white" meta-narrative of America, Parks's sustained focus on the individual simultaneously problematizes the establishment of a consistent counter-narrative, as apparent particularly in the discussion of *Venus* outlined earlier. Accordingly, Parks has always been very explicit in her refusal of the concept of the 'Black play' or a concept of African-American drama with a hegemonic agenda: as she put it in one of her essays, 'A black play does not exist. Every play is a black play. […] A black play employs the black not just as a subject, but as a platform, eye and telescope through which it intercourses with the cosmos' (Parks 2005, pp. 577, 582).

Parks's use of the grotesque is very much part of her overall strategy since its disruptive presence prevents *any* dominant narrative from arising. This is clearly evidenced in the grotesque mutability of central characters in her plays and the manner in which their appearance is examined in association with identity, from the Venus in the eponymous play to the imitation Lincolns of *The America Play* and *Topdog/Underdog*, and Hero/Ulysses and Smith of *Father Comes Home from the Wars*. The grotesque in the work of Suzan-Lori Parks consequently serves not only as a 'weapon of choice for social protest' that gives voice to the oppressed (see Connelly 2012, p. 18) but also as a device that helps defuse hegemonic counter-discourse.

Notes

1. The interventions of the Negro Resurrectionist are paralleled in the work of other experimentalist followers of Brecht, such as the celebrated Argentinian playwright Griselda Gambaro who has used extracts from contemporary newspapers to a similar effect in *Information for Foreigners*, a powerful drama about state terror written in the early 1970s (not published or performed until the early 1990s due to fear of repercussions).
2. The technicalities of the hustler's handling of the cards in three-card monte are explained in detail in Maley 2013, pp. 189–90.

Works Cited

Anderson, L. H. (2008). *Black Feminism in Contemporary Drama*. Urbana: University of Illinois Press.
Cassuto, L. (1997). *The Inhuman Race: The Racial Grotesque in American Literature and Culture*. New York: Columbia University Press.
Colbert, S. D. (2011). *The African American Theatrical Body: Reception, Performance, and the Stage*. Cambridge: Cambridge University Press.
Connelly, F. S. (2012). *The Grotesque in Western Art and Culture: The Image at Play*. Cambridge: Cambridge University Press.
Fuchs, E. (2001). Clown Shows: Anti-Theatricalist Theatricalism in Four Twentieth-Century Plays. *Modern Drama, 44*(3), 337–354.
Gantz, J. (2015, January 29). Suzan-Lori Parks's "Father" Is a Timeless Tale, review of *Father Comes Home from the Wars (Parts 1, 2 & 3)*, by Suzan-Lori Parks. *Boston Globe*. Retrieved August 28, 2015, from https://www.bostonglobe.com/arts/theater-art/2015/01/29/suzan-lori-parks-father-timeless-tale/gvPzkNIJrlhyVXIXv174hP/story.html
Geis, D. R. (2008). *Suzan-Lori Parks*. Ann Arbor: The University of Michigan Press.
Innes, C. (1999). Staging Black History: Re-Imaging Cultural Icons. In B. Reitz (Ed.), *Race and Religion in Contemporary Theatre and Drama in English* (pp. 95–107). Trier: Wissenschaftlicher Verlag Trier.
Isherwood, C. (2014, October 28). Ulysses as an American Slave, review of *Father Comes Home from the Wars (Parts 1, 2 & 3)*, by Suzan-Lori Parks. *New York Times*. Retrieved August 28, 2015, from http://www.nytimes.com/2014/10/29/theater/father-comes-home-from-the-wars-by-suzan-lori-parks-at-the-public-theater.html?_r=0
Keizer, A. R. (2011). "Our Posteriors, Our Posterity": The Problem of Embodiment in Suzan-Lori Parks's *Venus* and Kara Walker's *Camptown Ladies*. *Social Dynamics: A Journal of African Studies, 37*(2), 200–212.

LeMahieu, M. (2012). The Theater of Hustle and the Hustle of Theater: Play, Player, and Played in Suzan-Lori Parks's *Topdog/Underdog*. *African American Review*, 45 (1–2), 33–47.
Maley, P. (2013). What Is and What Aint: *Topdog/Underdog* and the American Hustle. *Modern Drama*, 56 (2), 186–205.
Miller, G. (2002). The Bottom of Desire in Suzan-Lori Parks's *Venus*. *Modern Drama*, 45 (1), 125–137.
Parks, S.-L. (1994, Spring). Interview by Han Ong. *BOMB Magazine*, 47. Retrieved September 10, 2015, from http://bombmagazine.org/article/1769/suzan-lori-parks
Parks, S.-L. (1995a). From Elements of Style. In S.-L. Parks, *The America Play and Other Works* (pp. 6–18). New York: Theatre Communications Group.
Parks, S.-L. (1995b). The America Play. In S.-L. Parks, *The America Play and Other Works* (pp. 157–199). New York: Theatre Communications Group.
Parks, S.-L. (1998). *Venus*. New York: Dramatists Play Service.
Parks, S.-L. (2002). *Topdog/Underdog*. New York: Theatre Communications Group.
Parks, S.-L. (2005). New Black Math. *Theatre Journal*, 57 (4), 576–583.
Parks, S.-L. (2015). *Father Comes Home from the Wars (Parts 1, 2 & 3)*. New York: Theatre Communications Group.
Saal, I. (2005). The Politics of Mimicry: The Minor Theater of Suzan-Lori Parks. *South Atlantic Review*, 70 (2), 57–71.
Saal, I. (2014). Suzan-Lori Parks. In M. Middeke, P. P. Schnierer, C. Innes, & M. C. Roudané (Eds.), *The Methuen Drama Guide to Contemporary British Playwrights* (pp. 243–260). London: Bloomsbury.
Warner, S. L. (2008). Suzan-Lori Parks's Drama of Disinterment: A Transnational Exploration of *Venus*. *Theatre Journal*, 60 (2), 181–199.
Wilmer, S. E. (2000). Restaging the Nation: The Work of Suzan-Lori Parks. *Modern Drama*, 43 (3), 442–452.
Worthen, W. B. (2010). *Drama: Between Poetry and Performance*. Chichester: Wiley-Blackwell.
Young, J. (1997). The Re-objectification and Re-commodification of Saartjie Baartman in Suzan-Lori Parks's *Venus*. *African American Review*, 31 (4), 699–708.

CHAPTER 6

Imagine This: Tim Crouch

I

Tim Crouch was a relative latecomer to playwriting, having produced his first full-length drama *My Arm* (2003) in his late thirties; this was when he also started writing shorter pieces for young audiences. Crouch trained as an actor and formed the Public Parts Theatre Company with his fellow graduates in Bristol in the late 1980s, where he developed devised productions for almost a decade. Following a subsequent postgraduate course in acting at London's Central School of Speech and Drama, he worked as a freelance actor in the UK and in the United States for approximately seven years while also becoming an Education Associate at the National Theatre in London. He was growing increasingly bored with the predictability of theatre at the time and was frustrated with the passive role that conventional forms of theatre ascribed to the spectator. His involvement in teaching provided an impetus for his radically experimental creative practice.

Crouch's work as a dramatist and performer, in which he has consistently collaborated with his co-directors Karl James and a smith (Andy Smith), may be viewed alongside the programmatic dismantling of realism by many of his contemporaries, such as Martin Crimp, Sarah Kane, and indeed virtually all the authors discussed in this book. However, Crouch has gone further in his absolute refusal of illusive theatre: his work has been stripping bare the fundamentals of theatre and articulating a rejection of verisimilitude in favour of an active employment of the spectators'

© The Editor(s) (if applicable) and The Author(s) 2016
O. Pilný, *The Grotesque in Contemporary Anglophone Drama*,
DOI 10.1057/978-1-137-51318-2_6

imagination. Crouch's profound concern with genuine audience engagement has been further attested by his long-term interest in conceptual art on the one hand, and the writings of contemporary thinkers on theatre on the other; as a matter of fact, the first collection of his plays bears an epigraph from Jacques Rancière's *The Emancipated Spectator* (see Crouch 2011a, p. 6).

As already apparent from Crouch's first play, which replaces actors with objects and tells about a boy who raises his arm and refuses to put it down for the rest of his life, the grotesque plays a seminal role in Crouch's work. Describing how meaning is created in *My Arm*, Dan Rebellato has asserted that 'the audience fills the gaps in performance with their own associations, experiences and ideas' (Rebellato 2013a, p. 131). This imaginative interpretation directly corresponds to what John Ruskin identified as the fundamental requirement of the beholder of the grotesque as a 'bold and fearless connection of truths' which it would be difficult to make in a more conventional form (Ruskin 1903, p. 132; see Chap. 1). As I will attempt to demonstrate, not only *My Arm* but the entire dramatic oeuvre of Tim Crouch may be seen as engaged in the use of the grotesque with the aim to involve the spectator in imagining the realities of others.

There are a number of features of Crouch's work that have brought it close to performance art, not least the fact that, apart from his most recent play, *Adler & Gibb*, his own presence as a performer has been crucial to its meaning. Moreover, two of his major works have signalled a strong affinity to site-specific practice: *ENGLAND* is a piece that is intended to be played in galleries, and the controversial drama *The Author* is performed as if set at the Royal Court Theatre, regardless of what the actual venue is. Nevertheless, all of Crouch's plays are crucially based on scripted text and involve a strong narrative element, which is also what justifies their inclusion in a study focused on text-based drama.

More so than any of the authors discussed in the present book, the work of Tim Crouch is that of paradox: not only is it characterized by frequently foregrounding conflicting propositions, but it occasionally seems to voice scepticism regarding the impact that art may have on what really matters, such as loss, grief, and death—an issue that Crouch raises within what are highly innovative aesthetic creations. As such, Crouch has been recently hailed as 'one of the most daring, playful and challenging theatremakers to emerge in the 2000s' (Rebellato 2013a, p. 125) and the author who has asked the most 'compelling set of questions about theatrical form, narrative content, and spectatorial engagement' in the twenty-first century to date (Bottoms 2011c, p. 11).

II

Crouch wrote *My Arm* in response to a crisis he experienced as an actor in representational performance and 'put it out as a statement' concerning his frustration (Crouch and Sierz 2014, p. 64; Ilter 2011, p. 398). He initially performed the play in people's front rooms in Brighton where he lives (Crouch and Sierz 2014, p. 64); following a preview at the Hayward Gallery in London in February 2003, which was directed by the author together with Karl James and Hettie MacDonald, *My Arm* officially premièred at the Traverse Theatre in July of the same year, becoming one of the highlights of the Edinburgh Festival. The subsequent tour of the play effectively ended Crouch's other acting engagements.

At the beginning of each performance of *My Arm*, Crouch asks the audience to lend him random items that they may have on them, and then uses the resulting assortment of objects as characters in the story he tells. His narrative follows the life of a boy whose apparently senseless gesture conceived at the age of ten initially confuses and exasperates his family and everyone around him, and gradually becomes the reason for the young man's appropriation as an icon by the art world. He becomes the subject of a variety of art works, and his dying as a result of the necrosis of his arm is followed in the manner of a freak show.

Seemingly absurd acts of defiance are relatively abundant in modern literature of course, from Herman Melville's Bartleby the Scrivener's preference 'not to' to Oskar Matzerath's decision never to grow up in *The Tin Drum* by Günther Grass, to name but two. As a rule, such acts are presented as a revolt against confinement by society. But although the boy's raising of the arm in Crouch's play may initially involve an element of dissent with the monotony and lack of parental attention in his typical middle-class childhood, his determination to keep his arm raised over the remaining thirty or so years of his life remains essentially unexplained and puzzling, and forms the central grotesque figure in his story. As Crouch has asserted, 'His arm becomes the ultimate inanimate object onto which other people project their own symbols and meanings' (qtd in Freshwater 2013, p. 172), and this crucially includes the audiences of the performance.

The story is performed by Crouch in a detached manner, involving minimal acting and consciously avoiding the expression of emotion. Parts of it are enacted with the objects solicited from the audience and projected onto a large screen. This grotesque technique is reminiscent of puppet theatre; however, Crouch has repeatedly stated that 'puppetry' is not really an appropriate term for it, since not only does he perform relatively little action with the objects but also the objects in no way resemble what they stand for, with the exception of the Action Man doll used to enact the role of the boy (Ilter 2011, p. 401; Crouch and Sierz 2014, p. 65). The emphasis on non-resemblance is also maintained on another level of the performance, that of the narrator: although Crouch speaks in the first person, he never raises his arm. Moreover, at an important point in the performance, he lets the audience look at his back, which is supposed to bear a large scar caused by a suicide attempt, and there is no scar there to be seen; similarly, when the protagonist has to have one of his fingers amputated, Crouch lifts his hand with the finger in question intact.

The puzzlement created by the contrast between the story and the images and actions seen on stage is further enhanced by the impression that the play may be autobiographical. This impression was particularly strong in the early performances of *My Arm* when Crouch was still relatively unknown, and the production team in fact capitalized on his relative anonymity by issuing two different press releases for the 2003 Edinburgh Festival, one of which announced 'a play by Tim Crouch' and the other spoke about 'a man who has lived with one arm above his head coming to Edinburgh to tell his story' (Crouch qtd in Ilter 2011, p. 398). As Helen Freshwater has observed, even in more recent performances, many audience members still believe at the end of the show that the story is Crouch's own, despite all the evidence to the contrary (Freshwater 2013, p. 173); such is the power of the habitual suspension of disbelief in the theatre.

It is clear that while the play is based on a coherent, chronologically ordered narrative and may be regarded, in the words of its author, as 'a storytelling piece' (Crouch and Sierz 2014, p. 65), it raises a complex set of questions about the nature of theatrical representation. This subject has since become a central part of Crouch's work as a dramatist. As pointed out both by Stephen Bottoms and Emilie Morin, it has evolved from Crouch's familiarity with and admiration for the richness of the critical debate about representation and its adequacy in the realm of conceptual art from Marcel Duchamp to the North American arts scene of the 1960s (see Bottoms 2009; Morin 2011). Crouch's use of mixed-media technology in *My Arm*, such as the live projection of objects or the inclusion of a home video of a small boy (created by film-maker and photographer Chris Dorley-Brown) that is projected onto a screen at the back of the performance space several times during the show, points to the same source of inspiration. Most importantly, however, Crouch shares the conceptual artists' belief that the work of representation is to be done by the spectator. By disallowing straightforward mimesis on the stage, Crouch delegates the audience an active role in the creation of meaning. Crouch is relentlessly intent on soliciting the spectators' involvement; at the same time, he has repeatedly voiced his dislike of participatory theatre. He has asserted: 'I am interested in audience participation, but I am not interested in members of the audience getting up on the stage and being made to look embarrassed and awkward. I want it to be a more genuine active participation whilst retaining the aesthetic or art aspect of it' (Ilter 2011, p. 401).

In terms of aesthetics, *My Arm* definitely became one of the strongest and most innovative theatrical works of the decade. Paradoxically perhaps, this was also due to the way in which Crouch has foregrounded seminal issues concerning the value of experimental art. For one, the 'boy with the arm' (Crouch 2011a, p. 31) is repeatedly exploited by artists who make him an object of their work; most prominently, it is his friend Simon Martin who shamelessly generates profit from his story. Simon promotes the device that 'Art is anything you can get away with' (p. 36). To him, this implies that he is free to display his friend among a series of nude photographs in an exhibit entitled *Man-i(n)festation* and present him as a symbol of injustice—only to sell parts of the exhibit for a significant amount of money. Unsurprisingly, Simon eventually goes on to sell the ailing man himself to an American gallerist, who intends to display his arm 'in an aesthetic context' after his death (p. 46). The assertion by which Simon abides, however, was originally not at all intended as an expression of opportunism: as Crouch has pointed out, the above statement comes from Marshall McLuhan, and was later quoted by Andy Warhol as part of a creative re-drawing of the boundaries of art (Ilter 2011, p. 403). Given the aesthetically unorthodox nature of *My Arm*, the sentence becomes clearly self-referential, too, questioning the play as a work of art; this is made explicit by the device being displayed on a placard for the entire second half of the show.

The play proceeds to discuss other motivations for artistic practice. The boy's brother Anthony eventually finds his way to politically engaged art through his work with refugees and dismisses Simon as a usurper. Moreover, a figurative painter carefully produces an empathetic representation of the dying man; by serving her as a model, he feels for the first time that his life has become meaningful (see Crouch in Ilter 2011, p. 404). The different attitudes to art are provocatively pitched against one another for consideration. Ultimately, the play indicates that anything *may* indeed become art but what matters is the ethics of the transformation; on a bleaker note, Crouch simultaneously demonstrates that no art proves able to save the protagonist from his tragic end. Again, there is a vital self-referential element to the uncomfortable intimation: as is apparent from the reports of reviewers, the impression of immediacy of the here and now created in *My Arm* is so strong that it has left many spectators profoundly moved (see Freshwater 2013, p. 174). Nonetheless, the notion of immediacy is explicitly undermined by the narrator at the end of the play, as he reveals that what the audience have witnessed was actually set five years into the future in a gallery in Manhattan, where the arm-man is delivering one of the talks arranged by Simon. Not unlike Suzan-Lori Parks in *Venus* (see Chap. 5), Crouch thus links his play with exploitative freak show, while simultaneously prompting the audience to consider the voyeuristic nature of their spectatorship.

III

Crouch's second play, *An Oak Tree*, examines the power of theatre in relation to trauma. *An Oak Tree* was co-directed by its author, Karl James, and a smith, and premièred at the Traverse Theatre in Edinburgh in August 2005, following a preview at the Nationaltheater Mannheim in Germany in April of the same year. It is the story of a man (Andy) whose daughter was killed by a stage hypnotist in a road accident. Trying to come to terms with the loss, the father attends the hypnotist's performance and volunteers as one of his subjects; on the stage, he reveals his identity to the artist and expresses his hope that talking to him might possibly help. The father also describes how, in his effort to overcome the trauma, he has transformed an oak tree at the place of the accident into his daughter.

The play is performed by Crouch as the hypnotist and by a different second actor every night, either male or female, who has not read the script and has only met with Crouch shortly before the performance to discuss the logistics. A short note is sent out by Crouch to the other actor beforehand, including a warning that if the loss of a child is an experience that is personally close to him/her, it is advisable not to be involved in the play. (The note is reproduced in Crouch 2011a, p. 55.) Crouch guides the actor through the performance, providing lines of the play on clipboards and issuing instructions either loudly through a microphone or, inaudibly to the audience, into a set of earphones that the other actor is wearing.[1] The grotesque enactment of the story of *My Arm* with inanimate objects is thus replaced in *An Oak Tree* by using a live actor as a puppet. The enacted events include not only the hypnotist's act the father volunteers to participate in, but also a conversation between the father and his wife, who is played by Crouch with his back turned to the audience, conversations between the two actors, and, finally, a rendering of the tragic accident.

As Wolfgang Kayser has pointed out, the reduction of characters into puppets became commonplace in a particular brand of Romantic drama and was further developed by a wide range of authors who have used grotesque elements in their plays, from Alfred Jarry to the *teatro del grottesco* (Kayser 1966, pp. 41–4, 91–2, 135–9). In these works, however, the main point was to indicate that the world was operated by an uncanny, incomprehensible force (see Chap. 1), a concern that is alien to *An Oak Tree*. We have also seen that puppet-like manipulation is central to the mechanism of the dark comedies of Martin McDonagh, where the principal purpose is that of providing thrills and laughs to the audience (see Chap. 1). Characters are also operated by others as puppets in a number of plays by Enda Walsh, where this action is subject to ethical judgement on the manipulators (see Chap. 4). *An Oak Tree* differs from all these works in that it presents an actor being operated almost like a robot—a feature that is most apparent in Crouch's loud instructions such as 'Ask me what I'm being. Say, "What are you being?"' (Crouch 2011a, p. 59)—but without passing judgment on the puppeteer. At the same time, Crouch strongly foregrounds the humanity of the puppet: as Helen Freshwater has observed, *An Oak Tree*'s 'celebrated affective impact appears to be realized by and through watching this actor struggling to read the script and follow Crouch's instructions' in a reflection of the father's perturbed state of mind (Freshwater 2013, p. 175). As the second actor is invited onto the stage from the auditorium at the beginning of the play, the audience are encouraged all the more strongly to picture themselves in his position as a bereaved father.

As in *My Arm*, the audience are propelled to bridge the gaps in the grotesque performance by using their imagination, a task that is made more challenging in *An Oak Tree* by the complex overlapping of the different levels of the plot, which often produces momentary disorientation. Moreover, the audience appear to be fictionalized (Ilter 2011, p. 396) because Crouch informs the spectators that they are 'upstairs in a pub near the Oxford Road', it is 'this time next year', and that when he wants volunteers from the audience, he will not be asking them (Crouch 2011a, p. 60). While a similar moment of alienation occurs at the end of *My Arm*, which discloses that although the audience have been addressed directly throughout the performance, the action was actually taking place elsewhere and in the future, Crouch uses this device right at the beginning of the play this time and is much more explicit about it. A practical reason for distancing the audience of *An Oak Tree* by announcing their fictional status may appear to be the desire to prevent the performance from turning into participatory theatre; indeed, any time spectators might volunteer, '*they are gently thanked and guided back to their seats by the* HYPNOTIST' (Crouch 2011a, p. 64). However, as Seda Ilter has argued, the chief purpose of questioning the status of the audience is rather to enhance the effect of '[d]ifferent realities and ontologies of fictional and "actual" people and space dissolv[ing] and reconfigur[ing] throughout the play' (Ilter 2011, p. 396) and make the spectators consciously consider their role in the performance from the outset.

One of the most convoluted matters that the audience are to ponder in *An Oak Tree* is Crouch's use of the hypnotist. For many, the associations conjured up by the notion of the hypnotist would primarily concern trickery and sham; these are encouraged in the play by the presentation of the Hypnotist's show as a bombastic spectacle and by having the Hypnotist wear a silver waistcoat (the only ostentatious item in terms of costuming, props, or stage decoration) throughout. Such negative connotations might insinuate culpability as regards the accident in which Andy's daughter is killed; nevertheless, the accident is never presented as anything other than an accident, and Andy never blames the Hypnotist for it.

Moreover, a hypnotist may be perceived as a particular kind of theatremaker, whose task it is to make people behave as he suggests. Given Crouch's views on theatre, it is easy to make an analogy between the Hypnotist's show in *An Oak Tree* and illusive theatre, in which the essentially manipulative nature of the latter in relation to the audience is highlighted. Yet, Crouch is very much aware that it is fundamentally the hypnotist's subject who enables hypnosis to succeed; one of the notes he made in the process of creating *An Oak Tree* affirms that 'All hypnosis is self-hypnosis' (Crouch 2013, p. 235). The word 'suggestion', which the Hypnotist uses several times with reference to his act, functions as a pun:

it indicates not only falling under the spell of theatre and rescinding one's own will but also an urge to actively imagine something. The conflicting double meaning is foregrounded by the role of the stage Hypnotist being played by the author of the drama, whose position would traditionally be associated with springing an illusion on the audience but that is here connected simultaneously with attributing an active role to the audience. This opens up the way towards a consideration of all art as a form of hypnosis, and even more importantly, towards the question of what power art may have in relation to personal tragedy. Indeed, the Hypnotist in *An Oak Tree* is said to have lost his ability to hypnotize anyone after the fatal accident, while, conversely, the father has performed a creative act by transforming a tree into a human being.

The notion of art as a creative process in which one thing is transformed into another is very much at the heart of *An Oak Tree* (see Rebellato 2013a, p. 133). Crouch emphasizes this by involving several celebrated art works in his play that revolve around the notion of transformation, such as Bruce Nauman's *Instructions for a Mental Exercise* (1969/1974; see Morin 2011, p. 73; Crouch 2013, pp. 239–41), which advises a prostrate human being how to merge with the ground. Nauman's *Instructions* is transposed by the playwright into a hypnotic text that is presented by Andy as a recipe for relief (see Crouch 2011a, pp. 97–9). Most apparently, Crouch engages with the eponymous installation by Michael Craig-Martin, which is detailed in the front matter of the published text: Craig-Martin's *an oak tree* (1973) consists in a glass of water placed on a shelf, accompanied by the title 'An Oak Tree' and a series of printed questions and answers where the artist asserts that the glass of water has disappeared and has been replaced by an oak tree. The father's act of transformation in Crouch's play develops the idea further, in that it suggests a transformation of an oak tree into a human being. However, the pivotal issue that the unorthodox two-hander explores is whether art may perform a liberating transformation in people who have suffered severe trauma.

The answer offered by Crouch is ambivalent. What *An Oak Tree* demonstrates is the ability of art to engender profound and deep-felt sympathy with other people's grief and loss. The 'affective impact' (Freshwater 2013, p. 175) is carefully built up over the course of the drama and is given a powerful coda in which the actors describe the accident through the respective eyes of the driver and of the girl. Speaking directly to the audience, they deliver lines that are evocative and, at the same time, harrowing in their simplicity, producing a hypnotic effect by an extensive use of anaphora, as apparent in the following extract:

> FATHER: When I click my fingers, you're stepping off the kerb.
> HYPNOTIST: When I say sleep, a girl is there. Her eyes are wide open.
> When I say sleep, she looks at you.
> When I say sleep everything slows.
> FATHER: When I say sleep a car is coming towards you. [...]
> (p. 105)

Nevertheless, the fact remains that Andy's wife, Dawn, is breaking down under the strain of watching his inability to cope with their loss, and is threatening to leave him. His act of transforming the tree into their daughter may be akin to the creative act of an artist—but it changes nothing about the fact that the girl is dead. As Dawn points out, 'That is a tree, I am your wife, this is your daughter, that is a road. This is what matters. This. This is what we have to deal with. This' (p. 102). Consequently, *An Oak Tree* may seem to be in harmony not so much with Craig-Martin's assertive gesture but rather with Magritte's famous images of a pipe, which insist on a fundamental difference between art and reality regardless of how strong the illusion of verisimilitude may be.

Still, a measure of hope in the healing power of art is proffered through Crouch's use of music in the play. Music is particularly vital to the impact of the final scene, which opens with a loud rendition of Carl Orff's 'O Fortuna', the monumental final cry of despair over the cruelty of fate from *Carmina Burana*. Nonetheless, Orff's music cuts out as the actors embark on their rendition of the accident, and it makes way for the subtle lyrical beauty of the Aria from Bach's *Goldberg Variations*. The Aria has already been heard at a number of points in the performance but as an initial stage direction stipulates, it has been 'a flawed rendition: faltering but ambitious, failing to resolve' so far (p. 56). It is only now, when the accident has been replayed, that the Aria is finally accomplished and as the Hypnotist and the Father prepare to open their eyes, the Aria moves into the spirited and joyful First Variation (p. 106). The two men will be left gazing at the catastrophe, and Andy's daughter will remain dead, but the lyrical, mesmeric re-presentation of the tragedy may indicate a way out of inconsolable grief, and potentially a new beginning.[2]

IV

ENGLAND, subtitled 'A Play for Galleries', continues Tim Crouch's concern with the value of art: it returns to the link between art and exploitation discussed in *My Arm*, and like both of Crouch's earlier plays, it questions the relevance of art in the face of death. *ENGLAND* was commissioned by the Traverse Theatre in Edinburgh and opened in Edinburgh's Fruitmarket Gallery in August 2007, performed by the author and Hannah Ringham, a founding member of the Shunt performance collective. The production was directed by Karl James and a smith. Following its Edinburgh run, the play was toured in the UK and globally, and it was presented in translation by several theatres in Continental Europe.

Act I of *ENGLAND* is performed as a guided tour through a gallery, regardless of what the current exhibition may be. The guides—one male and one female—alternate in delivering the lines of a first-person narrative uttered by an English person who suffers from a severe heart condition and lives in a designer duplex apartment with an art dealer boyfriend. The audience are provided with extensive information about the protagonist's life, including details of the swiftly deteriorating heart disease. However, they are never told the protagonist's gender. In the words of Dan Rebellato, 'This creates a fascinatingly paradoxical stage character, someone who is rounded and vivid and individual, yet with a key marker of their identity suspended' (Rebellato 2013a, p. 137).

In *ENGLAND*, Crouch's theatre becomes even more radically that of the imagination, since literally everything has to be conjured up in the minds of the spectators. Throughout Act I, the guides instruct the audience to look at the exhibited art works while describing them either as images or art works from the protagonist's life. The grotesque non-correspondence that is often involved challenges spectators to consider the nature of the performance in relation to reality, which is also true of the obvious non-correspondence between the two actors and the person they represent. The performance space functions as a particularly bountiful heterotopia (see Foucault 1984), a phenomenon that to an extent also emerges in *An Oak Tree*: the space is simultaneously the gallery where the play is performed, the protagonist's duplex, a doctor's surgery, Southwark Cathedral, and a series of clinics.

The protagonist's attitude to everything s/he discusses seems unremittingly positive. S/he is particularly enthralled by art, propounding its essential value for humans and encouraging appropriate aesthetic appreciation. Yet as the spectators simultaneously witness the rapid decline of her/his health up to a critical state, many of the statements about art are called into question. This applies to the therapeutic quality of art in particular, which the protagonist attempts to assert by pointing out how her/his GP's patients like looking at the paintings in his surgery because 'It helps them feel better about their illness' (Crouch 2011a, p. 124), or by stating that 'Art can make you feel better about going to die' (p. 128). The conclusive exclamation that art 'can make you live longer!' (p. 128), rather than turning into a query, has a distinctly ironic tinge in relation to the speaker's condition. By the end of Act I, the salutary role of art is in fact reduced to its commercial value: it is due to the affluence of the art-dealing boyfriend that the protagonist gains access to privileged medical treatment which saves her/his life. The play thus seems to be a somewhat cynical nod to the boyfriend's device that 'good art is art that sells' (p. 128).

For Act II, the performance moves to a more conventional theatrical space within the gallery, where the audience are seated. Here they are cast in the role of a veiled young Muslim woman. The two performers do not deliver their text to the audience as a whole, however, but to individual audience members, maintaining 'unwaveringly direct eye contact' (Bottoms 2011b, p. 458). One of the performers enacts the English person from Act I, who has now had a heart transplant and has travelled to an unidentified Third World country to thank the widow of the man whose heart s/he was given. The other actor plays the role of Interpreter between 'English' and the young widow, represented by the audience. Nevertheless, since the Interpreter speaks only English regardless of whose words are being translated, sometimes repeats English's words and sometimes not, and often speaks in the same speech on behalf of both of the interlocutors, the effect is strongly disorienting. The confusion is further underlined by the two actors exchanging their roles in the middle of the Act, without indicating this (in the original production, English was first played by Crouch and then by Ringham; Bottoms 2011b, p. 458).

The conversation discloses that the young woman's husband, Hassam, became a victim of a terrorist attack on a Marriott hotel, in which a US official was killed. It is gradually revealed that the heart was taken away for the transplant under shady circumstances, with Hassam still in a coma. Furthermore, Hassam's wife has seen very little of the money she was promised.

The gift that English has brought her as an expression of gratitude is a beautiful, expensive work of art. However, the widow is not at all interested and ignores even the commercial value of the gift: the one thing she would like is to have her husband back. English's final, repeated line, 'What's she saying?' (Crouch 2011a, pp. 158–9) signals not only a lack of comprehension but also the beginning of a realization that in this situation, art is utterly irrelevant. Moreover, the mere utility of art measured by its exchange value is tainted, since in this case art was used to purchase a vital organ in what was very likely an unsavoury operation.

The diseased heart—an image Crouch already used at the end of *My Arm*, as Morin has noted (Morin 2011, p. 83, n. 4)—clearly functions as a political metaphor in *ENGLAND*, as it is linked with Western intrusion in the Middle East and Africa. Crouch also associates this central image to the use of brain power and labour from poorer countries by Europeans, since English's GP, cardiologist, and heart surgeon are conspicuously of South Asian, African, and Middle Eastern origin, respectively (see Crouch 2011a, pp. 125, 134, 135; Bottoms 2011b, p. 457). The idea of Hassam's heart in a rich English person's body thus speaks volumes about what Morin euphemistically calls 'the shortcomings of global economy' (Morin 2011, p. 72). Nevertheless, the same image also relates to Crouch's predominant concern with art in the play. As Crouch's collaborator, a smith, has outlined, *ENGLAND* is one of the author's plays that puts something where it shouldn't be: just as Hassam's heart is inserted into another body, *ENGLAND* 'transplants' theatre into a gallery (smith 2011, p. 413). There it performs a critical intrusion into an art scene that—as John Berger has powerfully argued—we have endowed with a quasi-religious air that masks its essentially commercialized nature (see Bottoms 2011b, pp. 449, 457).

Considering that, as in his previous two plays, Crouch makes his critical scrutiny a part of an accomplished artistic creation, the apparent pessimism that *ENGLAND* voices concerning the relevance of art should not be taken at face value. Like *An Oak Tree*, Crouch's play amply demonstrates that art is capable of generating empathy with the plight of others; this relates both to the ailing protagonist in Act I and the bereaved woman in Act II. Rather than dismissing the work of artists, Crouch's 'play for galleries' ultimately aims to 'foster a new mode of looking' (Morin 2011, p. 81), one that requires fresh and thoughtful engagement on the part of the spectator.

V

Not many plays in theatre history have produced such a wide range of responses that they became the subject of a symposium within a year of their first production, as it was the case with *The Author* by Tim Crouch. Held at the University of Leeds in conjunction with performances of the play in November 2010, the gathering of theatre scholars and practitioners resulted in a thematic issue of *Contemporary Theatre Review*, the first (and, up to date, the only) collection of essays dedicated to the work of Tim Crouch. In the introduction to the volume, Stephen Bottoms reiterated the feeling of many reviewers by stating that *The Author* is the most challenging and, at the same time, the most puzzling of Crouch's dramas, and admitted that after two years' engagement with the play, he was still not entirely sure what he thought of it (Bottoms 2011a, p. 391).

The Author was commissioned by the Royal Court Theatre in London, where it opened at the Jerwood Theatre Upstairs in September 2009, directed by Karl James and a smith. The Jerwood Theatre Upstairs is also where the play is set. Following its relatively peaceful initial run at the Royal Court, the production had a much more controversial reception when it toured to the Traverse Theatre as part of the Edinburgh International Festival, and then to various venues across the UK, in Helsinki, Dublin, Budapest, Lisbon, and Los Angeles.

A fundamental defining feature of the play is its grotesque removal of the stage: the spectators are ushered into two sloping banks of seating that face each other, with only a small space in between. As Crouch indicates in a stage direction, 'This is a play that happens inside its audience' (Crouch 2011a, p. 164). The characters comprise an author, two actors, and an audience member who speak about the process of rehearsing, staging, and watching a play at the Royal Court Theatre. Like all of Crouch's other works, *The Author* involves a strong and consistent narrative but, given the unconventional arrangement of theatrical space and the subject of the narrative, the play is naturally almost exclusively and very radically metatheatrical. Indeed, Crouch may be seen to take a step further Pirandello's use of metatheatricality as a means of producing disorientation, having the performers use their real names and planting them as cuckoo's eggs among the audience.[3] The role of the performers is heralded in the actor Vic's early reflection: 'So, I'm, let's say, "provoking" you! Or maybe "rousing", or "stirring" [...]!' (Crouch 2011a, p. 171), a suggestion that is emphatically confirmed by the subsequent development of the drama.

The play discussed in *The Author* is an intensely violent fictitious piece by Tim Crouch. It focuses on a young woman who lives in an abusive relationship with her father, described with evocative precision; it is even hinted that the father ends up beheading the daughter (see Crouch and Sierz 2014, p. 71). Moreover, the actors and the author discuss their experiential preparation during rehearsals. This involved meetings with a man whose family died in a wartime massacre and with a woman who had been raped by her father, as well as watching videos of wartime atrocities and beheadings by terrorists. Much of the preparation process is again depicted in graphic detail, and the encounter with the rape victim is even replayed by the actress Esther and Tim the author.

Crouch's engagement with the use of extreme violence on the stage has a clear reference point in that he not only sets the play in the cradle of in-yer-face theatre, but he also cites several notorious scenes from the work of Sarah Kane, Mark Ravenhill, and Edward Bond, and repeatedly alludes to what Kane said in defence of *Blasted* in interviews (see Rebellato 2013a, pp. 139–40). *The Author* zooms in on the devastating effect that involvement in the staging of such visceral drama may have on actors: Esther ends up suffering a breakdown and finds it hard to be with her family and take care of her baby son, while Vic—who plays the abusive father—attacks a chef in a restaurant after a performance and, on the final night, almost kicks an audience member to death, mistaking him for an intruder. The detrimental impact on the spectators is in turn embodied in the metonymy of the eye wounded by theatre, which forcefully turns literal: in a deliberately hazy context, the audience character Adrian initially indicates that his eye was injured during a performance of Tim's play (see Crouch 2011a, p. 180); close to the climax of the drama, it is revealed that Adrian was the spectator attacked by Vic and his eye injury was inflicted during the savage battering.

Tim Crouch clearly does not favour violence or abuse on stage; as he stated in a letter to one upset audience member, 'One premise of my play (heartfelt by me) is that a representation of an act of violence is, on some level, still an act of violence. I have great difficulties with violent plays' (Crouch 2011b, p 416). *The Author* accordingly absconds from staging any violence whatsoever. Nevertheless, the degree of brutality, abuse, and self-harm that Crouch invites the audience to contemplate in the play is as high as in any in-yer-face production. The fact that the scenes are merely described by the performers does little to diminish their impact on the spectators. The reception of Mark O'Rowe's visceral monologue dramas discussed in Chap. 3, for instance, amply testifies that the effect of narrated violence is often as strong, if not stronger, than enacted violence. Indeed, the same conclusion may be drawn on the basis of the evidence pertaining to the reception of *The Author*. The shock and horror produced in the play are considerable, and when Tim moves into his final monologue, the play becomes positively monstrous (see Iball 2011, p. 441) as he discloses how, after a party with the cast members, he ended up casually watching child pornography and possibly sexually abused Esther's baby son. The closing monologue is the most profoundly disturbing part of the play and, as Freshwater observed, the fact that the only visual image present in the play is a photo of Esther's baby, circulated amongst the spectators halfway through the performance, makes the ending almost unbearable (Freshwater 2013, p. 179).

Crouch's assertion quoted earlier may be honest but, at the same time, it strategically de-emphasizes that in its critique of violent plays, *The Author* is itself no less violent. What I have outlined at various stages in the present book, moreover, is that playwrights such as Sarah Kane, Mark Ravenhill, or Philip Ridley have used extreme violence in their work in order to make a variety of important ethical points (see Chaps 1 and 2). The reason why Crouch chooses to ignore this is in my view mainly linked to how this type of drama has been consumed by audiences, particularly since in-yer-face theatre has become a celebrated strand of British culture in the eyes of the public. The unreflective reception of monstrosity is represented in *The Author* by Adrian, who enthusiastically enumerates the horrific things he has seen on stage. He concludes his list with a clear reference to Kane's *Blasted*, exclaiming: 'I've seen a dead baby get eaten! That was great! It's such an education!' (p. 192). Adrian's fervour demonstrates that what was originally a shock tactic aimed at rousing the audience is now commonplace, and that instead of changing the spectators' attitude to real atrocities, representations of extreme violence have become yet another commodity. Instead of engaging with how such representations relate to reality, audiences have begun to passively enjoy them as an approved form of art, and have regularly been attracted to them by the casting of stars—as reflected in Tim's acknowledgment in *The Author* that many people came to see his play because of Esther, who had recently appeared on television and starred in a film (pp. 193, 197). Noting the detrimental role of collective judgement that is emphasized by Crouch here, Stephen Bottoms has asserted that perhaps, 'corruptibility lies most readily in contexts where we hand our responsibility for individual judgement to collective opinion, or to supposed experts and specialists, allowing them to determine what is valuable *for* us' (Bottoms 2011c, p. 19). In effect, *The Author* suggests that uncritical consumption of violence in the theatre is not much different from watching online videos of atrocities or the use of child pornography, as it involves the same kind of dazed voyeurism (see Iball 2011, p. 438).

Apart from the unqualified glamorization of in-yer-face theatre, Crouch focuses his critique on the glorification of the author. The admiration that we tend to feel for artists who have achieved fame is vigorously undermined by the revelation that Tim is the perpetrator of child abuse. The discovery is deliberately unexpected and hence all the more shocking: although Tim depicts a number of gruesome details from his plays and from the writing and rehearsal process alike, he is consistently friendly, approachable, and communicative, coming across as a generally sound and "normal" individual. Crouch is merciless in not giving the spectators who have not walked out earlier much of a choice not to hear the disturbing final monologue—or at least the most abhorrent part of it—because the unravelling of the story is gradual, riveting, and occurs with the lights being slowly dimmed.[4]

Helen Freshwater has written in detail about how Crouch exploits the role of social conventions in *The Author*, pointing out that the play 'depends upon audience members observing the unspoken rules of social interaction', including 'the conventions which govern appropriate behaviour in a theatre' (Freshwater 2011, p. 408). This is why when spectators are initially asked about their life by the performers, they tend to answer, out of basic politeness and because of the expected willingness to play along. The same holds true of when the performers ask whether it is okay for them to proceed with the play following a particularly gruesome or offensive moment, such as Tim's early account of his sexual fantasy concerning an assistant in a floatation centre—mostly, the consent to continue is readily given. Finally, the conventions of appropriate audience behaviour also play an important role in discouraging spectators from intervening or walking out during Tim's final speech, together with several other factors, such as simple curiosity about how the play ends, an unwillingness to judge a play without seeing the entire performance, or even the fact of having spent money on the ticket.

Considering all of this, Crouch may justifiably be accused of tricking his audience into experiencing the revolting details of child abuse. The trick is far from gratuitous, however, and Crouch approaches the moment with the utmost level of responsibility. This is evidenced in that he casts himself in the role of the paedophile and uses his own name. He also includes a sprinkling of autobiographical details for those who are familiar with him to enhance the impression that 'Tim' really stands for Tim Crouch. In the words of Stephen Bottoms, the playwright thus makes himself a 'willing scapegoat for those appalled or simply confused by his play' (Bottoms 2011b, p. 462), a gesture that requires a significant dose of courage. Indeed as Crouch has confessed, he often found delivering the final monologue at least as unbearable as the spectators did listening to it, and has lost a few friends as a result of writing the play. During one performance, he was even assaulted by a spectator (see Freshwater 2013, p. 179; Crouch and Sierz 2014, p. 73). The incident only confirms Freshwater's observation that making oneself a suspect of paedophilia bears a substantial risk of suffering physical harm, as apparent from the number of recent community attacks on alleged perpetrators of child abuse in the UK (Freshwater 2013, p. 180).

Besides compromising Tim in the eyes of the audience, the final speech returns to the opening image of the author climbing into a floatation tank and getting a blade ready.[5] It is now clear what exactly was happening and why: Crouch kills off the author by having him commit suicide because of his deed. When the spectators were imagining the action at the beginning of the play, they were unaware that the scene where the author is literally stripped naked first before he gets in the water bears a powerful figurative significance. As Crouch indicates by explicitly referring to 'The death of the author' in a closing stage direction in the published text (p. 203), he intends to follow Roland Barthes in relinquishing the glamorized figure of the author as the sole creator of meaning, and he hands the decisive role to the audience (see Barthes 1989). Tim's last words before he leaves the theatre are not as puzzling as they might seem: 'The writing is leaving the writer' (p. 203) is yet another reference to Barthes that invites the spectators to author the meaning of what they have just experienced.

The ending of *The Author* forcefully confirms that this indeed is 'a play that happens inside its audience' and that spectatorship is its core concern. As discussed, Crouch foregrounds the conventions of audience behaviour at the onset; yet, he quickly proceeds to confound the spectators' desire to play by the rules by not making it clear whether what the audience are watching is scripted or improvised (see Freshwater 2011, pp. 408–9). Consequently, members of the audience are left to figure out their position and role in the performance, which may prove to be quite an ordeal for many of them. Moreover, as in Act II of *ENGLAND* (or, for that matter,

Parks's *Venus*), the play implicates the spectators in what they are watching by its emphasis on the spectatorial gaze: as Bottoms has observed, the seating arrangement, combined with the fact that the lights are up for most of the performance, produces a situation in which we are constantly made to observe others looking, while being simultaneously 'watched in our watching' (Bottoms 2011b, pp. 458, 462). The unease that is created is also essential to the manner in which the play disrupts any customary sense of community in the auditorium: according to Crouch, the 'idea of being on our own is absolutely necessary to finding one's responsibility' (Crouch and Sierz 2014, p. 75).

Dan Rebellato is one of the several commentators to assert that Crouch's work has been consistently characterized by taking its audience seriously (Rebellato 2013a, p. 144). In light of how deeply unsettling the experience of watching *The Author* is, Crouch is aware that the play must be 'handled with extreme care' (Crouch 2011b, p. 421). The performance is therefore alleviated with a good dose of humour, and the disturbing moments are carefully interspersed with passages in which spectators are allowed to recover from the shock (in one such moment, Adrian offers Maltesers to those sitting around him, balancing on the verge of irony). About ten minutes into the play, a planted audience member walks out in order to indicate that leaving the performance is definitely an option; as Crouch has noted, walkouts do occur almost every night and at the Traverse Theatre run in August 2010, the spectators who left comprised at least 10 % of the audience (Crouch and Sierz 2014, pp. 72–3).

Finally, music is used as another 'release valve' in the show (Crouch 2011a, p. 164): unlike *An Oak Tree*, which employs music predominantly to convey ideas or emotions, *The Author* uses a variety of popular tunes to put the audience at ease. The one exception where the situation becomes more complex is with the song 'We're All in This Together' from *High School Musical*, which is first sung by Esther and then the music is played again when Vic describes kicking Adrian almost to death. The irony is more than palpable in the latter occurrence of the tune, but it also pertains to Esther's initial singing of the tacky musical number, since the lyrics simultaneously verbalize a fundamental point that *The Author* makes. As Crouch himself has summarized, there is a 'moral, traditional drive in the action of that play around our responsibility' (Crouch and Sierz 2014, p. 73); by making the performers dress casually, sit in the audience, and use their own names, Crouch points out that the perpetration of violence, abuse, and atrocity has 'everything to do with us, everything to do with people who look like me and people who look like you' (Crouch and Sierz 2014, p. 73). The performers may be cuckoo's eggs, but the cuckoos in question are actually of the same species (Iball 2011, p. 434).

When asked about the concept of witnessing in the theatre, which has recently become so popular with political playwrights and their commentators alike, Crouch has dismissed the notion as inadequate, arguing that witnessing is still merely a passive act (see Bottoms 2011b, p. 463). What *The Author* attempts to demonstrate is that if the spectator's imagination is to be truly engaged, and if he or she is to thoroughly consider the relation between watching an act and committing an act, the immunity provided by conventional theatre through the awareness of its nature as a fictitious representation may need to be removed (see Crouch and Sierz 2014, p. 73). This is effected in *The Author* by a grotesque conflation of the world of the auditorium with that of the stage, which occurs simultaneously at textual, material, and bodily levels.

VI

In light of the strain involved in performing *The Author*, it is not surprising that Crouch's next original work was a relatively quiet, slow-paced piece. *what happens to the hope at the end of the evening* is a meditation on theatre and community; it is also a play about friendship. Commissioned by the Almeida Theatre in London where it opened in July 2013, *what happens to the hope...* was co-written by Crouch and Andy Smith, who also performed the play. The production was directed by Karl James, and subsequently toured to Edinburgh, several venues across England, and to Athens, Lisbon, Dublin, and China.

The play concerns the reunion of old friends who have fallen out of touch, referred to as Andy and Friend; their meeting is detailed in a chronological sequence, which is interspersed with flashbacks to the time when Andy was waiting for his friend to arrive. There is a notable difference in the two characters in that Smith's Andy borrows many details from the performer's life (such as having a small daughter, pursuing a Ph.D. in theatre at Lancaster University, etc.), as opposed to the character played by Crouch, whose life story does not relate to the performer's life whatsoever (see Rebellato 2013b). The manner in which the two roles are enacted is also remarkably different: Andy is seated on a chair and reads out his lines from a manuscript placed on a music stand, while Crouch acts in the conventional sense of the term. Indeed, both Crouch's physique and his emotive performance were noted as essential to the impact of the play: for example, Dan Rebellato remarked upon Crouch's figure being 'physically quite forbidding' due to his considerable height and shaved head (Rebellato 2013b), and Lyn Gardner described his persona in the play as 'hectic, resentful' and reminiscent of 'an angry bluebottle trapped in a jar' (Gardner 2013).

In contrast to *The Author*, the scripted nature of the performance is clear from the very beginning, as Andy not only reads out all his lines, including those that are part of dialogues with Friend, but he also ostentatiously turns a page in the manuscript at numerous strategic moments in the show. The self-reflexive nature of the performance is accentuated by an explicit discussion on theatre, in which Andy refers to or quotes a number of ideas proposed by recent scholars and practitioners. Their assertions are subsequently examined in the context of the performance.

One of the central propositions that is brought up comes from Helen Freshwater's book *Theatre & Audience* (2009); in Andy's paraphrase, Freshwater 'suggests that the theatre is a place in which we can clarify thought around some of our expectations of community, of democracy, of citizenship' (Crouch and Smith 2013, p. 24). This is a notion that *what happens to the hope...* engages the notion in its depiction of children who are gathering in the street outside Andy's house while the two friends are spending the evening chatting. The area seems to be currently undergoing gradual gentrification from what used to be a poor suburb of the town (Andy's house is described as 'ex-council'; p. 30) and there is some debate between Andy and Friend as to whether it is a 'good neighbourhood' yet (p. 38). Consequently, the children who are seen loitering nearby, looking for entertainment, make for an ambivalent presence. Andy's friend regards them as a threat, and while he speaks about them as 'dispossessed' victims of the government's policies, he ultimately sees them as 'little cretins' similar to the neo-Nazis against whom he has just been marching in a rally (pp. 39, 44). Andy, on the other hand, considers the children to be harmless members of his community who are just 'hanging out' (p. 45). Despite his neighbourly attitude, he still has a Neighbourhood Watch sticker on the window of his house, however, which his friend is quick to point out. The argument is ultimately concluded by Andy's angry exclamation that if Friend is afraid of the children, he should draw the curtains.

The most exciting feature of their debate about what is likely the effect of social deprivation is how the play links what happens outside the window with the auditorium. The spatial arrangement of the performance has the actors watch the imaginary children as if they were in the audience space; because of that, the characters speak their lines into the auditorium looking at the spectators, who are thereby invited to consider their attitude to the issue. The partitioning of Andy and Friend from the children by the glass of the window is similarly related to the theatrical context, since the actors describe themselves as being watched like 'in a goldfish bowl' (p. 31; see also Rebellato 2013b).

The analogy with a fish tank clearly reprises Crouch's critique of naturalism in terms of the passive, voyeuristic position that it affords the audience. The domestic setting of *what happens to the hope...* may be conducive to naturalist representation and, in fact, the part of the stage where Crouch performs is furnished accordingly. However, mimetic realism is presented as deliberately clunky, since the props and the furniture—including a heavy sofa—are laboriously moved to the stage by Crouch himself some time into the play and removed in a similarly awkward manner before the performance ends. In the context of the play, the potential of theatre to radically engage with social inequality as referred to by Andy when he says that in theatre, 'we can see where we are [...] we can think about where we might be going' (p. 39) obviously does not lie in its ability to produce an illusion of reality on stage. *what happens to the hope...* proceeds to examine interventionist theatrical practice in its turn, exemplified by *Paradise Now*, the famous performance toured by The Living Theatre in the late 1960s. Andy tells the spectators particularly how the audience were led out onto the streets at the end of performances, shouting 'Paradise Now!' The actors and some of the spectators in The Living Theatre's production notoriously stripped off their clothes, and what poured out of the theatre as a result was a carnivalesque procession of people demanding freedom and justice.

what happens to the hope... concludes with the same slogan—'Paradise now. Paradise now. Paradise now' (p. 63)—but in most tranquil circumstances: it is read out by Crouch from Andy's printed text of the play after the latter has already left the stage. The idea of theatre as an anarchic, revolutionary force promoted by The Living Theatre is thus remembered and undermined at the same time. Crouch and Smith replace interventionist action with contemplation, and the carnival of *Paradise Now* gives way to a different form of the grotesque that—as in Crouch's previous work—consists primarily in blending disparate levels and styles of representation.

Discussing the play in his blog, Dan Rebellato has argued that the radical potential articulated in *what happens to the hope...* lies in its focus on the importance of 'spending a little time together' (Rebellato 2013b). From this perspective, the hope that the title of the play refers to would consist in the ability of theatre to forge a community in the auditorium, a belief that numerous practitioners and theorists have been going by. This conviction is actually cited by Andy in the opening speech of the play, which describes the theatre as 'A space where we can really be together, sit together and listen to a story' (p. 2). Andy encourages the spectators to shake hands with one another, and later also to collectively join Friend in taking off their shoes. The bond between the performers and the spectators is further indicated by Crouch and Smith entering the stage through the auditorium, using the same door as the audience.

Nevertheless, as Rebellato acknowledges, this is also a drama that 'theatrically embodies the distance between people', since each character performs in his own space and they are unable to really interact (Rebellato 2013b). The staging reflects the fact that the close friendship that the two men attempt to renew remains at a standstill; as a reviewer summed it up, *what happens to the hope...* offers 'self-reflexive food for thought' about the possibility to 'really connect' in the theatre, 'yet the irony is, within the world of the play, Smith is failing to even really connect with one of his oldest pals' (Williams 2014). The failure of Andy and Friend to re-bond shows the importance of their current personal situation: Andy leads the happy and relatively sedate life of a family man but his friend's marriage is falling apart and he has started drinking. Their attitude to the world is understandably somewhat different as a result, and this lesson is clearly related to the situation of the spectators through the self-reflexive nature of the performance. The notion of theatre as a collective experience that is conducive to solidarity and bonding is therefore qualified by a measure of scepticism, which also underlies Crouch's laconic final statement on the issue:

> We arrive here from some other place, but this is also a place. We listen and watch and we make. We do all these things together. And then at the end we get up and we leave and we do something. We move somewhere else. To someone or something else. We start again. (Crouch and Smith 2013, p. 63)

The concept of hope that can be associated with this depiction of theatrical experience is less ambitious, and ultimately pertains to the individual since the communality experienced in the theatre is merely temporary. It is in fact the simple hope that Adrian speaks of in *The Author*: the hope for 'something to happen [...] for someone to talk to us. Really talk' (Crouch 2011a, p. 168). Any radical transformation of reality that may ensue remains impossible to predict.

VII

Adler & Gibb, which was developed on the heels of *what happens to the hope at the end of the evening*, saw Crouch employ a considerably larger canvass, perhaps the largest up to date. At the same time, it was the first of his dramas in which he did not perform himself. *Adler & Gibb* was a co-commission by the Royal Court Theatre in London and Center Theatre Group, Los Angeles. It opened in June 2014 at the Royal Court, directed by the regular team of Tim Crouch, Andy Smith, and Karl James.

Adler & Gibb focuses on the commodification of art and the fetishization of the artist, themes raised in *My Arm*, *ENGLAND*, or *The Author*. Almost inevitably with Crouch, the play also revolves around issues of representation and spectatorship, with a particular emphasis on the obsession with the authentic that is so typical of the contemporary era. It tells of an American art history student, Louise Mane, who is intent on unravelling the mysteries surrounding the final years of her favourite artist, Janet Adler, and her partner, Margaret Gibb. Adler and Gibb, we are told in the promotion materials for the play, 'were conceptual artists working in New York at the end of the last century. They were described by art critic Dave Hickey as the "most ferociously uncompromising voice of their generation"' (Royal Court Theatre 2014). Louise has made Adler her idol and embarked on a decade-long exploration of her life that results in the shooting of a biographical film, with Louise starring as Adler.

The two women are said to have withdrawn from the New York arts scene in 1999 and moved to a quiet house deep in the country, where Adler died under unexplained circumstances in May 2003. Together with her acting coach, Sam, Louise travels to the artists' house to find out more about Adler's death and to draw inspiration for her acting from the atmosphere. There they unexpectedly discover the ageing Gibb, who they presumed to have passed away as well, eventually shoot some important footage in the grounds of the house, and later also discover the truth about Adler's death. Ultimately, Louise decides to involve Gibb in her film.

This is the basic plot but the way it is presented is far from straightforward. Although the story of Louise's exploration is largely conveyed in chronological order, the audience first encounter a young student who delivers an oral presentation on Adler, speaking at a lectern into a microphone and introducing 'slides' to illustrate her points. However, instead of real slides, the actors who play Louise and Sam enact individual stages of their trip to Adler and Gibb's house and the shooting of their film. They first appear in their underwear and merely speak their lines to the audience, without performing any action. As the play progresses, items of clothing are gradually added and eventually they are in full costume; similarly, movement is slowly supplemented, puppet-like and mechanical to begin with, and completely natural towards the end of the performance. Moreover, the play features two children who act as stage hands, occasionally impersonating animals and spending the rest of the time drawing or playing games. In the middle of Act I, the children start building, bit by bit, a set on the stage, and complete it for the final scene of Act II.[6] This is where it turns out to be a film set, representing the interior of a room in New York where Adler and Gibb kissed for the first time. In this setting, the love scene is enacted by Louise as Adler and Gibb as her young self, while being fed through an onstage camera onto a screen. More images from the completed film are shown at a fast sequence, and the play concludes with Louise's speech at an awards ceremony; it is only at this point that the audience learn that the student who gave the presentation was Louise, ten years earlier.

As is apparent from this outline, *Adler & Gibb* begins with a grotesque stage image and style of presentation that follows that of *My Arm* but supersedes it in terms of its complexity. When the actors playing Louise, Sam, and Gibb gradually start acting, the children facilitate further grotesque elements by exchanging appropriate props for a variety of incongruous and often comical objects: for instance, a sledge hammer is replaced with a plastic fish, a shovel is replaced with a plastic lobster, and a dog represented by a child is clobbered to death with an inflatable swim float (Crouch 2014a, pp. 39, 50, 56). Such hilarious moments aside, both the positive and the negative reviews document in unison that the overall effect in Act I is one of complete bewilderment; as Michael Billington bluntly put it, 'for much of the first half, we don't understand what is going on' (Billington 2014). Once the style of presentation begins to approach realism and as the story gathers momentum, becoming more sinister, the confusion largely disappears.

Nevertheless, Crouch's play simultaneously links the progression towards realistic representation with immorality and death. Louise's obsession with Adler and her desire to penetrate the most private aspects of her life involves a frantic search for Adler's notebooks, which eventually results in the disinterment of her corpse. Unlike the digging up of the dead in the work of Suzan-Lori Parks (see Chap. 5), the unearthing of Adler is an appalling, ghoulish act, the sole purpose of which it is to gain inspiration for the most true-to-life performance as the artist in the biopic. As part of her "preparation" at the open grave, Louise even plays a 'Hamlet riff' (Billington 2014) with Adler's skull. What Crouch demonstrates is that, in his own words, 'An obsession with the real can sometimes feel like an acquisitive or even capitalistic act: a desire to own someone else's reality' (Crouch 2014d). Indeed, the ultimate aim for Louise is that her film succeeds and she becomes celebrated as an actress and as a film artist. To this end, she also manipulates Margaret Gibb into acting in the film. Gibb reluctantly complies while indicating that putting her in the film is going to kill her—which she does not mind, since she will then finally rejoin Adler (see Crouch 2014a, p. 78). Because of that, her performance in the love scene that the audience witness is passive, the costume and make-up that are supposed to make her look as if she were in her twenties are ludicrous, and the final kiss—performed by Louise with vampiric vigour—is clearly a kiss of death; the last image of the film that the audience see is that of Gibb's corpse (see Crouch 2014a, pp. 73–4, 85–6).[7] The moral condemnation of Louise's desire to appropriate Adler is all the more 'emotionally piercing' (Taylor 2014) due to Gibb's disclosure of the truth about her partner's death: while Gibb was suspected by journalists of killing Adler, she was in fact taking care of her as she suffered a debilitating, terminal illness.

The artists whose life is discussed in *Adler & Gibb* are said to have spent the last part of their career practising 'dematerialisations', that is, 'erasing the traces of [their] artistic output' (Crouch 2014a, p. 16). Their effort to 'resist materiality' (Crouch 2014c) was guided by the desire to avoid capitalization and commodification of their work. As Crouch stipulated in an interview published prior to the opening of *Adler & Gibb*, his play 'charts the failure of their attempt' and forcefully demonstrates 'our culture's devotion to the act of acquisition' (Crouch 2014c) in Louise's fetishistic yearning to own her artistic idol. However, the play also shows that commodification is essentially inevitable. Try as they might, Adler and Gibb still left material artefacts instantiating their work, and the scarcity of these only made their monetary value higher: as Louise intimates, only a fraction of Adler's estimated 9,000 art works remained, and as a result, a series of drafted diagrams had sold at Sotheby's for $215,000 (p. 17). This situation indeed reflects what has happened to numerous radical conceptual artists who habitually left only instructions for the creation of their art works rather than the actual art objects so as to avoid commodification: these sets of instructions would regularly fetch their owners considerable sums of money.

In the same interview, Crouch spoke of his own work as '"dematerialised" theatre' (2014c). Given the relatively lush nature of *Adler & Gibb*, the designation may seem somewhat surprising. Nevertheless, the central trick that Crouch plays on the audience consists in making the artists whose life is being documented fictitious. The play never indicates so much, but the information is readily available outside it: Crouch mentioned that he invented Adler and Gibb both in advance interviews and in an article he wrote about his play for *The Guardian* (Crouch 2014d). Furthermore, the promotion material for the play included a link to the artists' website, which displayed on its opening the simple sentence 'Adler & Gibb do not exist' (see Royal Court Theatre 2014). Consequently, the lavish material presentation of the artists in the play should really be discarded as fake, which indicates that—as in Crouch's previous dramas—the actual meaning of the work does not reside in mimesis but is to be created in the minds of the spectators.

'Dematerialised theatre' may sound like the introduction of a new brand of avant-garde practice but the fact that Crouch uses the same idea in reference to the work of Adler and Gibb suggests rather a playful acknowledgment of the oxymoronic nature of the concept. As much as a theatrical performance may be an ephemeral event, it still needs actors, props, and so on in order to take place, and it will leave material traces that may become commodified. What Crouch signals by his use of the term then is an awareness that even work inspired by conceptual art which undermines the importance of its material aspects, such as *Adler & Gibb*, requires a good deal of materiality in order to make its point concerning the greed and fetishization that often dominate people's attitudes to art.

Tim Crouch's idea of a 'play that happens inside its audience' finally brings us to consider the mechanism of its relation to reality. In Peircean terminology, representation in Crouch's work is not iconic—which would be the case in naturalist theatre, based on resemblance—but symbolic. This is not to claim that Crouch is a symbol*ist* playwright, of course, but rather that the meaning of theatrical signs bears an arbitrary relation to what they stand for and must be negotiated solely by their recipients. Certainly, Crouch plays provocative games with resemblance: as outlined in this chapter, he uses, for instance, his own physical presence on stage in plays such as *My Arm, An Oak Tree, The Author*, and *what happens to the hope…* in order to foreground representation as an issue that must be resolved. (In the last two, the same applies to his fellow performers.) In *Adler & Gibb*, verisimilitude is strived for and eventually achieved, only to be exploded as fake and based on corruption. However, what all of Crouch's dramas share is a creative juxtaposition of elements of reality and fiction that bring with them apparently incompatible original referents. Their disorienting combination constitutes Crouch's brand of the grotesque, which pushes the spectators to use their imagination and determine the precise symbolic meaning of the signs for themselves. By doing so, the audience members will have exercised their human ability 'to see one thing inside something else', to quote Crouch's simple phrase (Crouch and Sierz 2014, p. 68). This creative engagement of the imagination really amounts to the construction of an alternative reality, and as such bears significant ethical potential; it is the activity that makes the spectator 'emancipated' in Jacques Rancière's sense of the term, and it may open up ways 'towards new forms of subjectivation' (Rancière 2011, p. 82). At the same time, it is an activity that is as playful as a children's game, since children need no resemblance to turn one thing into another (see Crouch 2014d).

Notes

1. Crouch seems to have arrived at the idea of having an actor repeat verbatim the lines that he/she hears in headphones by himself, unaware of any precedents. However, he has in fact joined a contemporaneous trend that had been gaining prominence in site-specific and site-generic performance and that found its way onto the stage in a new brand of verbatim theatre around 2005, which has been referred to by critics as 'headphone-verbatim' (see Haydon 2013, p. 51; Garson 2014).
2. It is fascinating to follow what Crouch's notes document of his thinking about grief and loss when writing the play; the two statements that Crouch highlighted in bold run as follows: 'It may be necessary/to recognize that/there is such a thing/as being inconsolable …'; and, '"The loss of meaning that comes with the death of our child is greater than any we could imagine, but we will have to invent new meanings"' (Crouch 2013, p. 237). It is also of note that Crouch himself has a daughter.

3. The simile is Helen Iball's, who in a brilliant article interprets the play's mechanism through the concepts of parasitism and mimicry. Her essay is inspired by Julia Crouch's design of the poster for *The Author*, which features an image of a large cuckoo chick being fed by a diminutive reed warbler (see Iball 2011).
4. Whenever people do decide to walk out during the final speech, Crouch pauses and lights are brought up so they can see as they are leaving (Crouch 2011b, p. 417).
5. The use of the floatation tank is distinctly ironic, considering that this contraption is typically used by affluent customers to release stress.
6. One possible source of inspiration can be found in Emilie Morin's list of seminal productions of the Fluxus network of conceptual artists: Ken Friedman's 'Theater Exercise' (1989) involving a reverse process in which 'the actors carry all scenery with them, put the stage set together, and then take it apart while the play is in progress' (Morin 2011, p. 78). *what happens to the hope at the end of the evening* in fact replicates Friedman's 'Theater Exercise' in Crouch's work with the furniture and props, discussed earlier in the present chapter.
7. This climactic scene was substantially revised in rehearsal after the play had gone to print: the alterations mostly simplify the stage action, remove the undressing of "Adler" and Gibb, tone down to the minimum the suggestion that Louise might shoot Gibb, and shorten and revise the student's final speeches. See Crouch (2014b), pp. 80–3 and Crouch (2014a), pp. 83–6.

WORKS CITED

Barthes, R. (1989). 'The Death of the Author' (1968). In R. Barthes, *The Rustle of Language* (Richard Howard, Trans., pp. 49–55). Berkeley: University of California Press.
Billington, M. (2014, June 20). Adler and Gibb Review—A High-Concept Satire on the Cult of the Artist. *Guardian*. Retrieved September 28, 2015, from http://www.theguardian.com/stage/2014/jun/20/adler-and-gibb-review-royal-court-theatre-london
Bottoms, S. (2009). Authorizing the Audience: The Conceptual Drama of Tim Crouch. *Performance Research, 19* (1), 65–76.
Bottoms, S. (2011a). Introduction: Tim Crouch, *The Author*, and the Audience. *Contemporary Theatre Review, 21* (4), 390–393.
Bottoms, S. (2011b). Materialising the Audience: Tim Crouch's Sight Specifics in *ENGLAND* and *The Author*. *Contemporary Theatre Review, 21* (4), 445–463.
Bottoms, S. (2011c). Introduction. In T. Crouch, *Plays One* (pp. 11–20). London: Oberon.
Crouch, T. (2011a). *Plays One*. London: Oberon.

Crouch, T. (2011b). *The Author*: Response and Responsibility. *Contemporary Theatre Review, 21* (4), 416–422.
Crouch, T. (2013). Notes on *An Oak Tree*. In D. Rebellato (Ed.), *Modern British Playwriting: 2000–2009. Voices, Documents, New Interpretations* (pp. 125–144). London: Bloomsbury.
Crouch, T. (2014a). *Adler & Gibb*. London: Oberon.
Crouch, T. (2014b). Adler & Gibb. Royal Court Version 24/6/14. Unpublished manuscript, 85 pp.
Crouch, T. (2014c, May 5). Interview. *Aesthetica*. Retrieved September 25, 2015, from http://www.aestheticamagazine.com/interview-with-tim-crouch-writer-and-director-of-royal-courts-adler-and-gibb/
Crouch, T. (2014d, June 18). The Theatre of Reality ... and Avoiding the Stage's Kiss of Death. *Guardian*. Retrieved September 28, 2015, from http://www.theguardian.com/stage/2014/jun/18/theatre-reality-adler-and-gibb-tim-crouch-playwright
Crouch, T., & Sierz, A. (2014). Navigating New Patterns of Power with an Audience: Tim Crouch in Conversation with Aleks Sierz. *Journal of Contemporary Drama in English, 2* (1), 63–77.
Crouch, T., & Smith., A. (2013). *what happens to the hope at the end of the evening*. In T. Crouch, *Adler & Gibb*. London: Oberon.
Foucault, M. (1984, October). Des espaces autres. *Architecture, Mouvement, Continuité, 5*, 46–49.
Freshwater, H. (2011). "You Say Something": Audience Participation and *The Author*. *Contemporary Theatre Review, 21* (4), 405–409.
Freshwater, H. (2013). Children and the Limits of Representation in the Work of Tim Crouch. In V. Angelaki (Ed.), *Contemporary British Theatre: Breaking New Ground* (pp. 167–188). Houndmills: Palgrave Macmillan.
Gardner, L. (2013, July 14). Review of *what happens to the hope at the end of the evening*, by Tim Crouch and Andy Smith. *Guardian*. Retrieved September 28, 2015,from http://www.theguardian.com/stage/2013/jul/14/what-happens-to-hope-review
Garson, C. (2014). Remixing Politics: The Case of Headphone-Verbatim Theatre in Britain. *Journal of Contemporary Drama in English, 2* (1), 50–62.
Haydon, A. (2013). Theatre in the 2000s. In D. Rebellato (Ed.), *Modern British Playwriting: 2000–2009. Voices, Documents, New Interpretations* (pp. 40–98). London: Bloomsbury.
Iball, H. (2011). A Mouth to Feed Me: Reflections Inspired by the Poster for Tim Crouch's *The Author*. *Contemporary Theatre Review, 21* (4), 431–444.
Ilter, S. (2011). "A Process of Transformation": Tim Crouch on *My Arm*. *Contemporary Theatre Review, 21* (4), 394–404.
Kayser, W. (1966). *The Grotesque in Art and Literature* (1957) (Ulrich Weisstein, Trans.). New York: McGraw-Hill.

Morin, E. (2011). "Look Again": Indeterminacy and Contemporary British Drama. *New Theatre Quarterly, 27* (1), 71–85.
Rancière, J. (2011). *The Emancipated Spectator* (2008) (Gregory Elliott, Trans.). London and New York: Verso.
Rebellato, D. (2013a). Tim Crouch. In D. Rebellato (Ed.), *Modern British Playwriting: 2000–2009. Voices, Documents, New Interpretations* (pp. 125–144). London: Bloomsbury.
Rebellato, D. (2013b, July 15). what happens to the hope at the end of the evening. *Blog*. Retrieved September 28, 2015, from http://www.danrebellato.co.uk/spilledink/2013/7/15/what-happens-to-the-hope-at-the-end-of-the-evening
Royal Court Theatre, The. (2014). *Adler & Gibb* by Tim Crouch. Retrieved September 28, 2015, from http://www.royalcourttheatre.com/whats-on/adler-and-gibb
Ruskin, J. (1903). *Modern Painters, Vol. III* (1856). In E. T. Cook & A. Wedderburn (Eds.), *The Works of John Ruskin, Vol. 5* (pp. 1–439). London: George Allen.
smith, a. (2011). Gentle Acts of Removal, Replacement and Reduction: Considering the Audience in Co-Directing the Work of Tim Crouch. *Contemporary Theatre Review, 21* (4), 410–415.
Taylor, P. (2014, June 20). Review of *Adler & Gibb*, by Tim Crouch. *Independent*. Retrieved September 28, 2015, from http://www.independent.co.uk/arts-entertainment/theatre-dance/reviews/adler-gibb-royal-court-review-memorable-and-rewarding-9551997.html
Williams, H. (2014, May 7). Review of *what happens to the hope at the end of the evening*, by Tim Crouch and Andy Smith. *Independent*. Retrieved September 28, 2015, from http://www.independent.co.uk/arts-entertainment/theatre-dance/reviews/what-happens-to-hope-at-the-end-of-an-evening-brighton-dome-studio-theatre-review-9323894.html

CHAPTER 7

Afterword: The Grotesque and Spectatorship

Commenting on the contemporary practices of theatre in 1990, Susan Bennett observed a 'common determination to increase the spectator's activity' on the part of theatre-makers across the globe (Bennett 1990, p. 185). While it can be argued that the arrival of any new form of modern theatre, starting with naturalism and ever since, involved the desire of practitioners to engage the audience in a consideration of vital social and political issues, Bennett is right to observe the growing and increasingly more varied effort from the late 1970s onwards.

As is well documented, one of the frameworks utilized by recent politically committed artists in particular has been that of participatory theatre, which has audience members step into the role of performers. However, participatory theatre has also been criticized by scholars and practitioners alike for its manipulative nature: apart from often making spectators feel awkward rather than intellectually involved (see, for instance, Crouch in Ilter 2011, p. 401), it essentially just presents them with ready-made choices. As Helen Freshwater has argued, 'Performances which seem to be offering audiences the chance to make a creative contribution only give them the choice of option A or option B—or the opportunity to give responses which are clearly scripted by social and cultural conventions' (Freshwater 2011, pp. 405–6). Apart from simply holding on to their craft, this is probably one of the main reasons why most contemporary playwrights have instead turned in their desire for greater audience engagement to new methods of producing estrangement in their work. Brecht's

© The Editor(s) (if applicable) and The Author(s) 2016
O. Pilný, *The Grotesque in Contemporary Anglophone Drama*,
DOI 10.1057/978-1-137-51318-2_7

epic theatre may have become completely absorbed into the mainstream and thus deprived of its edge—as Bennett has asserted (pp. 180, 182)—but Brecht's legacy has simultaneously been developed in numerous original ways. Indeed, the use of the grotesque discussed in this book may be regarded as a radical neo-Brechtian technique in a broad sense of the word, producing visions of an alienated world that is mostly terrifying, engendering attraction and repulsion alike, and soliciting an active use of the imagination in its interpretation.

It is noteworthy that at least one twentieth-century theorist of the grotesque attempted to interpret the occurrence of the grotesque as a symptom of the times. In his study entitled simply *The Grotesque*, Philip Thomson claimed that 'the grotesque mode in art and literature tends to be prevalent in societies and eras marked by strife, radical changes or disorientation' (Thomson 1972, p. 11). Given the enormous range of grotesque art works that Frances Connelly discusses in her comprehensive history of the concept, originating in a variety of Western cultures and dating from antiquity to the present day (Connelly 2012), I would be hesitant to make such a sweeping generalization. Nevertheless, Thomson's claim would appear to have some validity as regards the contemporary era, which has been characterized by increasing disorientation produced by the effects of globalization, new and often unpredictable occurrences of violence and atrocity, recurrent economic crises, and a general confusion of the criteria of value judgement, an era that has been aptly described by a number of philosophers and critical theorists as that of 'precarity' (see Wallace 2014, pp. 120–2).

At the same time, we should not forget that the grotesque has become a standard feature in contemporary popular culture and has been avidly consumed in comics, cartoons, horror movies, fantastic literature, or computer games. As philosopher Noël Carroll suggested, the strong taste for the grotesque may perhaps 'have more to do with the expanding market for leisure than with reflecting the spirit of the age. For the grotesque provides a ready source of intense emotion and novelty. There may be so much more grotesquerie available today [...] just because the entertainment industry has grown so dramatically in tandem with the accelerating pursuit of leisure' (Carroll 2003, p. 309). This, however, does not necessarily decrease the potential of the grotesque to solicit engagement in an ethical or political sense: as I attempted to demonstrate particularly with regard to the work of Philip Ridley, the keenness to be exposed to the thrill of what is simultaneously alluring and revolting may be exploited precisely to this end.

Václav Havel, whose absurdist moral dramas have involved the grotesque in abundance, spoke of humanity in his famous 1978 essay 'The Power of the Powerless' as being 'dragged helplessly along by the automatism of global technological civilization' and having lost control over its mechanisms (Havel 1978, p. 43). If a 'general ethical—and, of course, ultimately a political—reconstitution of society', either totalitarian or democratic, is to occur, Havel argued, what is needed first and foremost is the re-awakening of the individual as an intellectually active and morally conscious human being, exercising responsibility 'to and for the whole' (pp. 37, 43). I attempted to show in the present volume that many of the most original contemporary playwrights have used the grotesque as a means of soliciting deeper engagement of individuals with the moral, social, and political deficiencies of the present-day era. Their effort may be viewed in the context of what scholars such as Nicholas Ridout, Dan Rebellato, or Mireia Aragay have referred to as the current, slightly belated 'ethical turn' in theatre and theatre studies. In her most recent edited collection on the subject, Aragay summarized the manner in which current scholarship has almost exclusively used the framework of Levinasian ethics, foregrounding the unconditional responsibility of the individual to the Other as the foundation of all moral action (Aragay 2014, pp. 3–5).[1] The tendency reflects not only the suitability of the theatre as a space for staging 'an ethical encounter, in which we come face to face with the other' (Ridout 2009, p. 54), but also the actual practice of committed playwrights who—instead of resorting to agitprop or manipulating the audience into scripted choices—have sought to stimulate the imagination of the spectators. To use Helena Grehan's pertinent phrase, such work has aimed at challenging audience members to consider 'the importance of a commitment to response and responsibility and how such a commitment might be activated and sustained' (Grehan 2009, p. 175).

The role of individual response is particularly strong in the reception of the grotesque, since the grotesque presents the beholder with radical incongruity that is fundamentally puzzling. In order to assess the efficiency of the grotesque as a means of 'emancipating the spectator', to return to Rancière's term, research into actual responses of individual spectators seems imperative. The work of theatre semioticians such as Keir Elam, Susan Bennett, and, last but certainly not least, Erika Fischer-Lichte, has been exemplary in helping us better understand *how* meaning is created in theatre. Yet, engagement with *what* a performance might mean to a theatre-goer who is not a reviewer or theatre scholar has been minimal. In his early development of Prague structuralism, Elam observed that 'Every spectator's interpretation of the [theatrical] text is in effect a new *construction* of it according to the cultural and ideological disposition of the subject' and noted that empirical research in audience reception 'is an indispensable, though so far neglected component of any proposed theatrical poetics' (Elam 1980, p. 95). Ten years later, Bennett did an admirable amount of pioneering work on how the cultural context and material conditions shape an audience's response (which she further elaborated in the second edition of her book, published in 1997). While she noted the beginnings of research in the area of individual response and demarcated it as a field for future study, Bennett also made the contradictory remark that 'The description of an individual response to a particular production may not be possible or, indeed, even desirable' (Bennett 1990, p. 184).

Erika Fischer-Lichte's magisterial, three-volume *Semiotik des Theaters* (1983) has rightly been regarded by many as the authoritative study of meaning in conventional forms of Western theatre. In this book, Fischer-Lichte discussed in detail the methodological difficulties that stem from the audience being composed of individuals with different histories and 'personal biograph[ies]' and concluded that since a 'universally valid, overall meaning' of a performance cannot be stipulated, empirical research into individual audience responses is desirable. According to Fischer-Lichte, such research is practicable; it only has to wait for the development of a hitherto unavailable methodology that would enable us to capture the theatrical event in all its complexity (see Fischer-Lichte 1992, pp. 212–17, 253). Fischer-Lichte's wonderful subsequent volume dedicated to performance art and contemporary experimental theatre, *Ästhetik des Performativen* (2004), argues for the interpretation of performance as an event and for a complete reformulation of the approach to reception (see Fischer-Lichte 2008). Groundbreaking and insightful as the study is, Fischer-Lichte joins the overwhelming majority of other scholars in not supporting her observations about the effect of the selected performances on individual spectators by a large enough set of empirical data. This general shortcoming validates Helen Freshwater's recent complaint that as scholars, 'we very rarely know very much about what audiences think because we rarely ask them' (qtd in Bottoms 2011, p. 424).

In 2014, the results of the first relatively large, AHRC-funded research into how spectators value the experience of theatre were published in the UK. 'Critical Mass' was a pioneering team effort of the British Theatre Consortium, led by Janelle Reinelt as Principal Investigator. It surveyed audience responses to eleven productions at three English theatres over a period of nine to twelve months, using questionnaires, interviews, and workshops as the source of data provided by more than 300 spectators. One of the aims of the project was to examine how the interpretation of a performance changes over time and so, the subjects were asked about their experience three times: immediately before the show, within twenty-four hours after it, and then again two months or a year later (see British Theatre Consortium 2014, pp. 5–9).

As this was the first project of its kind, the focus of the researchers was understandably on more general issues that could be analysed in the comparative context of different genres and venues, rather than on an in-depth scrutiny of individual shows. Still, the results seem to confirm at least some of the assumptions that I have made in this book, similarly to other scholars who have dealt with audience engagement. For one, it is reassuring to see that cognitive aspects such as 'engagement' and 'thinking' have consistently ranked highest among the values attributed to experiencing a performance, gaining prominence over time elapsed after the theatre visit (British Theatre Consortium 2014, pp. 25–31). Related to this, 84 % of the respondents saw a connection between the performance and the times they lived in, with the figure decreasing to 67 % over two months; a connection between the performance and the respondent's own life was perceived by 67 %, with the figure decreasing to 52 % after two months (pp. 39–41). As regards the collective nature of experiencing theatre, valuation was relatively low shortly after the performance, reaching between 10 and 20 %, and this dropped to approximately 7 % after two months; however, the vast majority of spectators valued going to the theatre as a binding experience with partners, family members, and friends, with whom more than 84 % of the respondents discussed the performance (pp. 26–27, 43–51). These figures indicate that experiencing theatre is overwhelmingly individual, and that the sense of community seems to be created only after the performance, beginning with the people who are the closest to the spectator. What must be borne in mind in relation to the territory covered in the present book, of course, is that the numbers pertain to a sample of theatre-goers and plays in particular locations in England in 2013–2014 only, and that they might differ considerably in other contexts, especially in the case of confrontational work.

Needless to say, the British Theatre Consortium researchers themselves are aware of the limitations of their project and were very open about these in their final report. Reflecting on the methodology to be used in future research, they concluded that the information gathered from questionnaires is insufficient, and recommended the use of interviews and workshops in order to obtain truly elucidating results (p. 90). This clearly implies that if we wish to learn in depth about how individual spectators interpret performances in a given cultural and temporal context, the effort may become gargantuan and require a high level of funding; which of course takes us back to the likely reasons why scholars have been reluctant to get involved to date.

Without such research, however, my examination of how exactly the imagination of individual spectators may bridge the gaps opened by the grotesque, and how they might use the room that it opens to play (Connelly 2012, p. 12), had to face the risks summarized so bravely by Helena Grehan in the introduction to her book *Performance, Ethics and Spectatorship in a Global Age*: when discussing spectatorship and audience response, there is always the danger of 'becoming too personal, of interpreting responses from the position of an "ideal" spectator, or of making generalisations or assumptions that cannot be supported or proved' (Grehan 2009, p. 4). I would like to ask my readers for their kind indulgence with any of the moments where I may have slipped.

NOTE

1. The influence of Levinas also permeated Václav Havel's later thinking about ethics, particularly in his *Letters to Olga* (1979–1982).

WORKS CITED

Aragay, M. (2014). To Begin to Speculate: Theatre Studies, Ethics and Spectatorship. In M. Aragay & E. Monforte (Eds.), *Ethical Speculations in Contemporary British Theatre* (pp. 1–22). Houndmills: Palgrave Macmillan.

Bennett, S. (1990). *Theatre Audiences: A Theory of Production and Reception*. London: Routledge.

Bottoms, S. (Ed.). (2011). A Conversation about Dialogue (Symposium Voices). *Contemporary Theatre Review, 21* (4), 423–430.

British Theatre Consortium, The. (2014). Critical Mass: Theatre Spectatorship and Value Attribution. Retrieved August 23, 2015, from http://britishtheatre-conference.co.uk/wp-content/uploads/2014/05/Critical-Mass-10.7.pdf

Carroll, N. (2003). The Grotesque Today: Preliminary Notes toward a Taxonomy. In F. S. Connelly (Ed.), *Modern Art and the Grotesque* (pp. 291–311). Cambridge: Cambridge University Press.

Connelly, F. S. (2012). *The Grotesque in Western Art and Culture: The Image at Play*. Cambridge: Cambridge University Press.
Elam, K. (1980). *The Semiotics of Theatre and Drama*. London: Routledge.
Fischer-Lichte, E. (1992). *The Semiotics of Theater* (Jeremy Gaines & Doris L. Jones, Trans.). Bloomington: Indiana University Press.
Fischer-Lichte, E. (2008). *The Transformative Power of Performance: A New Aesthetics* (Saskya Iris Jain, Trans.). London: Routledge.
Freshwater, H. (2011). "You Say Something": Audience Participation and *The Author*. *Contemporary Theatre Review, 21* (4), 405–409.
Grehan, H. (2009). *Performance, Ethics and Spectatorship in a Global Age*. Houndmills: Palgrave Macmillan.
Havel, V. (1978). The Power of the Powerless (Paul Wilson, Trans.). *The Václav Havel Library Online Archive*. Retrieved May 1, 2014, from http://archive.vaclavhavel-library.org/Functions/show_html.php?id=158723
Ilter, S. (2011). "A Process of Transformation": Tim Crouch on *My Arm*. *Contemporary Theatre Review, 21* (4), 394–404.
Ridout, N. (2009). *Theatre & Ethics*. Houndmills: Palgrave Macmillan.
Thomson, P. (1972). *The Grotesque*. London: Methuen.
Wallace, C. (2014). Playing with Proximity: Precarious Ethics on Stage in the New Millennium. In M. Aragay & E. Monforte (Eds.), *Ethical Speculations in Contemporary British Theatre* (pp. 117–134). Houndmills: Palgrave Macmillan.

INDEX

A
Albee, Edward, 12–13, 119
Anderson, Lisa H., 105, 106
arabesque, 3
Aragay, Mireia, 165

B
Baartman, Sara, 104–11
Bacon, Francis (philosopher), 62
Bakhtin, Mikhail, 4, 6–7, 19–20, 21, 53, 59, 63, 92, 99, 105
Baraniecka, Elżbieta, 78n2
Barthes, Roland, 148
Beckett, Samuel, 9, 12, 13, 82–5, 88, 89, 93, 94, 100n4, 104, 109
Endgame, 10, 84, 93, 94
First Love, 83
Krapp's Last Tape, 84
Not I, 109
Ohio Impromptu, 83
Play, 66, 100n2
That Time, 84
The Trilogy, 60, 83, 88, 92
Waiting for Godot, 93

Bennett, Susan, 163–6
Berger, John, 143
Billington, Michael, 32, 38, 41, 83, 92, 155, 156
Blair, Tony, 33, 43, 50
Bond, Edward, 18, 145
Bonney, Jo, 124
Booth, John Wilkes, 23, 113–14, 115, 118, 122, 123
Borges, Jorge Louis, 114
Bosch, Hieronymus, 3, 4, 20, 65–6
Bottoms, Stephen, 132, 134, 142, 143, 144, 146–7, 148, 149, 150, 166
Boyle, Danny, 13, 17, 58
Bradwell, Mark, 57
Brantley, Ben, 119
Brecht, Bertolt, 104, 108, 128n1, 163–4
Brenton, Howard, 4
British Theatre Consortium, 166–8
Brontë, Emily, 46
Bruegel, Pieter the Elder, 3
Büchner, Georg, 8, 87
Buggy, Niall, 90

172 INDEX

Buñuel, Luis, 30
Burgess, Anthony, 41

C
Callot, Jacques, 3
capitalism, 20, 32, 98, 156
capriccio, 3
caricature, 3, 38, 95–7
carnival, 3, 4, 20–1, 59, 63, 65, 105, 117, 152
Carr, Marina, 81
Carroll, Lewis, 93
 Alice in Wonderland, 93
Carroll, Noël, 164
Cassuto, Leonard, 105
catharsis, 12, 39, 52, 75, 99, 112, 113
Cheadle, Don, 118, 119
Churchill, Caryl, 12, 21–2, 108
circus, 108
Colbert, Soyica Diggs, 115, 120
comedy, 4, 7, 10, 13, 14, 16, 21, 22, 58, 59, 71, 98, 116, 118, 126, 137
comics, 31, 34, 39, 164
commedia dell'arte, 3
commodification, 24, 105, 109–10, 146, 154, 156–7
community, 65, 148, 149–51, 153, 167
computer games, 69, 164
conceptual art, 132, 134–5, 154, 157, 159n6
Connelly, Frances S., 2–5, 7, 12, 23, 53, 74, 77, 113, 127, 164, 168
Conway, Denis, 90
Courtney, Lorraine, 98
Craig-Martin, Michael, 139, 140
Crimp, Martin, 12, 21, 131
Crouch, Tim, v, 13, 22, 23–4, 131–59, 163
 Adler & Gibb, 24, 132, 154–9

 The Author, 24, 132, 144–50, 151, 154, 158, 159n3
 ENGLAND, 132, 141–3, 148–9, 154
 My Arm, 24, 131–8, 141, 143, 154, 155, 158
 An Oak Tree, 24, 136–41, 143, 149, 158
 what happens to the hope at the end of the evening, 150–4, 158, 159n6
Cuvier, Georges, 106, 107

D
Dalí, Salvador, 4
Diamond, Liz, 113
Dickens, Charles, 38
Domus Aurea, 2–3
Dorley-Brown, Chris, 134–5
Druid Theatre, 81, 85, 90, 98, 100n5
Duchamp, Marcel, 36, 134
du Maurier, Daphne, 36, 93
dystopia, 20, 41, 42, 44, 62, 63

E
EastEnders, 38
Edwards, Justin, 3–4
Elam, Harry, 111
Elam, Keir, 165, 166
entrapment, 13, 84–5, 89, 91, 94, 95, 99, 115
Esslin, Martin, 10, 11, 13
ethics, 5, 6, 7, 13, 15, 18, 19, 22, 32, 39, 42, 44, 45–6, 53–4, 58, 72, 75, 88, 98, 105, 111, 136, 137, 146, 158, 164, 165, 168, 168n1

F
fairy tales, 34, 37, 40, 42, 53, 97
farce, 7, 14, 15, 21, 23, 51, 86, 93, 99
Faulkner, William, 104
Faust, 69, 74, 75
fear, 32, 35, 69, 92, 128n1
Fischer-Lichte, Erika, 165, 166
Foreman, Richard, 104
Foucault, Michel, 127, 141
freak show, 104, 105, 133, 136
Freshwater, Helen, 133, 134, 136, 137, 139, 146, 147, 148, 151, 163, 166
Freud, Sigmund, 88
Fricker, Karen, 60, 64, 65
Friedman, Ken, 159n6
Friel, Brian, 76, 95
Fuchs, Elinor, 116, 117
Fuseli, Henry, 4

G
Gambaro, Griselda, 128n1
Gantz, Jeffrey, 124, 126, 127
Gardner, Lyn, 41, 42, 50, 52, 67, 151
Garson, Cyrielle, 158n1
Gates, Jr., Henry Louis, 103
Geis, Deborah R., 103, 104, 108, 109, 110–11, 112, 115, 117, 119, 121, 123
Genet, Jean, 9, 10
ghosts, 38, 49
globalization, 34, 98, 143, 164, 165
Golding, William, 82
Goldman, Lisa, 46, 50
gothic, 2, 4, 34, 46, 49, 66, 96
Gould, Stephen Jay, 106
Goya, Francisco, 3
Grabbe, Hans Dietrich, 8
Grant, Ulysses S., 126
Grass, Günther, 133
Gray, Alasdair, 114

Graulund, Rune, 3–4
Grehan, Helena, 165, 168
grottesche, 2
Grossman, Jan, 10–12, 25n1

H
Harpham, Geoffrey Galt, 2, 12, 73, 74
Harpin, Anne, 41, 42, 45–6
Haughton, Miriam, 59, 63, 77
Havel, Václav, 10, 12, 99, 165, 168n1
Haydon, Andrew, 158n1
Heaney, Seamus, 116
heterotopia, 141
Hirst, Damien, 30
Hitchcock, Alfred, 36, 93
Hogarth, William, 3
Hollywood cinema, 38–9, 59, 61, 67
Homer, 90, 124, 127
  The Odyssey, 23, 90, 98, 104, 124
Horace, 2
Huber, Werner, 81
Hughes, Declan, 86
Huxley, Aldous, 42
Hynes, Garry, 64
hypnosis, 138–40

I
Iball, Helen, 146, 147, 150, 159n3
Ilter, Seda, 133, 134, 135, 137, 138
Innes, Christopher, 104, 105, 106, 108, 116, 117
in-yer-face theatre, 13, 19, 30, 68, 69, 78n2, 98, 145–7
Ionesco, Eugène, 9, 10
Isherwood, Charles, 124

J

James, Karl, 131, 133, 136, 141, 144, 150, 154
Jarry, Alfred, 8–9, 10, 11, 13, 82, 87, 137
Jarzyna, Grzegorz, 90
Jordan, Eamonn, 25n3, 62–3, 64, 66–7, 88, 96, 99, 100n6
Joyce, James, 104, 124

K

Kafka, Franz, 10, 11
Kane, Sarah, 1, 13, 20, 21, 25n4, 63, 66, 131, 145, 146
  Blasted, 4, 14, 17–19, 20–1, 40, 42, 145, 146
Kant, Immanuel, 73
Kayser, Wolfgang, 6–7, 8–9, 17, 18, 19, 21, 24, 31, 53, 69, 82, 86–7, 137
Keaton, Buster, 93
Keizer, Arlene R., 110, 112
Kelly, Aidan, 57
Kennedy assassination, 48
Kimmig, Stephan, 100n5
kitchen-sink drama, 46, 51, 58
Knabe, Tilman, 90
Kubrick, Stanley, 41
Kushner, Tony, 108, 119

L

laughter, 6, 7, 12, 13, 14, 15, 17, 20, 31, 63, 73, 74, 99, 105, 113, 116, 122, 137
Law, Jude, 36
Lee, Bruce, 60, 61
Lee, Robert E., General, 114
Leeney, Cathy, 62, 76–7, 78
LeMahieu, Michael, 120, 122
Lenz, Jakob Michael Reinhold, 8
Letts, Tracy, 1, 25n1
  Killer Joe, 13, 14–15, 17, 58

Levinas, Emmanuel, 165, 168n1
Lincoln, Abraham, 23, 104, 113–18, 119, 120–1, 122–3, 126, 127
Lincoln, Mary Todd, 114
Living Theatre, 152
Lloyd, Matthew, 29, 36, 37, 39
Loane, Tim, 21
Lonergan, Patrick, 76

M

MacDonald, Hettie, 133
McBrinn, Róisín, 64
McCafferty, Owen, 76
McDonagh, Martin, 1, 4, 13, 15–17, 21, 25n2, 25n3, 25n5, 71, 81, 137
  The Beauty Queen of Leenane, 96
  The Cripple of Inishmaan, 15, 97
  The Lieutenant of Inishmore, 15–16, 58
  The Pillowman, 16–17, 86–7, 88
McLuhan, Marshall, 135
McPherson, Conor, 60, 68, 74, 76, 81
  This Lime Tree Bower, 60
  Port Authority, 68, 74
Magritte, René, 140
Maley, Patrick, 119, 120, 122, 123, 128n2
Mamet, David, 21
Mandela, Nelson, 107
Marber, Patrick, 81
Marlowe, Sam, 49
melodrama, 86, 98, 104
Melville, Herman, 133
Miami Vice, 58
Midler, Bette, 72, 73, 78n3
Miller, Arthur, 120
Miller, Greg, 108, 109, 110, 112
Minghella, Anthony, 100n2
Minotaur, 44–5, 54n1
Mitterand, François, 107

monologue, 1, 22–3, 30, 32, 57, 60–78, 91, 94, 107, 113–14, 116, 145–6, 147–8
monstrous, 2, 3, 4, 5, 8, 9, 12, 18, 20, 23, 32, 35, 37, 44–5, 49, 70, 99, 146
Morash, Chris, 75, 97
The Morecambe & Wise Show, 93
moresque, 3
Morin, Emilie, 134, 139, 143, 159n6
Mos Def, 119
Mullen, Marie, 64
Murfi, Mikel, 85, 90, 92, 93, 100n5
Murphy, Cillian, 81, 92, 93
Murphy, Tadhg, 90
Murphy, Tom, 72, 96
  The Gigli Concert, 72–5
  A Whistle in the Dark, 96
Murray, Christopher, 72, 74, 75, 96
music, 93, 103, 106, 126, 149
  classical, 41, 72, 75, 140
  film soundtracks, 78, 93
  hip hop, 71, 110, 119
  jazz, 103, 118
  pop, 33, 78n3, 93, 149
  rock 'n' roll, 34, 37
myth, 23, 33–4, 37, 44–5, 60, 63–4, 69, 77, 98, 124, 126

N
Nádas, Péter, 90
narrative, 1, 12, 20, 23, 42, 43–4, 52, 53, 64, 75, 76–7, 83, 84, 87–91, 95–6, 100n4, 111, 113, 115, 117, 118, 121, 127, 132, 133–4, 141, 144
  and identity, 43–4, 64, 88–90, 96, 100n4, 127, 141
naturalism, 8, 18, 25n4, 31, 42, 57, 104, 108, 118, 122–3, 152, 157, 163

Nauman, Bruce, 139
Němec, Marek, 77
nostalgia, 33–4, 36–40, 68, 95, 117

O
O'Brien, Flann, 93
O'Brien, Harvey, 77
O'Rowe, Mark, 22–3, 57–78, 97, 98–9, 145
  The Aspidistra Code, 57–8
  Crestfall, 23, 60, 64–7, 68, 70, 75, 76–8
  From Both Hips, 58–9, 61
  Howie the Rookie, 22–3, 57, 60–4, 65, 66, 67, 68, 75, 76–8
  Made in China, 59–60, 61
  Our Few and Evil Days, 78n4
  Terminus, 23, 57, 60, 64, 67–75, 76–8, 78n3, 97
O'Sullivan, Aisling, 64
O'Toole, Fintan, 93, 94–5, 96
Özdamar, Emine Sevgi, 90

P
Pacino, Al, 59
Parks, Suzan-Lori, 13, 22, 23, 103–28, 136, 149, 156
  The America Play, 23, 104, 113–18, 120–1, 125, 127
  Father Comes Home from the Wars, 23, 104, 123–7
  Imperceptible Mutabilities in the Third Kingdom, 103
  365 Days/365 Plays, 124
  Topdog/Underdog, 23, 103, 104, 113, 118–23, 125, 127
  Venus, 23, 103, 104–13, 114, 115, 116, 125, 127, 136, 149
Picasso, Pablo, 44–5, 54n1
Pinter, Harold, 10, 18, 31, 82, 100n4

Pirandello, Luigi, 9, 13, 86–7, 118, 144
pornography, 38, 146, 147
Porter, Adina, 111
Presley, Elvis, 34, 40
puppets, 8–9, 10, 13, 17, 24, 87–8, 91, 123, 133–4, 137, 155

R
Raabke, Tilman, 85, 90
Rabelais, François, 6, 19–20, 63, 92
Raffo, Heather, 4
Rainer, Alice, 111
Rancière, Jacques, 5–6, 24, 99, 132, 158, 165
Ransmayr, Christoph, 90
Ravenhill, Mark, 1, 13, 19–21, 44, 46, 63, 145, 146
  Shopping and Fucking, 4, 19–21, 44
Rea, Stephen, 92
reality show, 98
Rebellato, Dan, 19, 30, 31, 32, 34, 35, 45–6, 98, 132, 139, 141, 145, 149, 150–1, 152, 153, 165
re-enactment, 17, 23, 38, 39, 84, 86–9, 91, 92, 104, 113, 114, 116, 117, 118, 119, 121, 123
Reinelt, Janelle, 166
Remshardt, Ralf E., 7, 8, 11, 13–14, 17, 74, 77, 99
Richards, Shaun, 75, 97
Ridley, Philip, 1, 13, 22, 29–54, 60, 63, 66, 68, 89–90, 94, 98–9, 120, 146, 164
  Dark Vanilla Jungle, 32
  The Fastest Clock in the Universe, 31, 32–4, 36–7, 53, 94
  Ghost from a Perfect Place, 31, 32–4, 37–40, 53, 89
  The Krays, 31, 33
  Leaves of Glass, 31, 32, 46–50, 51, 52, 53, 120
  Mercury Fur, 22, 31, 32, 40–6, 48, 50, 53, 83, 89, 120

  Piranha Heights, 31, 32, 46, 50–3, 54, 89, 120
  The Pitchfork Disney, 22, 29–30, 31, 32–6, 46, 89, 120
  The Reflecting Skin, 31
  Shivered, 32
  Tender Napalm, 32
  The Universe of Dermot Finn, 30
  Vincent River, 32
Ridout, Nicholas, 165
Ringham, Hannah, 141, 142
ritual, 32, 38, 94, 108
Romanticism, 3, 7, 8, 9, 17, 63, 69, 78n2, 87, 99, 137
Royal Court Theatre, 17, 132, 144–7, 154, 157
Ruskin, John, 5–6, 132

S
Saal, Ilka, 109, 111, 116, 123
Sacher-Masoch, Leopold von, 46
Sartre, Jean-Paul, 93
Schimmelpfennig, Roland, 90
Schlösser, Patrick, 77
Schongauer, Martin, 3
science fiction, 34
Shakespeare, William, 8, 16, 38, 41, 68, 116, 156
Shelley, Mary, 4
  Frankenstein, 4, 35
Shepard, Sam, 22, 120
Shiels, Karl, 57, 90
smith, a (Andy Smith), 131, 136, 141, 143, 144, 150–4
Sierz, Aleks, 13, 14, 17, 18, 19, 20, 21, 30, 32, 35, 36, 38, 39, 43, 44, 46, 83, 134, 145, 148, 149, 150
Singleton, Brian, 57, 61, 62, 64, 76
slapstick, 12, 23, 58, 59, 92–3, 99
The Sound of Music, 42

stage design, 8, 36, 74–5, 76–7, 85, 94, 133–5, 136–7, 141–2, 144, 150–2, 155, 159n6
Stanton, Edwin, 114
Stein, Gertrude, 104
story, *see* narrative
Stoppard, Tom, 82
sublime, 23, 72–5, 78n2
Švankmajer, Jan, 30
Sweet, Matthew, 41, 42
Synge, John Millington, 15

T

Tarantino, Quentin, 13, 15, 17, 58
Taylor, Paul, 41, 42, 156
Teardo, Teho, 93
teatro del grottesco, 9, 17, 86, 137
terror, 6, 7, 20, 39, 53, 69, 73, 74, 82, 105, 128n1
terrorism, 15–16, 42, 46, 48, 51–2, 142, 145
  attacks on London public transport, 48, 51–2, 54n2
  9/11 attacks, 15
Thatcher, Margaret, 20, 33
theatre of the absurd, 9–12, 13, 98, 99, 104, 165
Thomas, Dylan, 82
Thompson, Steve, 21
Thomson, Philip, 164
Thorson, Greg, 25n2
Tiffany, John, 41, 42
totalitarianism, 10, 16, 165
tragedy, 7, 23, 99, 105, 108
  Greek, 31, 41, 104, 112, 122, 126
  Jacobean, 14, 22, 36, 68–9, 72
trauma, 24, 32, 39, 46, 48, 49, 88, 115, 120, 136, 139

U

Urban, Ken, 19, 32, 33–4, 35, 36–7, 38

V

vaudeville, 108
verbatim theatre, 158n1
verse drama, 60, 70–2
violence, 4, 13–24, 30, 33, 35–42, 46, 48, 50–3, 57, 59–62, 65–9, 74, 77–8, 85–7, 91, 94, 105, 116, 122, 145–9, 164
  verbal, 13, 19, 41, 50, 53, 60, 85, 146
Vitruvius, 2
voyeurism, 77, 109–10, 111, 136, 147, 152

W

Wallace, Clare, 13, 18, 76, 82, 97–8, 164
Wallace & Gromit, 93
Walsh, Enda, 1, 13, 22, 23, 81–100, 137
  Ballyturk, 23, 81, 84, 85, 92–5, 96–7, 98, 99
  bedbound, 83
  Disco Pigs, 81, 84
  How These Desperate Men Talk, 83
  My Friend Duplicity, 89–90, 92
  The New Electric Ballroom, 23, 81, 84–91, 93, 95–6, 98, 100n5
  Penelope, 23, 81, 84, 85, 90–3, 97, 98, 124
  Room 303, 92
  The Small Things, 83, 84, 100n4
  The Walworth Farce, 23, 81, 84–91, 93, 95–6, 98, 100n5, 118
Walsh, Eileen, 64

war, 4, 18, 19, 32, 42, 44–5,
    46, 48, 145
  Bosnia, 19
  Hiroshima, 43, 48
  Iraq, 4, 42, 43
  nuclear, 43, 47
  Rwanda, 42
  US Civil War, 4, 117, 123, 125–7
  Vietnam, 40, 42, 43, 48
  World War I, 48
  World War II, 7, 9, 10, 43, 48
Warhol, Andy, 135
Warner, Sara, 105–7, 109,
  112, 113
Whishaw, Ben, 41, 46
White, Hayden, 127
Whitman, Walt, 46
Wilde, Oscar, 37
Williams, Holly, 153

Williams, Tennessee, 31, 50
Wilmer, S. E., 104, 117, 118, 127
Wilson, August, 120, 123–4
Wise, Louis, 53
witnessing, 37, 39, 40, 45–6,
  48, 72, 110, 136, 142,
  150, 156
Wolfe, George C., 118
Woo, John, 61
Wood, John, 38
Woolf, Virginia, 104
Worthen, W.B., 109, 110, 118
Wright, Jeffrey, 118
Wyllie, Andrew, 39, 42, 49

Y
Yeats, William Butler, 97, 126
Young, Jean, 105, 109–10

CPSIA information can be obtained
at www.ICGtesting.com
Printed in the USA
LVHW082309231020
669663LV00014B/340